Protest on Trial

The Seattle 7 Conspiracy

Also by Kit Bakke
Miss Alcott's E-mail
Dancing on the Edge

Protest on Trial

The Seattle 7 Conspiracy

Kit Bakke

WSU
PRESS

Washington State University Press
Pullman, Washington

Washington State University Press
PO Box 645910
Pullman, Washington 99164-5910
Phone: 800-354-7360
Fax: 509-335-8568
Email: wsupress@wsu.edu
Website: wsupress.wsu.edu

Library of Congress Cataloging-in-Publication Data

Names: Bakke, Kit, author.
Title: Protest on trial : The Seattle 7 Conspiracy / Kit Bakke.
Other titles: Seattle Seven conspiracy story
Description: Pullman, Washington : Washington State University Press, 2018. |
    Includes bibliographical references and index.
Identifiers: LCCN 2017047617 | ISBN 9780874223569 (alk. paper)
Subjects: LCSH: Seattle Seven--Trials, litigation, etc. | Trials
    (Conspiracy)--Washington (State) | Dissenters--Legal status, laws,
    etc.--United States--History. | Anti-war demonstrations--United
    States--History. | Seattle Liberation Front (Seattle, Wash.)--History. |
    Vietnam War, 1961-1975--United States. | Boldt, George H. (George Hugo),
    1903-1984.
Classification: LCC KF224.S43 B35 2018 | DDC 345.73/0243--dc23 LC record
available at https://lccn.loc.gov/2017047617

To Jack, Jean, and Peter.
Thanks for teaching me about
luck, choice, and responsibility.

In a democracy, dissent is an act of faith.
—Senator J. William Fulbright, 1966

Contents

What's It All About?

It isn't the rebels that cause the troubles of the world, it's the troubles that cause the rebels.
—CARL OGLESBY, PRESIDENT, STUDENTS FOR A DEMOCRATIC SOCIETY, 1965

U.S. Federal District Courthouse, Tacoma Washington
December 14, 1970
Seattle 7 Conspiracy Trial, Day 12:

DEFENDANT JEFF DOWD: "The thing that disappointed me most is every day coming in this courtroom and you, Judge Boldt, stand up and you salute that [American] flag. That flag was born in revolution and, your Honor, I honestly don't think that flag deserves to be up there. The flag that deserves to be up there is this one…the Nazi flag."
Dowd pulls out a large Nazi flag from under his shirt. The defendants throw it at Judge Boldt, who is visibly shaken.

DEFENDANT SUSAN STERN: "Give me back the people of My Lai,[1] Judge Boldt, because the onus is on you, their deaths are on your shoulders."
Judge Boldt orders defendant Stern to sit down. When she doesn't, he orders armed marshals to forcibly remove her. Defense attorneys and defendants jump to defend her. An attorney is maced. Chaos ensues.

———◆———

How do you tell your country that its democracy is looking less democratic every day? How do you protest when your elected government is killing civilians in undeclared wars abroad and allowing racism and bigotry to flourish at home? How do you stop the passage of laws that benefit the wealthy few at the expense of the basic health and welfare of the majority? How do you stop a train that you think is about to obliterate the basic tenets of a government meant to be of the people, by the people, and for the people? What can you do when none of this is up for a vote, and all the free speech in the world isn't changing anything?

Eight young people in Seattle faced these questions in the late 1960s. They were not especially heroic or brilliant, but neither were they narrow-minded or uncaring. Their answers led to vigorous dissent and activism as they invested their personal lives in a full-time attempt to tackle their nation's most challenging problems. They certainly didn't invent American dissent, and they certainly didn't act alone, but by choosing to do what they did, these eight people added their unique sparks to the story of our American democracy. Their arguments and their actions offer us several models for how to span the gap between our personal values and our public actions.

Democracy is never finished. It's in a permanent construction phase, and dissent is foundational to its architecture. By living beyond a wholly personal life, dissidents give the rest of us a chance to see additional sides to troublesome social issues, to evaluate and understand, perhaps to rethink our own positions.

Dissidents, by definition, are always a minority; it is unrealistic to expect otherwise. Nor are they necessarily democracy's saviors; some activists promote fear-inducing, anti-democratic, sectarian programs biased against the interests of their fellow human beings. No matter what their cause, though, dissidents are instrumental to America's evolving and conflicted conversation about our identity, our place in the world, and in history.

All protest begins with observation and thought—"I think that's wrong" or "That's not fair"—and then moves to action of some kind. It may be as simple as signing a petition or talking to friends. However it is expressed, protest, dissent, activism, resistance (the terms are used interchangeably throughout) takes time away from other activities and requires acceptance of a degree of individual risk. Depending on the action taken, dissent can be merely uncomfortable or personally danger-ous. Some actions turn protesters into terrorists or traitors; others trans-form them into patriotic heroes. Most activists, however, work in the less dramatic middle. The story of the Seattle 8 (later the Seattle 7) is one such case. Even so, the Seattle 8's dissent brought them federal conspiracy indictments, a tumultuous federal court trial, and stints in federal and state prisons. No protest is hazard-free.

How do the tactical choices and particular experiences of the Seattle 8 and other antiwar and civil rights protesters of the 1960s speak to the

United States today and its role on our planet? What can we learn from their successes and errors? The devil lurks in the details, but so do solutions. The tale lived by the Seattle 8 overflows with both warnings and encouragement for today's activists.

The questions today's dissenters raise about the health and integrity of our American democracy are both the same as and different from their 1960s incarnations. We twenty-first-century Americans face a smorgasbord of simmering issues. Climate change, electoral malfeasance, corporate "personhood," racial and religious discrimination and violence, economic inequity, the defense of innumerable personal freedoms, and the responsible role of the United States among all nations in the nuclear age are just some of the issues that occupy American activists today.

The pages ahead depict the confusion and immediacy of life on the front lines of mid-twentieth-century American protest. They unravel the Seattle 8's story and briefly suggest its association with four broad issues of today. The book is a case study with several present-day links sketched in; it is not a history of the 1960s and 1970s in America, nor an analysis of protest in general. Readers interested in more broad-spectrum discussions on these topics can refer to the bibliography.

This book is divided into three sections. Part One: Dissent, situates the eight Seattleites in the protest movements and social experiments of their day. Told primarily in their own words, their stories of dedication, ignorance, energy, and courage were captured in lengthy personal interviews with the author.[2] These seven men and one woman accused of federal conspiracy in 1970 brought varied motives and perspectives to their activism, and they look back on those times with both satisfaction and regret. Numerous FBI memos and files, personal interviews with attorneys and law enforcement officers, the trial transcript, depositions, appeals court documents, and stacks of news articles, pamphlets, and flyers help fill out the picture of their tumultuous days.

Part Two: Trial, recounts the defendants' courtroom tactics in the face of the American judicial system's puzzling combination of freedom and repression. As the prosecution, the judge, and the defense scrambled to make sense of each other, all soon reached the end of their patience and the trial ended with an unexpected judicial bang.

Part Three, Consequences, opens with stories of the legal and personal lives of the defendants since their release from prison to today. The closing chapter identifies threads of strategy, tactics, and motivation that connect the Seattle 8's world of protest with four broadly defined, high-profile, nationally focused activist efforts underway today in the early twenty-first century.

PART ONE

Dissent

Seattle Liberation Front flyer, 1970. *Author's collection*

1

The Lay of the Land

The Vietnam War unbolted us from the social contract—it broke the bond between us and our government.

—TOM BYERS, SEATTLE LIBERATION FRONT MEMBER

They were known as the Seattle 8 when they were indicted in April 1970, but became the Seattle 7 when one of their number went underground. Their combined federal conspiracy charges spread over six counts and eighteen overt acts, adding up to possible ten-year prison sentences and fines of thousands of dollars. The Honorable George H. Boldt, who presided over the twelve days of the Seattle 7 trial in the rainy winter of 1970, was accustomed to organized crime cases with savvy defendants and experienced attorneys on both sides. With the Seattle 7, he faced an unruly bunch of young activists fresh from their middle-class homes and their school civics classes where they had learned that American justice was fair and that the accused was guaranteed a jury of his or her peers.

Reality was to prove otherwise.

And then there was the woman. In 1970, women were rarely present in politics or business, let alone exhorting crowds of antiwar demonstrators to take to the streets. Men often didn't know how to act around the unusual woman who appeared in the masculine world outside the home. Judge Boldt had trouble with the indicted Susan Stern. Susan Stern, in turn, had trouble being the only woman among the defendants.

The other defendants were Michael Lerner, at twenty-seven the oldest of the group, an assistant professor in the philosophy department at the University of Washington (UW); Chip Marshall, a newly graduated political science major from Cornell University; Joe Kelly, a "red diaper baby,"[1] good friend of Marshall's, and also a Cornell graduate; Jeff Dowd, a high school graduate from Ithaca, New York, who later became the inspiration for The Dude in the 1998 Coen brothers' film *The Big Lebowski*; Michael Abeles, a Cornell freshman dropout, son of a Buffalo, New York, tavern owner; Roger Lippman, a Reed College chemistry major dropout and leftist organizer and theoretician; and Michael Justesen, a UW freshman from Seattle who decided not to stand trial and went underground. Susan Stern had a master's degree from the UW in social work and was recently divorced from a UW law student. Though not all of them were acquainted before the trial, all had been active in Students for a Democratic Society (SDS), the largest student antiwar organization in the country in the 1960s.

The conspiracy indictment against these eight activists hinged on a February 1970 Seattle demonstration to protest the anticipated guilty verdict coming to the Chicago 7 in the aftermath of antiwar protests held at the violence-infused 1968 Chicago Democratic National Convention. Unexpectedly, while the Chicago 7 jury was busy deliberating, Judge Julius Hoffman abruptly sentenced the still innocent-until-proven-guilty defendants and two of their attorneys to prison for a maximum of four years on 159 charges of contempt of court. Similar rash behavior would appear nine months later in the Seattle trial; in both cases, the judiciary had transformed a criminal trial into a political one.

Judge Hoffman's high-handed move in Chicago sparked immediate street demonstrations in dozens of cities around the country, including Seattle. The protests were called The Day After, or TDA. The Seattle 8 were accused of leading Seattle's TDA protest, and were indicted under the same federal "intent to riot" law that had been levied against the Chicago 7. Buried in the 1968 Civil Rights Act, and also called the Anti-Riot or Rap Brown Act (after black activist H. Rap Brown), 8 U.S.C. 2101 had been passed in a panicked flurry by Congress in 1968 in response to escalating riots in black neighborhoods after Martin Luther King Jr. was assassinated in April that year. This statute, still in force, makes it illegal to cross state lines or to use "any facility of interstate…commerce, including…the telephone…with intent to incite, organize, promote, and encourage a riot."[2] It has been repeatedly criticized in legal circles as vague, unconstitutional, and unnecessary, in part because it appears to make one's thoughts the crime, rather than one's deeds. As there are already plenty of existing state laws against rioting, critics see no need for a federal law aimed at people who might or might not be thinking about rioting as they (or their words) travel across state lines.

In response to TDA protests, the Department of Justice used the power of 18 U.S.C. 2101 very selectively. None of the other cities' TDA protest leaders, even those whose demonstrations were larger and more violent than Seattle's, were similarly accused. So why Seattle? Why these eight young people?

What made the actions of these particular Seattleites, nationally unknown and so distant from the media and political centers of the country, appear so potentially threatening? How and why did they draw the attention of the Department of Justice, so much so that their indictments were personally announced from Washington, DC, by Attorney General John Mitchell and FBI Director J. Edgar Hoover?

Perhaps because the Seattle 8 were neither your typical rowdy street demonstrators, nor was their organization hampered by tedious factional infighting, nor did they confine the scope of their dissent to the university campus. Instead, they were variously involved in building a region-wide, antiwar, anti-racist, and community service organization they called the Seattle Liberation Front (SLF).[3] They deployed multiple, layered tactics on many fronts aimed at many different constituencies—from gathering signatures for a statewide tax reform referendum, to providing doughnuts and coffee to people standing in line at the unemployment office, to disrupting classrooms, to fighting a freeway extension through the black neighborhood, to leading mass antiwar street demonstrations. However small and new, however fun-loving and adolescent, SLF was beginning to engage poor, working, and middle-class Seattleites with helpful alternatives and direct social services that had the potential to disturb the political and economic status quo of the city. Unlike most antiwar youth organizations of the day, SLF's political agenda extended beyond ending the war, and their circle of activity was growing beyond the college campus. In fact, some of the community service organizations founded by SLF collectives and members exist to this day, providing thousands of Seattleites with health care, legal services, and more.[4]

The Seattle 8 were among that crowd of babies born to parents who lived through or fought in World War II. Part of a strong and growing post-war middle class, many parents of these so-called baby boomers believed in patriotism, education, science, hard work, and vaccinations. They raised their children to love and trust their country—after all, America had just saved the world from Hitler and his storm troopers.

When some of these children, including the Seattle 8, reached high school age in the early 1960s, they began to pay attention to the national news. They saw television footage of black American citizens being attacked by police armed with vicious dogs, long batons, and powerful water hoses. They learned that both black and white people were being murdered for trying to legally register black citizens to vote.

These white teenagers had been taught that all those racial problems had been fixed by the Civil War and Reconstruction, but now it was blindingly apparent that they'd not been told the truth. Racism was alive and well, and was far more ingrained and brutal than they'd imagined possible. Upset at being lied to, many decided they couldn't "trust anyone over thirty." This was not the just and fair America their parents and teachers had promised them.

In a one-two punch on top of the shocking displays of homegrown racism came the horror of the war in Vietnam. The growing American military operations in Vietnam quickly became a major problem for these young students. The president of SDS said in 1965, "Most of us grew up thinking that the United States was a strong but humble nation, that involved itself in world affairs only reluctantly, that respected the integrity of other nations and systems, and that engaged in wars only as a last resort…the incredible war in Vietnam has provided the razor, the terrifying sharp cutting edge, that has finally severed the last vestige of illusion that morality and democracy are the guiding principles of American foreign policy."[5]

By 1968 over 500,000 American troops were deployed in Vietnam, and over a million Vietnamese and 30,000 American soldiers had been killed. By the time the Americans withdrew in the mid-1970s, the U.S. had dropped 7.6 million tons of explosives on Vietnam, Laos, and Cambodia (an area only slightly larger than Texas), which is over three times what the United States dropped in all of Europe and Asia during World War II.[6]

The Democratic National Convention in the sizzling Chicago heat of late August 1968 displayed the actions of both the war's opponents and the government's response in full view of the national press corps. Thousands of antiwar demonstrators of all ages with little experience in protest marches and no intention of committing violence or of being arrested came to Chicago. They came to support the nominations of Sen. George McGovern (who had inherited many of Robert Kennedy's delegates after his assassination), or Sen. Eugene McCarthy, both of whom advocated an end to the war. On the downtown streets and in the lakefront parks of Chicago the demonstrators were repeatedly set upon by armed and armored police and National Guardsmen. Over five hundred demonstrators were arrested during the convention week; many more were injured.

The television-watching public was horrified, either by seeing uniformed men wearing gas masks clubbing white college students amidst clouds of choking, nauseating gas, or by seeing unruly young people taking over the streets, yelling and throwing rocks. Opinion polls at the time gave law and order a sympathetic edge—chaos in the streets was not the way to end violence elsewhere. Later, however, the official investigation termed the events a "police riot."[7]

For some of the protesters, including several of the Seattle 8, this first taste of serious opposition, the tear gas and billy clubs in Chicago, ignited in them a rush of adrenaline and a feeling of comradery with rebels around the world. Susan Stern, for instance, felt as if the experience linked her directly to victims of oppression everywhere, from Auschwitz to the extermination of Native American tribes, and the assassinations of Malcolm X and Martin Luther King Jr.[8]

But none of this stopped moderate Hubert Humphrey from being nominated over McCarthy and McGovern, and then losing the election to Richard Nixon, whose policies and appointees continued to expand the war. By the end of 1968 as the death toll mounted, the young, idealistic foot soldiers of antiwar protests and staunch allies of the growing Black Power movement were frantic. How could their country be making such tragic mistakes? Why wouldn't their government listen to them?

Similar questions had been asked six years earlier, in 1960, by a small group of college students meeting at the University of Michigan in Ann Arbor. Two years later, in a United Auto Workers' conference facility in Port Huron, Michigan, they wrote down their thoughts about the problems faced by their country and themselves. Dubbed the Port Huron Statement,[9] the document established the foundation of SDS, which by 1969 had 100,000 members.[10]

The students wrote that they wanted to become agents of social change. What needed changing, they said, was racism, the Cold War, and poverty. The mechanism of change was something the students called "participatory democracy."

SDS National Council members meeting in Bloomington, Indiana, in September 1963. As it grew, SDS had four meetings a year, located on different college campuses around the country. In this photo, Tom Hayden is on the far left. *Photo by Clark Kissinger*

These fledgling SDS members, all white, mostly male, recognized that their generation was raised in "modest comfort" and that they were "looking uncomfortably at the world we inherit." The tone of the statement was idealistic, tentative, not strident or bombastic. It drew its strength from espousing traditional democratic values of fairness and justice, and by emphasizing the value of local organizing around local issues. SDS was to be a multi-issue organization, a new start, and it formed the core of what came to be called the New Left. The Old Left, the Communist Party, had lost its credibility among most American leftists when Soviet tanks crushed the Hungarian uprising in 1956. The students instead turned for their models to the black organizations in the American south, particularly the Student Nonviolent Coordinating Committee (SNCC).[11]

All eight of the indicted Seattleites were too young to have participated in SDS' founding, but all were involved in national and local SDS actions in their high school and college years. When SDS broke apart in late 1969, the Seattle Liberation Front was a local phoenix that rose from SDS's ashes.[12]

As if the war and racism weren't enough to keep activists occupied in the 1960s, attention to women's rights issues intensified in the mid-twentieth century. Women have been demanding equal pay for equal work, the right to education, the right to enter all professions, and the right to control their own income, property, and bodies for centuries. In the United States, from 1848 to 1920, women engaged in seventy-two years of activism, from civil disobedience to lobbying, before finally securing the right to vote.

But many inequities remained and the 1960s antiwar movement was not exempt from the turmoil caused by women's increasing demands for justice. Despite being able to vote, most women in their teens and twenties in the late 1960s weren't raised to consider themselves equal to the men in their lives. Most middle-class families still had only one wage-earner, and that was overwhelmingly the man. Married women, even those who did work, could not get credit cards in their names without their husband's signature on the application. If women were elected to anything, it was likely the local school board. Job ads specified "male wanted" or "female wanted" and women's jobs tended to be restricted to store clerk, secretary, typist, nurse, K–12 teacher, or, if you were unmarried and under 32 years old, flight attendant. Many employers expected women to quit their jobs as soon as they married, and pregnancy in many occupations was likely to result in dismissal.

Abortion was difficult, painful, and illegal in the 1960s. Legal abortion didn't become available until 1973. Readers not alive then might be surprised at how many horrific abortion stories their grandmothers or mothers may have hidden away in their pasts. Seattle 7 defendant Susan Stern was one of thousands of young women who paid dearly for one, financially, physically, and emotionally. Pregnant in 1964, she asked her boyfriend to drive her from their Syracuse University campus to Union City, New Jersey, where she had been told to wait on a street corner to meet the person who would do the procedure.[13] Because abortions were illegal, they often took so long to arrange that the process became more dangerous and often occurred without adequate medical back-up. And, of course, it was always a pay-up-front, cash transaction.

These three issues: ending the war, ending racism, and improving the status of women, jostled against one another throughout the 1960s, sometimes supporting and sometimes hindering each other. Tactics and strategies were freely borrowed among advocates of each of the three, and individual activists strengthened their organizing skills as they learned and moved from one issue to another.

A looming character in any story of the antiwar and civil rights movements of the 1960s is the Federal Bureau of Investigation (FBI). The primary job of the FBI since its inception has been to investigate and apprehend people who disobey federal laws. However, early in the twentieth century, under the leadership of J. Edgar Hoover, the FBI chose to take on the task of harassing people whom it thought *might* disobey a law at some unspecified time in the future, or *might* someday contribute to civil unrest.

For this open-ended chore, the FBI set up its Intelligence Division. By the early 1970s, the Intelligence Division had files on over half a million suspected contributors to unrest, crammed with information about their personal lives obtained by informants, undercover agents, and warrantless break-ins to install listening devices or steal papers. Other FBI work disrupted possible dissent by training and paying provocateurs, planting drugs in activists' apartments or cars, sending anonymous letters and press releases, making intimidating and slanderous phone calls, setting off car bombs, harassment arrests, and other "dirty tricks." The FBI titled this array of secret and illegal activities the Counter Intelligence Program (COINTELPRO) and aimed it specifically at black leaders and people opposed to the Vietnam War.[14]

COINTELPRO tactics were fully described in secret FBI memos; agents around the country, including those in Seattle, were ordered to implement them and to report regularly to "The Seat of Government," as FBI Director J. Edgar Hoover's office was known internally.

In full swing during the time of the Chicago 7 and the Seattle 7 trials, COINTELPRO was not widely known until years later, when a 1975 Senate committee pursued a major investigation of the FBI's illegal intelligence practices. However, every antiwar and civil rights activist had felt its presence on a daily basis, and various specific COINTELPRO activities came to light during the Seattle 7 trial.[15]

What drew four of the Seattle 8 from their Cornell University campus in Ithaca, New York, to Seattle? Chapter Two details their individual stories, but Seattle itself, like the FBI, was a leading player in this unfolding drama. Seattle, the largest city in the mountainous upper left hand corner of the United States, was not always the wealthy and worldly purveyor of software, airplanes, caffeine, and the online retail experience that it has become in the early twenty-first century. On the contrary—Seattle had an unruly adolescence of its own. Its politics have always tended to be a little rough around the edges, with a history of activism from both the right and the left.

Anti-immigrant campaigns were launched against Chinese laborers in the 1800s and early- to mid-1900s, sheriff-appointed citizen deputies spied on German-American citizens during World War I, and fake "licenses to hunt" Japanese-Americans circulated around town during World War II. Mirroring this vigilante approach, just a few days before the Seattle 7 trial began, a reporter asked people on the street what they thought about the upcoming trial. One woman responded, "I don't think there should be a trial. They should be shot."[16]

On the left, in the 1912 mayoral election, the Socialist candidate almost won. The Wobblies (Industrial Workers of the World or IWW),[17] the Socialist Party, and the Communist Party have been periodically large and active in both city and state politics. As World War I ended, Seattle's labor organizations led a large, non-violent action, the Seattle General Strike of 1919. A general strike involves far more than walking off the job or picketing one's work site to ask for better pay or working conditions. In a general strike, workers want to change the rules of capitalism. Strikers represent dozens of industries and businesses. They take over the utilities necessary to keep the city's population safe and functioning. Striking workers organize, manage, administer, and perform fire protection, food distribution, hospital services, police services, garbage collection, etc., and they do it using workplace and community democracy. Seattle's general strike was peaceful and lasted for almost a week in 1919.

Future Seattle 7 federal indictees Chip Marshall, Joe Kelly, Jeff Dowd, and Michael Abeles knew about and admired Seattle's history of resistance and its general strike. That is a large part of why, in the winter of 1969, they pointed their "People's Chevy" out of Ithaca and drove west.

Four months later, with their SLF organization in full swing, they, along with Michael Lerner, Susan Stern, and Roger Lippman, already in town, were in jail.

The Seattle 7 and two of their attorneys in the summer of 1970. From left: Michael Abeles, Jeff Steinborn, Roger Lippman, Jeff Dowd, Susan Stern, Joe Kelly, Michael Lerner, Michael Tigar, and Chip Marshall. Susan Stern is holding a photograph of Angela Davis. Missing is Michael Justesen, who went underground rather than stand trial. *Photographer unknown, courtesy Steve Hudziak*

2

Meet the Seattle 8

Seattle remains a frontier metropolis, a place where people can experiment with their lives, and change and grow and make things happen.
—TOM ROBBINS, AUTHOR

Political choices stem from personal experiences. Other than all being white and all but one male, the Seattle 8 were not an atypical group of mid-twentieth-century American teenagers and twenty-somethings. Some grew up in well-off families, others were not so well-off; some enjoyed stable parental marriages, others were children of divorce. A few had actively left-wing parents; the rest were raised in quietly apolitical homes. Most grew up in small to medium-sized cities, with fathers employed in business, social services, teaching, and the law.

SUSAN STERN

In the summer of 1966, Syracuse University graduates and newlyweds Susan and Robby Stern drove west across the United States on Interstate 90. The highway bridges the Mississippi, unrolls across the flat plains of South Dakota, up and over the Rockies in Montana and Idaho, and finally winds through the Cascades down into Seattle. The only major U.S. city named for a Native American chief, Seattle is precariously sited between earthquake fault lines and active volcanos. Perched on steep hills that slide down to mostly rocky beaches, edged with ancient conifers, glacial lakes, and the frigid waters of Puget Sound, Seattle was a blue and green revelation to the Sterns. "The rising and falling of the young and wild Pacific Northwest greeted my eyes like no scenery I'd ever seen," Susan wrote. "Everywhere were green-blue fir trees and lush golden-green foliage, endless mountains and valleys sparkling under a clear blue sky. It was vast and pure and vividly beautiful."[1]

Susan and Robby arrived in Seattle with little more than admission letters to the University of Washington law school for Robby and the UW master's program in social work for Susan. They knew nobody in town.

They had married a year earlier in New York in an elaborate ceremony documented by high-society photographer Bradford Bachrach, all paid for by Susan's alternately generous and abusive father. It was the same year she'd had her first illegal abortion. They could have attended graduate schools closer to home, but three thousand miles from family entanglements, Seattle offered the Sterns plenty of space and time to become the kind of people they wanted to be.

Susan Stern did not have a happy childhood. Born in 1943 in Brooklyn, New York, the eldest of two children, she grew up in New Jersey. Her father was a successful Jewish businessman with a "violent temper and a taste for manipulation."[2] Susan was nine years old when her parents divorced; her father continued to both abuse and spoil her, leaving her with an uncertain sense of self-worth and a lack of trust in other people. Her father raised her to feel "stupid and ugly."[3] Believing she belonged nowhere, she never lost that teenage desire to be part of the coolest gang around.

Robby Stern grew up in Charlotte, North Carolina, surrounded by harrowing stories of his parents' escape from Germany two weeks before *Kristallnacht*. His parents were survivors, but not his grandparents. Residual fear and timidity haunted his childhood and sensitized him to the racism he saw around him every day. Moving north to Syracuse University, he discovered that oppression and racism were not limited to the South. He had to respond, and in doing so, he learned that he had a knack for political organizing. He was good at encapsulating issues and engaging supporters.

Susan, admiring this tall and articulate man, watched and learned from his ability to draw a crowd, to sway people, to get their attention, to make a difference. She wanted to do, to be, the same. In the fall of 1965 she had a chance of her own when she taught sixth grade in a ghetto school in Syracuse. But it was chaotic and the children did not respond well to her uncertain methods. She left early, full of anger at a system that created such disastrous educational experiences for children and teachers alike. It was one more reason to get away.

As the couple settled into the Pacific Northwest, they noticed that Seattle had more than beautiful scenery. Hippies. Street people. Coffee shops. Hanging around University Way near the UW campus, these Seattle people seemed so relaxed, so happy, so non-judgmental. Susan was immediately entranced by their colorful tie-dyed clothing, their music and laughter, and the way the air around them was perfumed with patchouli and marijuana. She didn't yet know what kind of person she wanted to become in Seattle, but she liked the idea that there were choices like that.

She began sampling the hippie music scene. She joined a band called *Suspended Purple* (she had an excellent singing voice), and played small venues around town, once opening for *Big Brother and the Holding Company,* whose singer Janis Joplin hadn't yet become famous. As Robby became more involved in antiwar activities on campus and around town, Susan occasionally joined in, but not at the expense of her class schedule or her role as Mrs. Robby Stern. That didn't change much until early 1968, when she read Betty Friedan's 1963 manifesto *The Feminine Mystique.* She devoured the book: "It was the first time in my life that I'd ever taken a personal interest in anything."[4]

Stern was the first Seattle 8 alleged conspirator to arrive from out-of-town. The only woman among them, she weighed under a hundred pounds. Her dark, wavy, shoulder-length hair was sometimes cut shorter, sometimes with bangs, and sometimes not. She wore glasses with large frames that emphasized her tiny size. In her later mug shots she appears tired, spent, looking inwards, slightly troubled.

Susan Stern protesting the war shortly after moving to Seattle. *Photo by Fred Lonidier*

Roger Lippman

The least dramatic of the Seattle 8, and the one who least sought the spotlight, Roger Lippman is a native Seattleite. In 1963, when Lippman was sixteen, his father moved the family to Sacramento, California, where he became an advisor on policy issues related to children with cognitive disabilities (then referred to as "mentally retarded"). The move was an unpleasant eye-opener for Lippman: Sacramento was "soulless, awful, ugly, desert, four gas stations on the corner where we lived." Even worse, "California state requirements for high school graduation included a civics class. I'd already had the book in a previous course in Seattle so I objected when they wanted me to take it again in the summer. That opened my eyes. Teachers were stupid; I just hated the school. I fell in with the liberal kids and we became radicals together."[5]

In Sacramento, Lippman also was only eighty miles from the Free Speech Movement's large rallies, sit-ins, and mass arrests on the University of California's Berkeley campus, and even closer to the growing efforts of California farm workers to secure decent wages and working conditions. He became much more politicized there "than I would have been in sleepy Seattle."[6]

In 1965 Lippman entered Reed College, a small liberal arts college in Portland, Oregon. Reed is known for attracting smart, intellectual, self-motivated, often iconoclastic students, and it rewards those students with a great deal of academic and social latitude. Lippman, a chemistry major, found himself becoming less interested in chemistry and more interested in history. Like many college students in the late 1960s, he was opposed to the U.S. presence in Vietnam. Gradually, his antiwar work took more of his time than his classwork. He became editor of an SDS regional newspaper based in Portland called *The Agitator*. By the end of his junior year, he had dropped out of Reed and moved back to Seattle, where he worked full time on local and national antiwar activities including draft counseling and SDS organizing on and off the University of Washington campus. By this time, SDS had chapters on hundreds of campuses, fulltime organizers crisscrossing the country, a national weekly newspaper *New Left Notes*, and a busy central office in Chicago.

Like all young men not in school, he knew he'd soon be receiving his own draft notice. When he did, Lippman joined approximately half a million other young men who refused induction over the course of the Vietnam War. Doing so was a high-stakes form of protest, trumped only by those who joined the Army and then organized against the war from within, or who went AWOL (absent without leave) after becoming soldiers.[7] In Seattle, Lippman's draft counseling "brought in a lot of high school seniors, especially from working-class families, a number of whom ended up going to the university. And we

Seattle 7 defendant Roger Lippman (on right) advocating resistance to the draft in a protest at the Selective Service (draft board) office in Seattle in 1968. *Photo by Fred Lonidier*

worked with others from the community who were facing the draft who were not necessarily totally politicized, but were in the objective situation of facing the war in Vietnam. So we had a scene there with a good number of people."[8]

In the group photo of the Seattle 7 defendants, Roger Lippman is the thin, somewhat uneasy looking guy with black-framed glasses. He often wore a red bandana tied around his forehead to hold back his shoulder-length dark hair. One SLF member likened him to the nerdy, not-cool guy in high school, "he loved to slink around and be mysterious. Everything was hush hush."[9] He had a reputation for seriousness, and for understanding Marxism and Maoism better than anybody—people would take their political questions to him. He saw himself as an on-the-ground organizer with a strong theoretical foundation.

MICHAEL LERNER

In 1968, Michael Lerner, a hulking twenty-four-year-old with shoulder-length curly hair and black plastic-rimmed glasses, was in San Francisco. A Marxist philosopher working on his PhD in philosophy (dissertation title: *Justification for Democracy: The Marxist Perspective*), he'd been hired to teach at San Francisco State, but students there had shut down the school to protest the firing of a teaching assistant who was a member of the Black Panther Party and outspokenly opposed to the Vietnam War.

Lerner began to look for a campus that wasn't on strike and could offer him a place to teach and organize. He was eager to try out his specific ideas for creating a community-based, socialist-leaning antiwar movement. It would be an organization with strong roots among workers and middle-class families. Students would be an important part, but it would not be primarily a student organization. Nor would it be a traditional Marxist workers' organization. It would reflect what he wanted America to become, a sensible, committed, productive, middle-class model of social justice and responsible internationalism.

Lerner grew up thinking he was entitled to speak and be heard. His father was an Appeals Court Judge in Newark, New Jersey. Lerner attended both private and public schools, as well as Hebrew school. He was not shy about the fact that one of his college admissions recommendations was written by family friend John F. Kennedy. Lerner graduated from Columbia University in 1964, and then went west to UC Berkeley for graduate school.

At Berkeley in the mid-1960s, Lerner met Tom Hayden and Jerry Rubin, both of whom were nationally known antiwar activists. But Lerner wanted to be more of a top dog than he could be in activist-infested Berkeley. When the University of Washington offered him a one-year contract as a visiting assistant professor starting in fall 1969, he took it, not so much because he thought the UW was a good school but because he thought Seattle was just the sort of city to give him room to try out his organizing ideas: "I'd never been to Seattle. I had no idea what it was like. But I thought, well, it's a fairly good university. It's not sort of top tier. I was still thinking that maybe I would be a successful academic and use that position to influence politics. I had the intention from the start of trying to create something."[10]

Lerner's UW philosophy classes were hugely popular. As word of mouth spread about this radical young professor from Berkeley who talked about revolution and Marxism, students dropped other classes and rearranged their schedules to enroll. Women in particular gravitated to the smooth-talking, self-assured Lerner. One Seattle woman, whose previous claim to fame was as a Daffodil Princess in the Puyallup Daffodil Festival, recalls the start of her affair with Lerner: "We were watching TV with a bunch of people and the news was showing all these body bags being brought back from Vietnam, and I started crying. Lerner said something like 'How can you live your middle-class life with this going on?' I was hooked."[11] Another woman put Lerner's style slightly differently, "He pontificated—you didn't have casual conversations with him."[12]

Assistant professor of philosophy and about-to-become Seattle 7 defendant Michael Lerner addressing an antiwar rally on the University of Washington campus. *MOHAI, Seattle Post-Intelligencer Collection, 2000.107.112.21.01, Dave Potts, photographer*

Lerner had not yet met any of his future fellow alleged conspirators. He was, however, successfully building a base of students for his new organizational ideas. He was just waiting for the right moment, the right spark, to go public. He already knew what he wanted to call his new organization: the Seattle Liberation Front.

MICHAEL JUSTESEN

Michael Justesen chose to go underground rather than stand trial, reducing the Seattle 8 to the Seattle 7. He is only a shadow in this story. He represents another dissenting choice—one that many considered but only a few took.

Justesen grew up in Seattle and was raised by his mother when his parents split up. He was a 1968, B-plus graduate of a large public high school that drew from mostly white neighborhoods. With his short, light-colored hair and regular features, he looked no different from hundreds of other young Seattleites of Nordic heritage.

He was introduced to politics by the catcher on his school's baseball team. The catcher told him about black American revolutionaries such as Huey Newton, Eldridge Cleaver, and other Black Panthers. Justesen was impressed by the fact that there were such people in the United States. The more he learned about racism, the more he began to see connections among racism, capitalism, and the American presence in Vietnam.[13]

Justesen entered the UW in 1968 and quickly became good friends with Roger Lippman—comrades may be the better word—as they bonded over their serious study of historical and contemporary anti-capitalist, anti-imperialist revolutions around the world. They were not as focused on personal growth, drugs, or sex as many of their peers were. They were more occupied with the global political picture and wanted nothing more than to act decisively on the side of the oppressed.

Justesen lived for a time in the Wallingford neighborhood house rented by Susan and Robby Stern. Robby found Justesen "very young, very serious, smart and somewhat gruff. He never washed his socks. He just got swept up in all this. I liked him."[14] Another activist remembers Justesen as "quiet, studious, intelligent."[15] He wasn't so quiet, though, as to avoid the notice of both the FBI and the SDS national office leadership. When he spoke up in meetings, he, like Lippman, came across as shrewd, informed, and militant. The FBI added him to their COINTEL-PRO watch list and SDS leaders saw him as a potential rising star.

One way SDS cultivated its leadership was to send individuals abroad to learn from activists in other countries, and to alert those movements that they had allies inside the United States. This exchange helped cement the perception of a connected global uprising of the oppressed, which, in those days, seemed to many young, optimistic American radicals to be the world's inescapable destiny. Justesen was sent to Tokyo in August 1969 to attend the Second International Anti-Imperialist Conference. He met with a number of student activists and workers who were engaged in violent street demonstrations and huge student strikes at over two hundred Japanese university campuses. Justesen learned that the Japanese students were copying tactics from the Chinese Red Guard, including mentally brutal criticism/self-criticism sessions that were shortly to be adopted wholesale by Weatherman when SDS splintered apart.

In Japan, Justesen also saw some of the street fighting tactics the students there had developed, including wearing helmets, carrying sticks, and performing a snake dance move in which protesters linked arms and whipped around in snakelike patterns, making it difficult to separate and arrest individuals. Justesen came back to Seattle where he wrote and gave talks about the good work being done across the Pacific. Eight months later, when he was indicted for conspiracy, he was nineteen years old.

◆

Susan Stern, Roger Lippman, Michael Lerner, and Michael Justesen were living and working in Seattle before the rest of the Seattle 8 arrived from Ithaca at the end of December 1969. Seattle and Ithaca, 2,700 miles apart, are hardly sister cities, nor are their respective universities, the UW and Cornell, twin material. Yet in late 1969 and into 1970, dozens of college and high school students from Ithaca drove their used Chevys, Fords, and VW vans west to Seattle. They were were attracted by stories of Seattle's mountains and waters, its friendly bars, hippie culture, its left-wing history, and its economic reliance on Boeing's military contracts, a ripe target for antiwar protests. Besides, as the Sterns had noticed, it was far off in that northwest corner, thousands of miles away from the strictures of one's upbringing.

For many of these young people the trip out west included a detour south to check out San Francisco's fabled music, drug, and protest scene. But, as Michael Lerner had discovered, San Francisco was already too crowded. As one of the Ithaca-to-Seattle migrants said, "Part of the attraction of Seattle was that the antiwar scene there was not as ideologically hidebound [as San Francisco's] and might benefit by an injection of new blood."[16]

The vanguard of the Ithaca emigrants were two Cornell graduates—draft resisters, wannabe cowboys, SDS organizers, and good friends Chip Marshall and Joe Kelly. The timing was providential—Ithaca had become a good place for them to leave.

Kelly, Marshall, and their high school buddy Jeff Dowd had criminal trespass charges pending against them for scaling a chain link fence on the Cornell campus and painting antiwar and peace slogans on a Navy ROTC artillery gun.[17] They asked the judge if they could cut a deal—erase the charges and they'd leave Ithaca for at least a year. The judge thought he was doing his town and his court docket a big favor, so he agreed to the plan. The travelers used their returned bail money to buy gas for the trip west.

JOE KELLY

Joe Kelly grew up in rural upstate New York, where his father worked as chauffeur and manager on Random Farm, a five-hundred acre country estate. Kelly has happy childhood memories of living there, "It was a great place to grow up and where I started hunting with a .22 and terrier dogs."[18]

Kelly's parents were both Irish immigrants and neither graduated from high school. Kelly senior was a self-educated, inveterate reader who had been a member of the Communist Party, but quit over a doctrinal disagreement. His son recalls, "It was very easy for me to be involved in the antiwar movement. [My dad] always encouraged a social conscience… He told me at a young age, 'Son, you're not military material. You don't take orders very well.'"[19] A friend later described Kelly as "Irish, like his dad. Revolution is in his blood."[20] Smart and friendly, with blue eyes and curly hair, he was affable and caring, enthusiastic without being preachy, like a favorite big brother. One woman SLF member described Kelly as "outgoing, with a big feminine side" but "stronger than you can ever imagine. He just keeps going."[21]

As a young teenager, Kelly once had trouble with the mechanics of his hunting rifle, so he took it to his middle school shop class to see if his teacher could help him fix it. No one batted an eye, and the gun was repaired as part of a class project. Kelly thought a major plus of moving to Seattle was its proximity to large animal hunting opportunities in the forests and mountains of Washington State, British Columbia, and Alaska.

While at Cornell, Kelly, like Roger Lippman at Reed, was struck by the organizing potential presented by the existence of the draft and the overwhelming likelihood of draftees ending up in the swamps of Vietnam. He quickly became part of a long-standing and active New York draft resistance movement. When he returned his own draft card to the Selective Service with a letter explaining his refusal to enter the armed forces, he attracted FBI notice and was called before a grand jury, where he recalled realizing the gravity of his situation:

> Oh shit, this is getting serious. The grand jury process sucks. You lose all of your rights right away. We had legal advice saying, 'Don't tell them anything. Take the Fifth Amendment. Don't tell them anything.' It made me realize that there were going to be consequences for what we were doing, but I wasn't afraid. My father taught me a lot about 'No Fear.' Once I made the commitment to turn my draft card in, I mentally prepared myself, I'm probably going to do eighteen months to two years in jail. Once you come to that conclusion in your own mind and your own heart, it's a kind of freedom, like, 'Okay, now what have you got? I'm not really afraid anymore.'[22]

Continuing to publicly protest the war at Cornell, Kelly was contacted by two local FBI agents. Could they come talk to him? Kelly said fine, and arranged a meeting outside the Cornell library, where he had hidden friends with cameras behind nearby bushes. When the agents showed up, his laughing friends jumped out and began snapping pictures of the agents. Confused and angry, the agents hurriedly retreated. Their memo about the incident characterizes Kelly as uncooperative and hostile.

MICHAEL ABELES

Michael Abeles (pronounced "Ables"), the bright and sociable nineteen-year-old son of a Buffalo, New York, tavern owner, entered Cornell as a freshman in 1968, Kelly's junior year. In high school Abeles had been editor of his school paper and governor of the New York State Kiwanis Key Club. The Key Club's pledge, recited seriously and ceremoniously by Abeles, was:

> I pledge, on my honor,
> to uphold the Objects of Key Club International;
> to build my home, school and community;

to serve my nation and God;
and combat all forces which tend to undermine these institutions.

Abeles showed up on campus short-haired and as conventional as they come. That didn't last long, as he began partying with the other guys in his dorm, including Huey Lewis, soon to form his band *Huey Lewis and the News*. Abeles also became friends with Jeff Dowd, the other teenager among the Ithaca-to-Seattle crowd. Always ready with a joint and a joke, they were both tall, sturdy teenagers with loud voices and curly hair, like Kelly's, that corkscrewed out into imposing afros.

Abeles has been frequently described by his friends and comrades as a sweet guy, a term not applied to any of the other Seattle defendants. There aren't long stories about him, he wasn't a front man or a strategic thinker. But he was quick to identify injustice and to speak out against unfairness. He was also funny and impetuous, always around and ready for action, "a kid, the sidekick, a good-spirited foot soldier."[23] His political style didn't progress much beyond "wav[ing] his fists in the air and advocate[ing] total mayhem."[24]

He also liked the seemingly unlimited access to women and to drugs, recalling, "I was a really smart kid and then drugs got in the way, I was really smart and then really stupid. I thought I was pretty cool, but then the whole women's liberation stuff came up."[25] After Lerner, Abeles is the most criticized for his male chauvinism and taking endless advantage of the women in the movement, although one woman SLF member noted that it wasn't hard to ward off his advances with a sharp elbow to the ribs.

JEFF DOWD

Jeff Dowd, like Joe Kelly, has a radical parental pedigree. Dowd's stepfather was Paul Sweezy, the Harvard-educated Marxist economist and founding editor of *Monthly Review* magazine. His father was Douglas Dowd, an economics professor and author of the 1997 *Blues for America*. Dowd senior was outspokenly against the Vietnam War. When Black Panther Eldridge Cleaver ran for president in 1968 on the Peace and Freedom Party ticket, the elder Dowd was one of Cleaver's vice-presidential running mates (he had several, running in different states).

Jeff Dowd is big enough to be physically intimidating (as Judge Boldt was to discover during the Seattle 7 trial) and could shift from friendly to intimidating and back again in an adolescent minute. He had, and still has, a creative, theatrical, goofy bent that allows, even encourages, him to say and do things in public that most people wouldn't consider, let alone actually do. A friend described Dowd as "brilliant in flashes, other times idiotic. He was the wild idea guy."[26] One of his girlfriends said, "Jeff never envisioned himself having an ordinary life. He had two speeds, full speed ahead or comatose."[27] A raconteur who lives his good stories as well as tells them, it is not surprising that he inspired The Dude in *The Big Lebowski*.

Dowd has this slant on why he and his Ithaca buddies decided to go to Seattle:

> We wanted to go to the West Coast for the reasons many of us are on the West Coast, from decades of people going to the West Coast, right? We went to a rundown farmhouse in upstate New York for a weekend trying to figure out where we'd go. We wanted to go someplace where we could organize and also live. So we went through a bunch of cities. We didn't consider San Diego very much. On paper, San Jose was very good—working class, this, that and the other thing. But we'd heard the Dionne Warwick Bacharach song and we didn't want to go to San Jose. Portland, we somehow didn't consider.
>
> The great place on paper was Honolulu. Working class. Military bases. Partially Third World, etcetera. But we couldn't picture it, going to Hawaii to organize, and sending postcards back saying, 'Okay, we're ready to go. Let us know when the revolution is ready and we'll kick in our shit.' You know, we just couldn't justify saying we were organizing in Honolulu.
>
> So Seattle on paper looked really, really good. We knew nobody there, though, there was zero personal connection. But on paper…Of course, you had the whole working class Wobblies background and the Seattle Strike. But small enough town, you know. That's the other thing. Seattle wasn't intimidating like the Bay Area. And Los Angeles was out of the fucking question.
>
> We decided to go to Seattle. Knew nobody. Arrived on December 30, 1969, with ten cents, which we blew on a wrong number.[28]

Chip Marshall

Charles Clark Marshall III grew up in a liberal family in conservative, suburban Camp Hill, Pennsylvania, just across the Susquehanna River from downtown Harrisburg. His first fistfight was on his elementary school playground—as a second-grader defending his right to support the Democrat Adlai Stevenson over war hero Republican Dwight Eisenhower in the upcoming presidential election.

In the local high school, he partied and hung out with black kids because he liked their music. In 1963 he went to the rally in Washington, DC, where he heard Martin Luther King Jr. give his "I Have a Dream" speech: "And that had a pretty big impact. [But at Cornell the next year, it] was pretty much just a jock/party boy kind of thing. I was still sort of interested in things, but not much had happened. I saw one demonstration—probably in 1965—about six people walking around complaining about Vietnam, and I had no idea what they were talking about. So I started looking into it."[29]

Marshall joined VISTA in his sophomore year, where he was trained in community organizing by Saul Alinsky to do voter registration in the South.[30] He became friends with Stokely Carmichael, then the national chairman of SNCC. "I think I was the last white person to actually work with SNCC," he joked. Marshall was attracted to articulate leaders and became one himself. One of the SLF women later said that Marshall created a "hierarchical distance" between himself and her; she didn't know if he discounted her because she was a woman, or because he was so wrapped up in being The Leader.[31]

Marshall grew out his dark hair and had a droopy mustache that gave him a slightly Che Guevara appearance. He and Joe Kelly cut their antiwar and anti-racism teeth on the Cornell campus. They supported the California farmworkers' strike and boycott and physically helped protect black students as they occupied Willard Straight Hall to demand an end to the university's discriminatory practices.

Seattle's history of Wobblies and strikes was attractive to Marshall:

> Like I say, one of the reasons we picked Seattle was because we knew it had a history. And, of course, being New Lefties, we loved the Wobblies, because they seemed a little cooler than just regular Commies. And, as you know, unfortunately in the 1960s, being cool was just about as important as being politically correct.

We'd never actually been to Seattle. We got there on the last day of 1969, and we had the name of Susan Stern and the Blue Moon Tavern. So, on New Year's Eve, we went to the Blue Moon Tavern. There were hippies dancing naked on the bar. And we went, "Hmmm. This looks like a good place to start." So that's how we got to Seattle...We wanted to break away and do something different from what Weatherman was doing.[32]

The distinction between Weatherman and the Seattle Liberation Front was clear to some, but not to the Department of Justice or the FBI. This misunderstanding was to hang over the Seattle 7 conspiracy trial like a never-ending Pacific Northwest rain cloud.

3

Seattle Needs Liberating

The Seattle Liberation Front was one of the last New Left organizations, drawing hundreds of new people into the Movement at a time when almost everywhere else in the country was falling apart.
—ANN FARRAR, SAN FRANCISCO AREA ACTIVIST AND JOURNALIST, 1970

The news media called summer 1967 the "Summer of Love," as cities around the country sprouted free clinics, head shops (selling marijuana and hash accoutrements), free concerts, peace rallies, underground newspapers, natural food grocery stores, and whole neighborhoods filled with long-haired young people, hippies dressed in tie-dyed clothes, sandals, and beads. Hippies were also moving to the countryside, trying their hands at farming and communal living. Hitchhiking was a common and accepted mode of travel. Travelers could easily find the hippie part of town and a temporary couch or a mattress in a friendly house. Sex was called "free love" as the use of contraceptives spread. HIV did not yet exist and heroin, cocaine, ecstasy, and their many derivatives were not hippie drugs of choice. Utopia was clearly at hand.

But it was not to last. The year 1968 brought the assassinations of Robert Kennedy and Martin Luther King Jr. Nonviolent protesters were tear-gassed and clubbed at the Chicago Democratic National Convention and student strikes and building occupations disrupted dozens of university campuses. The following year was riven by the violence of SDS/Weatherman's October "Days of Rage" demonstration, the police killings of sleeping Chicago Black Panther leaders Fred Hampton and Mark Clark, the killing by Hells Angels security guards of a fan at the Rolling Stones' Bay Area free concert, and the murder spree by Charles Manson's followers in Los Angeles. It was no longer possible to pretend that flowers, beads, music, and marijuana could prevent seriously bad things from happening.

When SDS leadership christened themselves Weathermen and gravitated to more violent action in late 1969 and early 1970, they abandoned the tens of thousands of their members who were still active in campus and mass-based antiwar work, and who had no intention of becoming underground bombers or street fighters. Joe Kelly and Chip Marshall, initially loyal to the new direction of Weatherman, spent the summer of 1969 helping to organize what was to be the group's last aboveground action—the October 8–11 Days of Rage in Chicago.[1]

By summer's end, Kelly and Marshall were more convinced than ever that an entirely different strategy was needed. Kelly described their experience:

> So the Weathermen approached Chip and me about coming to Chicago to help organize for the Days of Rage demonstration, "Come and help us organize gang kids, white gang kids in Chicago."
>
> We said, "Boy, that sounds great. Yeah, we can do that."
>
> So, at first we were in, in for a nickel, in for a dime. We didn't realize what we were getting hooked into. We were in the collectives and, you know, collective discipline and criticism/self-criticism. And some pretty crazy politics, which we termed "fight the people."
>
> The idea was that we'd prove ourselves by getting into a big fight with some blue-collar kids, as if that would show what tough revolutionaries we were. It made no sense to me. But that's what Weatherman did. They thought they were training themselves to be a white fighting force inside America. They had delusions of grandeur about how many people were going to buy into this idea.
>
> You've got to give them an awful lot of credit for guts and courage, but I just didn't agree with where they thought the whole thing was going.[2]

The decision about whether or not to engage in violence may be made, unmade, and re-made over the life of a movement, and over the lives of individual dissidents. Those like Mahatma Gandhi, Fathers Daniel and Philip Berrigan, or Martin Luther King Jr., who maintained a nonviolent stance throughout their long struggles are much admired but rarely imitated. More common is a protest movement that begins peacefully, but as frustration mounts over lack of progress, some members are swept into angry violence.

Many but not all Weathermen have since written and spoken against their own turns to violence. Mark Rudd, an early Weatherman, noted in a 2016 interview, "Given that Americans have been taught that all non-state violence is either mentally ill or criminal, it's hard to argue that it helps build the mass movement we need…My general take is that anyone advocating political violence is either very stupid or a cop, or both."[3]

Future Seattle 7 defendants Jeff Dowd, Chip Marshall, and Michael Abeles drove to Seattle in December 1969 in The People's Chevy, a blue 1962 Chevrolet Biscayne that Joe Kelly bought in Ithaca with $250 in pooled money. After all the planning, Kelly couldn't make the trip because he had court dates in Chicago from an arrest that summer.[4] He wasn't able to join his comrades in Seattle until early spring 1970, after which he had to go back to Chicago in June and July to serve jail time.

The People's Chevy acquired its name after someone broke off the key in the ignition so anyone could start it. The gas gauge didn't work, so the rule was that every driver had to put two dollars of fuel in the tank. With its big fins and orange and black New York license plates, it was easy for the FBI to keep tabs on its drivers and locations, and they did. Later, parked in front of a known SLF house, it was firebombed, possibly by Seattle police, either rogue or not. The fire department put the fire out, but not until the upholstery was a charred and smoking mess. Still, the car ran, so Kelly threw out the smoldering seats, drove it through a car wash with the windows open, tossed in a few cheap Army surplus mattresses and everyone kept on driving.

Marshall, Abeles, and Dowd shared the ride out west with Jane Smith, who had been recruited into the Seattle move by Marshall and Kelly. She was to become Susan Stern's best friend and a key member of the defense collective during the Seattle 7 trial.

The crew drove first to Chicago, where Smith's parents lived and where they dropped off Kelly for his court dates. Smith's parents, who had paid for the insurance on The People's Chevy, cried as they saw their daughter off, upset about the boys' appearance, "Those boys had hair out to *here!*" Later, when the FBI visited the Smiths to ask them where their daughter was, they responded, "That's your job."[5]

To Chip Marshall and the other Seattle newcomers, the Pacific Northwest still had a whiff of the Wild West to it. On the drive out, Michael Abeles had picked up a stray puppy that he named Etta, after the Katherine Ross character in their favorite film, *Butch Cassidy and the Sundance Kid,* a charming and romantic 1969 tale of two cheerful but doomed (fans always skip over the "doomed" part) outlaws. "We were East Coast boys who related very heavily to cowboys," Marshall said. "We all had earrings, long hair and boots."[6] A Seattle Liberation Front collective member later said "It was like these people were living their images, not their own lives."[7] Their afros and leather jackets made even the teenaged Abeles look frighteningly revolutionary and terminally cool.

After detouring to San Francisco for a few days, the group arrived almost penniless in Seattle at the end of December 1969. The travelers discovered that Abeles, with his cheerful smile and awkwardly large plaster cast (he had broken his leg hiking on Mount Tamalpais while tripping on LSD), was perfectly dressed for street corner panhandling, especially since it was the holiday season. Having the puppy Etta around added to his charm, and to the take.

Jane Smith, though, was disgusted with their living arrangements, crashing on the floor of a tiny apartment occupied by a movement contact who was none too happy to have them around. Poor Etta had diarrhea and was vomiting all over; she had distemper and wouldn't survive long. After a few days, Smith went home to Chicago where she worked at the People's Law Office before returning to Seattle several months later.

Roger Lippman, from his perspective as a full-time antiwar organizer already in Seattle, saw the winter arrival of his future fellow alleged conspirators in the context of SDS' split and subsequent disintegration: "So they fell into that vacuum, which was a lot of people looking for something they could do. Plus they were charismatic. Plus things were even more intense than they had been in terms of the political and the war situation, so it all came together rather nicely for them. That's not to deny them credit for what they did, but just to say they were there at the right moment."[8]

Another Seattle organizer, a woman, was particularly sensitive to the Ithacans' macho behavior. She remarked, "Well, I was, of course, very tuned in to the way they treated women, particularly the way they treated me…They didn't respect the people who had been around for a long time. They came in with their group and their ideas and just planted themselves here."[9]

Susan Stern, meeting them in early January 1970, may have agreed with some of that, but to her, Marshall, Dowd, and Abeles "waltzed through a room and left it careening, throbbing with energy and excitement. They were cataclysmic, Chaplinesque, hedonistic and brilliant; young and impetuous, strong, fearless, prudent and irresponsible."[10]

In early January 1970, with the exception of Joe Kelly who was still in Chicago dealing with arrest issues, all of the alleged Seattle conspirators were now in the same metropolitan area. They still hadn't all met each other, and they held conflicting ideas on a few strategic and political issues, but they were all energetic, experienced organizers dedicated to fighting racism and ending the war. Before the month was out, most of them would become founders of the Seattle Liberation Front.

The Seattle Liberation Front's birth (and Count One in their federal indictment) occurred in the student union building on the UW campus, called the Husky Union Building, or the HUB. The HUB was packed that Saturday, January 17, 1970, with hundreds of people—students, police, FBI agents, and informers—all there because Jerry Rubin, Chicago 7 co-defendant and co-founder of the Youth International Party, or Yippies, was in town. Michael Lerner had invited his old Berkeley comrade Rubin to Seattle to speak, hoping it would light a new fire of activism on campus and in the city. Rubin would update the crowd on the news from the Chicago 7 courtroom, including the shackling and gagging of defendant Bobby Seale,[11] and generally galvanize the crowd. Lerner was hoping Rubin's appearance would kick-start his own organizational plans. "I was waiting for the right moment to bring people together, and to form an organization around some of the ideas that I had…The meeting was definitely the biggest political event that wasn't a demonstration that had happened in Seattle for a long, long time."[12]

Hearing that Chicago 7 defendant and Yippie leader Jerry Rubin was going to speak, Abeles, Dowd, and Marshall, having been in town not quite three weeks, decided to attend. They also had a good idea about what they wanted to do in Seattle and this seemed like the right place to start. Marshall noted, "We were not into Weatherman's violence or terrorism and stuff like that. I mean, I always felt it was kind of chickenshit myself. If you're going to fight somebody at least go fight them face-to-face. Don't do a bomb and run away…Here in Seattle we wanted to go wide. We were not interested in being the vanguard. We wanted to be the majority."[13]

Rubin, known for presenting his politics in a creative and provocative wrapping, succeeded in entertaining and re-energizing much of his large audience with statements like: "if you're still in college today, you haven't done enough. Because if you had, you'd have been thrown out by now."[14]

Everyone was fired up, and agreed to meet again two days later to plan some local action. Jeff Dowd recalled the meeting:

> We didn't know anybody, at this point, in town. And the Weathermen people were there, too, and they sang this stupid song about pigs to a Beatles' tune and they're just like pathetic children making fools of themselves.
>
> So Chip [Marshall] gets up there and gives a speech about this is what we should all do and how we should come together. Rubin was talking about planning these demonstrations called The Day After around the country…What Chip tried to do that day in the HUB was to raise the bar about what a movement could be.[15]

Michael Lerner and his adoring students were no competition for the protest-hardened cowboys from Ithaca. Lerner was blindsided by Marshall's persuasive clarity and friendly manner. In retrospect, he described Marshall as a "people-pleaser," a person who gave Lerner the impression that he supported his ideas, but who in fact had very different plans for organizing in Seattle.

For his part, Marshall thought Lerner's Marxist perspective was "pretty interesting":

> But a lot of our people thought he was just too liberal, not hardcore enough. But I was thinking this guy seems to have something going. So he and I started chatting and became kind of friends. And then, as a group, a bunch of us formed this thing called the Seattle Liberation Front…and unlike most SDS people, we definitely pushed the lifestyle and the music. And all our publicity and everything was focused so it would appeal more to the masses, the people who were growing their hair long and so on.[16]

Lerner remembers meeting Marshall:

> I was approached at the end of the event by a Chip Marshall. Chip had just arrived in town, he said, a few days before…and he convinced me that he had something to offer to this whole thing, and that he could possibly be my ally in it.

He reassured me that everything I said was totally what he wanted to do. But unfortunately, he turned out to be like many liberal Democratic politicians I know, who say yes to everyone. But a lovely person.

He also said, "Oh, and I've got some other people that I came with." And I said, "Terrific."[17]

And so the Seattle Liberation Front was born. Lerner envisioned it as similar to an SDS chapter with hundreds of members, but better and smarter than what he'd experienced in Berkeley:

But Marshall convinced me that we should do collectives, in which people would be more closely connected with each other, and work together. And I thought, well, I don't really have anything against that idea, even though I had been in this collective with Tom Hayden [in Berkeley] and it didn't work out too well for me, because Tom had all the power...On the other hand, Marshall's idea of small groups could be a way of intensifying people's commitment.

So the first SLF collective was called Sundance after the revolutionary energy of the Sundance Kid in that movie *Butch Cassidy and the Sundance Kid*. And I said, "Wait a minute. That's not exactly what I had in mind."

But Chip and his friends' response was, "You want to have something that excites people in their own culture. You can't just be into your own ideas, Michael." And so I thought, all right, Sundance. We're calling ourselves Sundance. So then we have this first meeting. About 200 or 250 people showed up...people were very excited and they formed all these different collectives. So it seemed like, great, something is happening.[18]

An FBI agent present summarized the meeting: "A strange new unity had been formed among campus radicals at this meeting. SDS Weathermen were replaced by the Seattle Liberation Front in the eyes of the great majority of campus radicals. They were looking toward LERNER, MARSHALL and DOWD [capitalization in original] as the vanguard of the revolutionary movement in Seattle." Roger Lippman, a Weatherman supporter who could see which way the wind was blowing, knew it too, and he "made a successful effort to ally the Weathermen with the SLF," noted the agent's memo.[19]

Marshall's friendly but firm communication and debating skills would come to the fore ten months later in the Seattle 7 courtroom. As one friend put it, Marshall "knew when to use logic and when to put his foot on the gas." He also worked well in small groups; he "knew how to convince people that this [antiwar work] was something worth getting involved in."[20] He knew how to rouse a crowd and how to calm it down, and he would deftly use humor to defuse the opposition. "Sometimes, though," one SLF woman member noted, "he was so smooth that I questioned his sincerity."[21]

Many of Lerner's students found themselves attracted more to Marshall's vision than to Lerner's. They liked the idea of forming and naming their own collective, and then defining and running their own projects. One of Lerner's philosophy students remembers:

> [I felt] way over my head in being asked to help found this new organization. When Chip [Marshall] and Jeff [Dowd] showed up, it was an immense relief…But one of our first meetings of the Red Avengers collective was a complete fiasco. Lerner had proselytized that collective members needed to get over their sexual hang-ups and secret longings for one another by having some sort of group sexual experience. After that, with secret sexual longings out of the way, one could get down to business better. I thought this was a pile. The collective meeting degenerated into an aborted game of strip poker. What a joke. I've heard that the Weatherman took this nonsense seriously, with bad psychic results for them.[22]

After a few missteps like that, the SLF collective structure gained momentum and its margins became looser, more diffuse. Collectives popped up in old houses and student apartments on Capitol Hill, Eastlake, around the University District, and in North Seattle. They adopted political names like Red Avengers, East is Red, The West is Dead, Stonerage, Tupamaros, Long Time Coming, and more. One woman SLF member recalled, "It was very chaotic a lot of the time. There's a whole learning curve on how to live and work with a lot of people. It was a very interesting time for all of us. And a lot of us were still in school and/or had jobs."[23]

The collectives' projects overlapped the living arrangements, so some people who participated in a project didn't necessarily live in that collective's house, and others who lived in collective houses didn't participate in their project. The more SLF broke away from Weatherman's sternly militaristic line, the more inviting and vigorous it became. It was this, perhaps, that particularly attracted the attention of the Department of Justice people in the other Washington—no other campus-based antiwar movement had a strategy to address the needs of its city's unemployed or those without healthcare or housing in addition to protesting the war and supporting the local black community. SLF approached this broader constituency with seriousness, humor, and energy.

A fifteen-point program for the launch of the Seattle Liberation Front was hastily written after the January meeting at the UW student union. Lerner was surprised to find that the version he thought he had approved was not quite the version that came back from the printers:

> We announced that we were going to create this organization—and I had developed a program of 10 or 12 points...Meanwhile, these two young people from the group that Chip had brought from Ithaca, said, "Oh, we'll take the program and we'll get it printed up."
>
> And I said, "Fine."
>
> And they said, "And yeah, we'll put some graphics on it and like that."
>
> They were Jeff Dowd and

Front cover of SLF Program for Action. This mimeographed twelve-page, two-color version swings between hardcore revolutionary icons and hippie cartoons, marijuana references, and song lyrics of the times. *Courtesy Zels Johnson*

Michael Abeles, two young kids. So about two weeks later, they come forward with this program, and suddenly, there's points in there that I had not ever agreed to and had not been presented to the people at that first meeting; and with drawings on it that were exactly the opposite of the message that I wanted. There were guns and there was all this super-macho bullshit.[24]

The printed Program for Action of the newly launched Seattle Liberation Front read as follows:

> The people of Seattle desire human solidarity, cultural freedom and peace.
> 1. We shall create our revolutionary culture everywhere.

2. We shall resist the destruction of our physical environment.
3. We must turn the schools into training grounds for liberation.
4. We will destroy the university unless it serves the people.
5. We will struggle against imperialism.
6. We must show working class people that the international struggle for socialism is their struggle as well.
7. We will struggle for the full liberation of women as a necessary part of the revolutionary struggle.
8. We will take communal responsibility for basic human needs.
9. We must protect and expand our drug culture.
10. We must break the power of the landlords and provide beautiful housing for all.
11. We will tax the corporations, not the working people.
12. We will defend ourselves against law and order.
13. We must transform ourselves into more loving and more committed human beings.
14. We must begin to create the machinery for a people's government.
15. We will unite with blacks and other movements throughout the world to destroy this motherfucking racist capitalist imperialist system.

Power to the Imagination
All Power to the People

Each of these points was followed by an accompanying paragraph of illustrative text in florid revolutionary jargon. *The Seattle Times*, fascinated, reprinted the entire SLF program and devoted many inches to the explanatory detail.[25] Chief prosecuting attorney Stan Pitkin later recited them word for word at the Seattle 7 trial, to the delight of the SLF supporters in the spectator seats. Pitkin told the jury that the Fifteen Points were the "first manifestation that a conspiracy was developing."[26]

4

TDA—The Day After: Stop the Courts!

*Eighty-nine people were busted with your routine police brutality and half
the people busted were innocent spectators.*

–Jeff Dowd, Seattle 7 defendant

Back in Chicago, Judge Julius Hoffman had had enough. It was
February 1970. The Chicago 7 jury had been deliberating for four
long days and Hoffman was incensed. He couldn't bang his gavel and
shout "Off with their heads!" like the Queen of Hearts in Lewis Carroll's
Alice in Wonderland, but he could summarily order the defendants to
jail for contempt of court. Never mind that the jury hadn't yet decided
on their guilt or innocence, Hoffman certainly had. He called in the
defendants and their attorneys and ruled: 159 counts of criminal
contempt, adding up to two and a half to four years in federal prison for
each one of them, starting immediately.[1]

When news of the sudden jailings spread, antiwar activists in cities
around the country quickly put their organizing skills into high gear.
They'd been preemptively planning to demonstrate against the expected
guilty verdict. Now they would protest the contempt sentences, still
using the acronym TDA for The Day After.

Shock and outrage ran deep among activists on the UW campus as
it had been only a few weeks since Chicago 7 defendant Jerry Rubin's
appearance there. For Michael Lerner and Chip Marshall's fledgling SLF,
organizing a TDA demonstration was a perfect way to publicly show off
its gathering strength. A date and a place were set: Tuesday, February 17,
1970, 2:00 p.m. at Seattle's federal courthouse. SLF sent a telegram to
Mayor Wes Uhlman and Governor Dan Evans announcing the action:

> The Seattle Liberation Front will hold a demonstration tomorrow in the
> Federal Courthouse…We intend to enter the courthouse and focus the
> attention of the Federal Courts on the suppression of blacks and the anti-
> war movement….we have no intention of introducing violence into the
> demonstration…we [hope we are] allowed to enter the courthouse to
> exercise our rights as citizens by having the courts speak to the needs of

the people and our justified fears of a renewed McCarthyism and incipient fascism.[2]

Seattle's federal courthouse in 1970 was on the block between Fifth and Sixth Avenues and Spring and Madison Streets, a few streets north of Seattle's historic Pioneer Square, and on the southern margin of the city's retail core. The building's neoclassical, buff-colored, undecorated stone exterior had few windows and its blocky design gave it a foreboding, Stalinesque look. In addition to courtrooms, in 1970 its ten stories housed the FBI, the Secret Service, the probation office, the U.S. Marshal's offices, a local office for the Ninth Circuit Court of Appeals, the local offices of Washington state's two powerful Democratic senators, and holding cells for federal prisoners awaiting transportation to other facilities. (Today the building is named after Seattle native William Kenzo Nakamura, a World War II Medal of Honor winner who was killed defending his U.S. Army unit in Italy. As a UW student Nakamura had been incarcerated with his family at the Minidoka War Relocation Center, one of several internment camps where U.S. citizens of Japanese ancestry were held during the war.)

Quickly spreading the word about TDA was a matter of leafletting street corners, school campuses, record shops, head shops, and hippie hangouts. The city's daily newspapers also carried stories about it. SLF members led by Jeff Dowd announced the demonstration by breaking into a UW economics class taught by feisty and politically conservative Professor Henry Buechel, age sixty-two. As Dowd and others ran up and down the classroom aisles, handing out leaflets about TDA, Buechel took them on. He loudly asked his class to vote on whom they'd rather hear, himself or them. He took off his coat and offered to fight Dowd in the hall.

News of this relatively small incident (no fistfight occurred) made it to the White House and Professor Buechel received a congratulatory note from President Nixon, dated the day after TDA:

> The White House, Washington, February 18, 1970
> Dear Professor Buechel:
>   Today I read a news report of your vigorous defense of the right to teach in your own classroom. You have my personal admiration for it.
>   Nor should you be too surprised by the reception you are getting in the rest of the country and in the State of Washington. The patience of the people of this country is wearing thin with arrogant hooligans who intimidate and harass and bully speakers they disagree with, whether in

the public forums of the land, or in the classrooms of our universities. In addition, they tend to respond instinctively and warmly toward a man who stands up for what he believes is right in a tough situation.

The kind of instinctive fortitude you showed we can use more of, not just in the classrooms of our universities, but through every segment of American life.

Best personal regards,

(signed) Richard Nixon[3]

The crowd that massed in front of the Seattle federal courthouse along Fifth Avenue that rainy and cold Tuesday afternoon in February numbered about two thousand. That was big for a Seattle demonstration; veteran protesters were thus a minority—which meant less control and more uncertainty.

Seattle police, protecting the federal building that housed the Selective Service, during an earlier antiwar demonstration. *Fred Lonidier.*

Law enforcement took notice, particularly U.S. Marshal Charles Robinson, the man in charge of the security of this courthouse and the courthouse in Tacoma where the Seattle 7 would be tried nine months later. Robinson, a seventeen-year FBI veteran before becoming U.S. Marshal for western Washington, brought in the Seattle Police Department, the King County Sheriff's office, and the Washington State Patrol to defend the building on this protest day. He prepared for violence, stuffing a hundred tactical squad and riot police in the public library across the street, ready to reinforce another crowd of troops stationed inside the courthouse building. FBI agents with cameras were positioned at windows on the ninth floor of a hotel across from the courthouse, taking both still and video shots of the people attending the protest. Robinson had perhaps over-prepared, and the government's force likely escalated, rather than diminished, the violent skirmishes over the next three hours.

TDA in Seattle was billed "Stop the Courts." Michael Lerner proposed that demonstrators should enter the courthouse, stop any trials, and, he said:

> [They should] conduct a teach-in to the judges, with the intent of help-ing them understand how the federal courts in Chicago had been mis-used…I thought that what was likely to happen would be civil disobe-dience of a non-violent sort. I thought we would be able to get into the building and sit in the hallways…We would be shutting it down, but not through any particular acts of violence.
>
> But this was their [the government's] call, in a way, of how they wanted to deal with it. And they decided to deal with it in a repressive way … Their choice was to confront.[4]

As the crowd grew, the SLF leadership didn't know quite what to do. Lerner recalled:

> So I get there. I'm one of the organizers. People are asking me, "What are we going to do?" The doors are locked and there are police inside and I'm thinking, I don't know. Maybe we'll conduct something out here, but we hadn't brought sound equipment. I don't know why we hadn't thought about the possibility that the doors would be locked. Stupid, but anyway, we hadn't. And then, all of a sudden, from the other side of the street hundreds of police appear in riot gear and started attacking the demon-strators. And that's how it started. There was no violence up until that point, until they started attacking us with violence.[5]

One demonstrator, a graduate student in European history at the UW who was new to antiwar protests, recalls briefly chatting with U.S. Mar-shal Robinson, who was initially circulating in the crowd, asking people who was in charge. But when a rock was thrown from the edge of the crowd Robinson quickly switched gears and ordered his courthouse-based troops into action. They poured out into the crowd of demonstrators.

The graduate student who had been peacefully talking with Robin-son was hit repeatedly with police batons and thrown to the ground.

"Eventually the medics picked me up, bleeding, and took me out of there before I got arrested… talk about 'instant radicalization,' that was me."[6] Another relative newbie who came to a different conclusion was a pacifist woman who was also roughed up by police. She said later that "fighting for peace is like screwing for chastity: it's insane."[7]

Robinson returned to the courthouse doors and ordered the building locked down. Quickly, a demonstrator picked up a spewing tear gas canister and threw it back toward the police and the courthouse entrance. Just before the doors closed, the canister rolled into the building, along the lobby floor and through a closing elevator door, gassing both Robinson and U.S. Attorney Stan Pitkin as they ascended to their offices. By this time, Robinson's phone was ringing off the hook with calls from the Department of Justice, wanting to know what was going on out there in Seattle. Neither Pitkin nor Robinson realized that they had just been launched onto one of the strangest cases of their careers.

Unable to get inside, the crowd on the building's front lawn listened to speakers and chanted "Free Bobby" (referring to Black Panther Bobby Seale), "Hog Hoffman" (Judge Julius Hoffman), "Off the Pigs," and "Peace Now." Some demonstrators threw rocks and balloons filled with paint (supplied, though they didn't know it yet, by an undercover FBI

Protester at TDA demonstration on February 17, 1970, being subdued and arrested. *Courtesy Paul Dorpat; Doyal Gudgel, photographer*

informer and provocateur) at the building. Glass was broken and a red flag was raised on the courthouse flagpole. In white lettering, it read "End the War and Free the [Chicago] Seven."

Although Robinson thought the demonstrators who "seemed interested in violence were relatively few in number," he also noted that some were deliberately "outrageous" in order "to foment a reaction that brought the kind of publicity that they seemed to be interested in—they being the Seattle 7, ultimately, as they were known."[8]

What, in fact, were the future Seattle 8 doing at the courthouse on that Tuesday afternoon? Although eighty-nine people were arrested that day, Kelly, Marshall, Dowd, Stern, Lerner, Lippman, Abeles, and Justesen were not among them. Apparently their outrageous fomenting had not been illegal enough to attract police attention. In fact, two of the eight were not even in the state: Lippman was in the Bay Area at the time with Robby Stern and others, and Kelly was visiting friends in Colorado.

Marshall, who was present, gave a speech, but didn't advocate trashing buildings or breaking windows—Weatherman's use of those tactics was the main reason he had left SDS. He was delighted and stunned, however, at the size and diversity of the Seattle turnout; he read it as a sign that their SLF organizing was going well, and was reaching well beyond the UW campus.

Susan Stern, who had fully embraced Weatherman's anger and style, intended to bring a more violent approach than what Marshall, Lerner, and the others anticipated. She was also depressed, distracted, and, she wrote, "consumed with murder and suicide and violence." The day before TDA, she had flown to Chicago for a court date stemming from her arrest at the Weatherman Days of Rage demonstration. Arriving back to Seattle that night, she and Justesen made plans for the following day:

> We decided to carry iron pipes with us…We decided not to wear helmets, because we wanted to blend in with the rest of the crowd. I was excited and on edge, prickling with energy as I always was before a demonstration…the impression that Justesen…gave me was that the Sundance [collective] people…were not interested in a militant demonstration. It was up to us to up the ante.
>
> [But, instead] just as Chip [Marshall] began to speak, the pigs attacked. They suddenly reached a point where they could no longer restrain themselves and went wild. They rammed into the crowd and attacked viciously using their clubs indiscriminately upon older people and street kids, men and women, against curious onlookers and passers-by caught

in the mob, against people standing dumfounded or blinded by tear gas. People trying hysterically to escape the smashing clubs were thrown against others on the crowded streets.[9]

Stern gave as much as she got, and, although not arrested, her militancy earned her expulsion from the SLF collective house she was living in—she was too much of a Weatherman to fit in with Marshall and Lerner's visions for creating a mass movement.

One SLF demonstrator was Zels Johnson, a Seattle kid still sporting his military haircut because in February 1970 he was an AWOL National Guard radio telephone operator. Johnson had recently walked out of military life after a war games assignment. The game's scenario was to put down a demonstration of antiwar and black militants in Seattle's Volunteer Park. Sited in the middle of a historically wealthy residential neighborhood on a hilltop overlooking Elliott Bay and the Olympic Mountains, this popular Olmsted-designed park spreads its calm greenery over almost fifty acres. Johnson was so appalled at the tactics being practiced

The TDA demonstration at the federal courthouse in Seattle. Clouds of tear gas drifted over the downtown core and up the hill toward several local hospitals. *Photo by Barry Sweet*

in the drill—firehoses, snipers, helicopters spraying tear gas—that he went AWOL, joined up with SLF, and became part of their high school organizing efforts.

Johnson went to TDA: "In all the fighting, I was arrested and dragged into the courthouse building where they were holding the arrestees. When they figured out I was AWOL the military police stepped in. It was incredible overkill. They hustled me into a car and on to the interstate with a caravan of cop cars front and back, and on both sides of me, helicopter overhead. And off we went to the Ft. Lewis lock-up, where I met a bunch of other resisters, which was great."[10] He spent over a year in the U.S. Penitentiary at Leavenworth, which also housed gangsters, mass murderers, drug traffickers, spies, and a few corrupt politicians. In retrospect, Johnson said, "My life was changed forever, for the good. I had a belief of what my life would stand for."[11]

At the other end of the TDA participant continuum was a second grader at a parochial school near the courthouse: "A group of us stumbled on a protest in front of the U.S. Courthouse. Somebody in the crowd bet us $5 we wouldn't throw rocks at the building. We were little street urchins and took it as a challenge. Plus $5 was a lot back then. We

Policemen in gas masks guarding the broken front door of the Seattle federal courthouse at TDA. *Courtesy Paul Dorpat; Doyal Gudgel, photographer*

unleashed our rocks but our little second-grader arms didn't really connect. We didn't get the $5 either. People started yelling and we hightailed it."[12]

As the tear gas and clubbings intensified, terrified and angry protesters were forced away from the courthouse. The police hadn't expected that some would move, en masse, north toward the downtown core, which had been left unprotected and unpoliced.[13] The running protesters broke windows in stores and cars in an orgy of mayhem and rage. Tens of thousands of dollars of damage was done before the afternoon was over.

Lerner described the scene:

> I was with other groups spreading into downtown Seattle, thinking that this is unfortunate, but this is the way we're going to make our point. We're going to demonstrate in the streets.
>
> As [the police] are throwing tear gas, they're effectively enlarging our demonstration from a one-block thing into at least half of downtown Seattle. And the whole place is filled with tear gas, and everybody has to be sent home from work…So it becomes a huge event, none of which we had thought of or planned. The last thing I wanted was for the antiwar movement to be perceived or portrayed as against the people, because that was precisely the problem that we had been having all along, that we were being portrayed that way.[14]

One dark-haired high school girl, who later became a girlfriend of Jeff Dowd, was at work at the downtown Coliseum Theatre during TDA. She was selling movie tickets in a little booth on the sidewalk. It was a double bill: *Jenny* starring Alan Alda and Marlo Thomas, about a woman helping a man to avoid the draft, and *Point Blank* with Lee Marvin and Angie Dickinson, a gangster revenge movie that's been remade several times.

Suddenly the TDA crowd surged around her booth, closely followed by pursuing police: "When I looked down on my little shelf where I'd place the tickets for people, there was this card. On the card it said 'The system does not work.' And I turned it over and it said 'You lose.' I could see the police with their batons out, waving them up and down, up and down, and going 'Hup! Hup! Hup! Hup!' in unison. They really seemed inhuman, very like a machine, just moving down the street. Scary… within a month I had joined the SLF."[15]

Not all the demonstrators, however, went downtown. A few, rightly guessing that the downtown scene would include trashing windows and cars, chose to move with their friends west toward Elliott Bay to escape the choking tear gas. One was an attorney named Dan Smith. He'd been a law student with Robby Stern, and had worked with him on campus SDS actions. Smith remembered:

> So we went down the hill toward the waterfront. Between Third and Second Avenues, maybe on James Street, we were followed and then attacked by rough-looking burly guys wearing plaid wool jackets. We thought they were right wing counter-demonstrators. They grabbed my friend and dragged him into an alley and started punching and kicking him. So I went after them, jumped on one to try to pull him off [my friend]. Then someone jumped on my back. Suddenly our attackers identified themselves as police officers. We stopped fighting and were handcuffed and taken to jail.[16]

A similar incident was reported by John Chambless, a UW lecturer who attended the demonstration in his additional role as news director for a local FM radio station. He reported his TDA experience on the radio. He and his wife Dorothy stood near the library entrance, across the street from the courthouse, where they watched demonstrators being clubbed even as they were lying prone on the concrete. As the violence moved across the street toward the Chamblesses, they saw a stocky man in plainclothes choking and dragging a young woman with one arm around her neck and the other wrenching one of her arms backwards. Dorothy Chambless, in tears, begged the man to stop. He ignored her, and tightened his hammerlock on the woman. Both husband and wife then noticed other men attacking and holding other women in the same way. Eventually, after their verbal pleas were met with nothing but silence and no change in behavior, Dorothy, a petite woman, tried to intervene between one of the women and the man. When another plainclothes man grabbed her, Chambless jumped in to free his wife. He was summarily seized and dragged into the library where he was told he was under arrest. It was only then that the men identified themselves as policemen.

Chambless concluded his radio report with a disquisition on the uses of violence by those who want radical change and those who are protecting the state. He opposed both, but worried that pacifism might be unrealistic in the face of such government behavior.[17]

The daily *Seattle Times* headlined their front page article on TDA: "Police Use Tear Gas with Demonstrators Outside Courthouse." Demonstrators were described as "young, long-haired and bearded," and the paper marveled that some among those arrested were "young women."[18] Next day's front page followed up with "Police Deny Use of Tear Gas." Seattle's acting police chief Frank Moore busily issued statements that TDA was the worst and most vicious example of property destruction ever visited upon the city. He also denied using tear gas, but photographs showed clouds of it rising from the area. Then he said that the protesters must have brought it with them. Finally, he admitted deploying tear gas against the crowd.

The *Seattle Times* coverage of TDA played into the hands of President Nixon, Attorney General Mitchell, FBI Director Hoover, and others who tended to view opposition as criminal if not traitorous. The *Times* hashed over TDA for days with headlines like "Revolution Wears a New Face in Seattle." Articles emphasized SLF's increased presence in high schools as well as its involvement in community issues such as trying to block a plan to build a freeway through black neighborhoods.[19] Antiwar dissent was escaping its college campus boundaries and that was worrisome to many in government.

In addition to the unlucky AWOL Zels Johnson, most of those arrested were in their early twenties. The youngest was fourteen, the eldest was fifty-two. Fourteen people were charged with federal crimes, the rest with municipal offenses, usually failure to disperse, failure to obey a police officer, or disorderly conduct. Three were charged with profanity.

While a number of TDA protesters were nursing head injuries and being booked into jail, Mayor Uhlman began receiving irate letters. People were angry that streets had been blocked, that crime was going unpunished, and that tax-supported institutions like the UW were harboring "un-American people." One employee at a retail store near the courthouse wrote to ask the mayor to "convey my appreciation and congratulations to the Seattle Policemen for their conduct and aggressive handling of the so called demonstrators. Too bad the night sticks couldn't have been used more freely and effectively." One woman wrote, "Please use any means necessary to stop any violent demonstrators." A group of sixteen people from Tacoma—where the Seattle 7 trial would be held—wrote to commend the Seattle police for their "forceful restraint of the unruly mob that roamed the streets of Seattle on Tuesday, February 17, 1970. If this problem developes [*sic*] in Tacoma, we are hopeful that our officials will act with equal vigor."[20]

A group signing themselves "The Seattle Patriots" wrote:

> We are sick and tired of the riots, marches, and bombings that plagued Seattle during the past twelve months…These Communist-led swine don't understand talk, Mr. Uhlman…the time for action has come. They've wanted it for a long time, and you have held back your police due to the charges of "police brutality" that you knew would have resulted. Mr. Uhlman, we don't feel the same way. They want action and believe me, we'll give it to them. Give us the word, Mayor. Just withdraw your police, and we will take over. And I will make a personal guarantee that the niggers and hippies will give it a lot of thought the next time they decide to riot.
>
> Remember, Mr. Uhlman, we await your word. But a warning is in order. If <u>ONE</u> march, or disturbance goes by without 'suitable' police action; <u>WE</u> will take action!
>
> Thank you for your time. We remain,
> Sincerly [*sic*],
> The Seattle Patriots
> The White Mans' [*sic*] Organization
> We support our local police; do YOU?[21]

Uhlman did not respond to the vigilante Seattle Patriots, and though he had initially been fully supportive of his police department, he was also trying to educate his jumpy city on Americans' right to publicly dissent. He responded to another letter several months later: "I see a clear difference between protests, demonstrations and riots. Common to all definitions of a riot are violent actions which destroy property or harm persons. Demonstrations and protests clearly stop short of this violence and would not be called riots. Therefore, I am a strong defender of the individual's right to protest and to demonstrate."[22]

Uhlman added, "The student involvement in environmental issues is but one area in which students have been quite influential." The first Earth Day in the United States was in April 1970, two months after TDA. Seattle students participated in neighborhood trash cleanups, a "car smash," "pro-ecology pep talks," and other festivities. Some SLFers—including Seattle 7 defendant Joe Kelly, who spoke at Seattle's first Earth Day rally—participated in this effort to understand and protect our planet—tasks which have become increasingly critical in the twenty-first century.

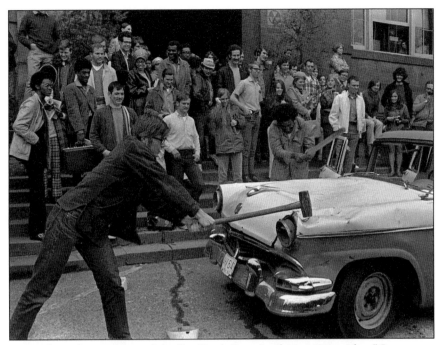

Seattle students celebrated the first Earth Day, April 22, 1970, with a "Car Smash," demonstrating against fuel-guzzling automobiles. *MOHAI, Seattle Post-Intelligencer Collection, 1986.552119.3, Phil H. Webber photo*

SLF distributed its summary of TDA in a single-issue magazine *Discover America* shortly after TDA. The non-bylined article read:

> [The demonstration] could have come off a lot better, but the good effects of the demonstration far outweigh the bad points...the movement isn't dead, not even dying...The minor property damage that occurred at the courthouse, while not inflicting any real material damage, posed a political threat; violence is becoming more and more recognized as a legitimate, and possibly the sole means of change. Peaceful demonstrations don't move anybody; they're mostly an appeasement for sore consciences...Obviously a lot of people were pissed off by the demo. That's good. It's a reaction.[23]

Lerner told the *Seattle Times* political reporter that TDA "gave our people experience in how to deal with the tremendous brutality of the police—a horrible reality that can't be dealt with by merely sitting down and saying 'peace, peace' in one's living room."[24]

In a prologue to the bigger trial to come, supporters swamped the Seattle courtroom as the charges against those arrested at TDA were heard. Over fifty spectators were denied admission by U.S. Marshal Robinson who said, "Frankly, on the basis of past performance, I distrust any group related to the demonstrators."[25]

Teenager Michael Abeles and U.S. Marshal Charles Robinson in front of the Seattle federal courthouse three days after the TDA demonstration as some of those arrested were being arraigned. None of the future Seattle 8 were among those arrested. *Courtesy Paul Dorpat; Doyal Gudgel, photographer*

5

Action and Reaction

The federal grand jury is not a forum in which the government tries to present any real solid evidence. They just want to summarize things and get the indictment. The FBI already had some paranoid fantasy about what the Seattle Liberation Front was or could be.

—MICHAEL TIGAR, SEATTLE 7 DEFENSE ATTORNEY

Learning of Seattle's TDA demonstration from his Washington, DC, office, Assistant Attorney General Will Wilson quickly sent a memo to FBI Director Hoover ordering him to launch an investigation of SLF (which he had already done). Wilson added that Guy Goodwin, chief of the Special Litigation section of the Internal Security Division of the Department of Justice, would shortly be arriving in Seattle to arrange a grand jury.[1] When Goodwin arrived in Seattle a few days later, Hoover had already slapped the Weatherman label on TDA, despite what his agents had reported to him about the January meetings at the UW HUB. Hoover told the Seattle FBI office that SLF "is dominated by the Seattle Weatherman faction of SDS" and that SLF is "in reality nothing but a Weatherman front."[2]

Meanwhile, unaware of the strength of the federal forces gathering against them, SLF was off and running. As more than a single-issue, student antiwar group, the burgeoning collectives found the Seattle landscape littered with community issues demanding their organizing attentions. Unemployment was a big one; it reached double digits in 1970, twice the national average. Boeing, the economic engine of the region, was collapsing—the company had laid off 50,000 of its 80,000 employees, mostly highly skilled technicians and engineers. Food stamp and unemployment applications skyrocketed.[3] So many people were moving away that U-Haul dealers ran out of trailers. A locally famous billboard appeared near the airport, "Will the last person leaving SEATTLE—Turn out the lights." A suicide net was placed around the 605-foot-tall Space Needle, just in case.

There were other problems too. The *Wall Street Journal,* reporting on Boeing's massive layoffs, labeled Seattle the country's "Food Stamp and Bomb Capital." Mayor Uhlman had counted ninety incendiary and explosive devices set off in Seattle in the first half of the year, some by Weatherman, some not, the vast majority unsolved. Law enforcement was not working at its best—the department was being pummeled over several well-publicized police corruption scandals. The police chief position changed hands six times during 1969 and 1970. Officers were working twelve-hour shifts, their patrol cars filled with squads of six men in full riot gear.

The SLF, however, did not embrace bombing as an organizing technique. Jeff Dowd explained: "We were very into being safe, but we wanted to be in the media. We organized and worked with everybody, did publicity stunts to get the word out, but we were willing to go to jail. We put our asses on the line. We're united front guys, not vanguard guys. But the federal authorities thought we were vanguard guys because we were loud."[4]

High unemployment provided SLF with a golden opportunity to move their brand of radical politics into community neighborhoods. SLF members got up early to talk to the lines of people at the unemployment office about capitalism and the war, and to hand out free coffee and doughnuts. This work even rated a mention in *Time* magazine's coverage of Seattle's woes: "a church-sponsored volunteer organization called Neighbors in Need is distributing free food, as is a small commune of the left-wing Seattle Liberation Front."[5]

Other SLF collectives visited dry cleaners around the city to collect clothing that hadn't been picked up by the cleaners' deadline. They took the clothing to their Georgetown Free Store in south Seattle where it was given away to needy customers. Another collective supported a strike of mostly women workers at a photo developing shop. The mother of one of the SLF members on this project told him "Well, I knew you must have really believed in this to get up at 5:00 in the morning."[6]

The *Seattle Times* interviewed SLF members a few days after TDA: "Chalked on the blackboard were possible areas for action—water and air pollution, abortion, the proposed Interstate 90 freeway, Boeing…It could well have been a session of the legislature. But a further reading of the blackboard might dispel that notion—revolutionary art, free rock concerts, nude stage productions."[7]

One of the most lasting and valuable projects launched by SLF collectives or their spin-offs was the founding of Country Doctor, a thriving Seattle community medical clinic that today serves over 68,000 patient visits per year in two high-needs neighborhoods. Another was the founding of what has become the Northwest Immigrant Rights Project, which provides legal services and advocacy to thousands of people and families caught up in the complexities and uncertainties of the U.S. immigration system. The successor of a food co-op the group started several blocks from the Country Doctor clinic still flourishes today.

SLF members also collected signatures to qualify a tax reform measure for the fall state ballot. Initiative No. 35, written by Michael Lerner, called for shifting the overall tax burden from the lower end of the income scale to large corporations and businesses, with fines and jail terms for corporate executives whose companies transferred their increased tax expense to consumers. An elected state commission would withhold all state citizens' federal income tax payments until the federal government "ends all foreign wars and spends the savings on statewide environmental and social programs."

Some of Lerner's UW philosophy students participated in the tax initiative signature gathering as a class project. One wrote, "Surprisingly enough we got quite a few signatures at the food stamp office at seven in the morning. Most of the people were receptive to our ideas...However, a lot of them wondered why the war was included on the same initiative, which is difficult to explain. Most agreed the tax idea was good but had been so mindfucked that they could not conceive of it ever passing."[8]

Lerner viewed the tax initiative as SLF's most important organizing tool but also didn't expect it to win. Although somewhere between 30,000 and 40,000 signatures were collected, the effort lost steam in the face of the more urgent need to prepare for trial. In June, shortly after his arrest for conspiracy, Lerner filed suit against the state's attorney general, charging that disparaging remarks made by the A.G. about the initiative could prejudice the conspiracy trial's jury against him.

SLF members also actively supported the UW's Black Student Union's demands that the school cancel its sports competitions with Brigham Young University. This was a protest against BYU's affiliation with the Mormon church, which at that time was racially discriminatory in both practice and doctrine. The protests became so heated that by mid-March the administration called in over two hundred Seattle and King County police to essentially occupy the campus, precipitating both injuries and arrests.

SLF members also rallied around Seattle's black community to oppose the construction of Interstate 90 through the predominantly black Central District neighborhood. The collectives supported the Seattle Black Panther chapter's community organizing work, including a free medical clinic, busing people to visit friends and family members in prison, and a neighborhood breakfast program.

All these efforts were spiced with frequent partying. Led by their Sundance collective leadership, SLF members freely shared their beer and marijuana with any long-haired kid who showed up. Like The People's Chevy, collective houses were wide open—their food, drink, sofas, and beds were available to one and all. They wanted to live the culture their flamboyant Fifteen Point program outlined.

The most dramatic incident in the national antiwar movement in 1970, however, occurred in March in New York City, just three weeks after TDA. A lovely and expensive four-story brownstone house on a leafy, high-end Manhattan street was leveled in a horrific explosion. The rubble revealed an enormous cache of dynamite, boxes of nails, and three dismembered bodies of Weatherman leaders. Soon the whole country knew that Weatherman was not only building large bombs but, like the U.S. Army in Vietnam, they were embedding shrapnel in them to create exquisitely terrible antipersonnel weapons. The target of the New York bombers was discovered to be a dance for soldiers at nearby Fort Dix.

Many surviving Weathermen were as appalled as the general public, and deserted the group. A small number quickly moved underground as the FBI and police ramped up their national efforts to find them. Calling themselves the Weather Underground, these ex-SDS Weather leaders were articulate, militant, and few. Shell-shocked by the three deaths, they still wanted to overthrow the U.S. government, but publicly declared that they weren't yet ready to kill people to do it. They would target buildings, not people.

Over the next five years, the Weather Underground planted dynamite in several dozen government and corporate buildings around the country without being caught and without additional deaths. The placement of the bombs was always announced in advance, both to explain why that particular building was a target and to allow time for people to be safely evacuated. At the same time, however, they maintained their hardcore rhetoric, studded with talk of guns, rage, and phrases like "war without terms."

Meanwhile the Department of Justice and the FBI continued to focus on Seattle, but the local agents weren't coming up with enough malfeasance to satisfy their DC superiors' need to catch Weathermen and quash the increasing strength of the antiwar movement. Hoover told his agents to find evidence that SLF violated anti-riot laws, but in a February 24 memo, just a week after TDA, Seattle agents reported that their findings "failed to indicate a violation of Federal Antiriot Laws." U.S. Attorney for Western Washington Stan Pitkin, who was to lead the eventual prosecution of the Seattle 7, told the FBI on February 27 that "he could not render a prosecutive opinion in this matter at this time because of insufficient information."[9]

However, none of this on-the-ground intelligence derailed Special Investigator Guy Goodwin's mission upon arriving into Seattle: to disrupt antiwar activists and catch Weathermen, or at least people who could be called Weathermen. Goodwin's tool of choice for this work was the grand jury—an instrument often used to intimidate and distract, bully and jail perceived enemies of the government.

Grand juries, however, were not originally designed to do this. Their existence harks back to twelfth-century England, when they acted as a check-and-balance mechanism to give citizens some small control over the capriciousness of sheriffs, barons, princes, and kings. The idea was that grand jurors would be regular citizens, i.e., male landowners over a certain age, who would act as watchdogs as they listened to a prosecutor's evidence against a particular person. If the evidence was entirely flimsy, the jurors could refuse to allow the charges to be brought. Presumably this would reduce the number of arbitrary and unfair accusations brought by powerful people against less powerful people.

In contrast, grand juries today meet in secret to listen to subpoenaed witnesses handpicked by prosecutors to support a planned indictment against specific people, and then jurors rubber stamp it. In a further twist, the process stacks the cards against both the targets and the subpoenaed witnesses.

Intimidation is the name of the grand jury game and it is an extremely effective weapon against dissidents. No judge is present at grand jury proceedings, subpoenaed witnesses are not allowed to have an attorney present, and their Fifth Amendment rights against self-incrimination are waived (disallowed). Witnesses are called, one by one, into the grand jury room. They are not told the nature or scope of the allegations, or whether or not they themselves are the targets of the investigation. No press, no spectators, no legal representation, no other witnesses are allowed in the room.

If a witness chooses not to respond to a prosecutor's question, he or she faces jail time for the duration of the grand jury. This was, and remains, most dissidents' preferred approach. Grand juries are empaneled for eighteen months, but if the grand jury is looking into riot-connected offenses, it is doubled to three years. The witness is jailed instantly upon refusal to answer a question; no appeals are allowed. If you serve that time, a subsequent grand jury could call you again and if you still refuse to answer, you go back to jail for the life of that jury. And so on.

In addition to intimidation and distraction,

i don't talk to grand juries

Advice for those subpoenaed by a federal grand jury. *Artwork by Ricardo Levins Morales, www.rlmartstudio.com*

grand juries are used to fish for information that could compensate for sloppy or illegal police or FBI work. Solomon Wachtler, chief judge of the New York Court of Appeals in the late 1980s and early 1990s, said, "A grand jury would indict a ham sandwich, if that's what you wanted."[10]

Grand jury subpoenas can be issued wholesale to groups of people, and so they were in 1970. The Department of Justice reshaped and heavily funded its Internal Security Division to use the grand jury process as a way to extract information, frighten, and drain energy and money from antiwar and civil rights organizations. It often succeeded in these purposes without bothering to secure convictions or even issue indictments. Grand juries are used as a weapon against dissent very much like the House Un-American Activities Committee (HUAC) was in the 1940s and 1950s, but updated to allow secrecy, denial of Fifth Amendment rights, and immediate imprisonment for uncooperative witnesses.

In the early 1970s, strike forces of Washington, DC-based federal attorneys summoned witnesses and conducted grand juries all over the country including Seattle, New York, Los Angeles, Tucson, Detroit, and other cities where Black Panther and Weatherman activity was believed to be high. Local U.S. attorney's offices thus were no longer in control of what federal cases were brought in their districts. The most well-known member of this federal attorney posse, who flew around the country to convene dozens of grand juries targeted at radical political activity, was Special Investigator Guy Goodwin. He subpoenaed two thousand witnesses and brought over four hundred indictments during his tenure. Goodwin's zeal earned him the name "Witch-Finder General" from noted political columnist Jack Anderson.[11]

Seattle 7 defense attorney Michael Tigar recalls one pretrial meeting of the attorneys on both sides in which he "made some joke [to Goodwin] about, you know, 'If you had your way, you'd just shoot the defendants.' Goodwin replied, 'Well, I'd have to use a squirrel rifle.'"[12]

Goodwin crisscrossed the United States, running grand jury after grand jury, issuing subpoenas that fished for dubiously relevant information and asked broad but minutely detailed questions that were essentially impossible to answer. The next step was to jail uncooperative witnesses and throw clouds of distracting fear over all the local activists. What his indictments generally failed to do was result in a trial, because in the end the government wasn't willing to admit in court that its evidence relied on the FBI's illegal surveillance and provocateur work.

But in Seattle's case, they decided to go for it. The need to catch a Weatherman, combined with SLF's growing reach into a receptive community beyond the campus (not a model the White House wanted to see spreading to other cities), was too strong to ignore. The fact that SLF maintained an unusually cordial and collaborative relationship with the local Black Panthers was also a factor. To the Nixon administration, if anything was worse than the Weathermen, it was the Panthers.

So Goodwin charged into Seattle shortly after TDA, worked his grand jury mischief to secure conspiracy indictments against the eight Seattleites, and then quickly left town. In essence, Goodwin had scored a triple play in Seattle. His grand jury frightened and distracted SLF, the charges relied on poorly understood and rarely used conspiracy and intent laws, and he secured indictments in a city thought not to be sophisticated enough to defend the case.

Conspiracy statutes are controversial in the legal community. Many of their theoretical and practical difficulties surfaced during the Seattle 7 trial. A conspiracy is an agreement between two or more persons to commit a crime. The crime itself need not occur. Nor need it be attempted—existing laws already handle attempt (attempted murder, attempted theft, etc.). The government couldn't use attempt or other charges against the eight indicted Seattleites because not one of them had been arrested for attempting or committing any criminal act at TDA. But that's also the conspiracy law's strength. As U.S. Marshal Robinson noted later, "[conspiracy charges] are easier to proceed with than a 'who swung the hammer, who broke the window' sort of approach" because no one has to be caught in the act.[13] But during conspiracy trials, the distinction between conspiring and attempting or committing often gets lost: "Even in the cases in which conspiracy alone is charged, many prosecutors and half of the trial judges believe that the defendants had completed or attempted the object crime."[14]

Goodwin never prosecuted the cases himself, leaving that to the local federal attorneys, who didn't always understand that was Goodwin's modus operandi. In Seattle it was U.S. Attorney Stan Pitkin who made that mistake. A month after the indictments against the Seattle 8 were announced, Pitkin was still saying, hopefully, that Goodwin would lead the prosecution.[15] Pitkin didn't believe the government had a strong case, and he wanted Goodwin to have his back. He was "not optimistic" about a "reasonable and orderly trial" and wrote repeated memos to

Washington, DC, emphasizing his hope that Goodwin would be in town to help the prosecution go as smoothly as possible.[16]

Pitkin was one of the youngest U.S. attorneys in the country—a native of Minneapolis and a graduate of Vanderbilt, he'd been admitted to the bar in 1966 and was appointed by President Nixon to the U.S. attorney position just three years later. Pitkin's experience was slim but dramatic: he and William Erxleben, another attorney who would prosecute the Seattle 7, had worked on a previous case that convicted an assistant chief of police in Seattle of lying to cover up the department's widespread practice of shakedowns at illegal gambling clubs around town. It was Pitkin's first case in federal court, and his successful and aggressive conviction was likely noticed by John Ehrlichman and Egil Krogh, both Seattleites, and by 1970, part of President Nixon's internal circle tasked with domestic spying, planting false news stories, wiretapping, and burglarizing citizens' homes or offices.

Ehrlichman and Krogh had worked in the same Seattle law firm before being recruited by Nixon to White House advisor positions; both would later spend time in prison for their roles in Nixon's criminal activities. For a few years though, they were riding high, and were happy to help Nixon squelch the antiwar movement. Perhaps they thought Seattle's young prosecutor would be up to the task of showing the rest of the country how to do it. On the other hand, Pitkin worried that the case was so slim that prosecuting it would bring "bad publicity…to Seattle and his office; not to mention that it might well make radical 'martyrs' of the eight."[17]

It was reasonable for Pitkin to assume that Goodwin would try the Seattle conspiracy case because the indictments were announced on April 16, 1970, not in Seattle, but in Washington, DC. With great fanfare Goodwin's boss Attorney General John Mitchell linked the indictees to "the militant Weatherman faction of the Students for a Democratic Society (SDS)."[18] Subsequent news articles all emphasized the Weatherman connection and always included the words "militant" or "radical."

The Department of Justice was so excited about the indictments that their announcement inflated the figures, trumpeting that they'd arrested people whom in fact they hadn't yet captured. A second, accurate press release was issued a few hours later; rather than ten (including a few unindicted co-conspirators) arrests, they'd succeeded in nabbing only five. The local morning paper explained the federal bungling: "Although the indictments were secret—to allow the FBI time to arrest those charged before they were alerted, news of the secret indictment was leaked by the Federal Bureau of Investigation and Department of Justice in Washington, D.C."[19]

In early April 1970, nine days before the indictments and eight weeks after TDA, the daily *Seattle Post-Intelligencer* ran a series of three articles chock-full of fear-provoking details about the Seattle Liberation Front. Four names appeared repeatedly: Michael Lerner, Chip Marshall, Joe Kelly, and Jeff Dowd. All four were described as violent revolutionary trouble-makers from out of town. In fact, the articles were likely part of the FBI's stealth COINTELPRO media strategy to create and cement a negative impression of the about-to-be-indicted defendants amongst the citizenry and potential jurors.

The first article, dated April 5, was headlined "SLF: Seattle Is the Target of Revolutionaries."

> Seattle and the University of Washington began the Seventies as the primary target of an experienced band of hard-core revolutionaries... the revolutionaries of the SLF have been fervently at work fomenting rebellion in the heretofore 'remote' northwestern corner of the U.S.... Most are from the East. At least one is from the torn campuses of California. They are in Seattle because they presumably consider the city and the university ripe for revolution...The SLF holds in contempt many aspects of American society. It aims to rally under one revolutionary banner every possible dissident group and individual.[20]

The second histrionic article, "The SLF: Fiery Credo Mirrors All Discontent. Familiar Calls to Revolution Seek to Fuse Other Groups," appeared the following day. It reminded readers that "most of the hard-core SLF leaders are not from the Pacific Northwest—they came here from other strife-torn campuses and cities because they regard the [Seattle] area as territory ripe for revolution." The SLF is described as a "rebirth...an *enfant terrible*" of Students for a Democratic Society and Weatherman.[21]

The articles help explain why the Department of Justice had become so interested in Seattle. The sentence, "It aims to rally under one rev-olutionary banner every possible dissident group and individual," and the headlined phrase, "Seek to Fuse Other Groups," indicate the level of political threat the government felt about SLF's work to become a multi-issue, community-based organization. Perhaps, like the founders of SLF, a few government staffers remembered the Seattle general strike from their own college U.S. history classes.

In the short time between the likely FBI-planted newspaper articles about the SLF, and the arrests of most of the Seattle 8 a week later, the SLF leadership mobilized. They held a press conference to charge the newspaper with endangering their lives. They demanded equal time; *Post-Intelligencer* editor Louis Guzzo complied and ran a remarkably factual description of many of the SLF's community organizing projects, including their tax initiative, providing coffee and doughnuts to people in the unemployment office line, starting a free medical clinic, running a free store, and more.[22] Once the trial began, the local press continued to provide a generally balanced and detailed account of its contentious and often chaotic proceedings.

What were the actual criminal charges brought by Goodwin's grand jury against the seven Seattle men and one woman? There were six counts and eighteen overt acts, falling under four federal statutes. The legal wording is slippery, as the defendants, jurors, and prosecutors were soon to find out. The first count references three statutes (18 U.S.C. 371, 18 U.S.C. 1361, and 18 U.S.C 2) relating to damaging or conspiring to damage U.S. government property. This count referred directly to the February 17 TDA demonstration at the Seattle federal courthouse. It charged that the defendants "did willfully, knowingly, and unlawfully conspire, combine, confederate and agree together with each other…to commit offenses against the United States" and that they did "willfully and unlawfully injure, and aid, abet, counsel and procure others to willfully and unlawfully injure the property of the United States."[23]

This charge was accompanied by a list of eighteen overt acts dated between January 10 and February 17, 1970, only two of which note actual courthouse damage, and neither of those names any of the defendants. The remaining sixteen overt acts refer not to conspiratorial planning to damage the courthouse, but to public meetings containing standard antiwar organizing speeches, usually well-covered by the mainstream press.

The second charge, delineated in the remaining five counts, is the previously mentioned "Rap Brown Law" (18 U.S.C. 2101), named after a veteran of both SNCC and the Black Panthers whom Congress believed was driving from state to state fomenting riots in black ghettos. The statute was included in an effort to get the needed votes to pass the 1968 Civil Rights law. It was used against white antiwar leaders for the first time on the Chicago 7, and for the second time in Seattle. This law makes it illegal to use interstate commerce, including highways, telephones, radio, or the mail "with intent to incite, organize, promote, and encourage a riot."

Counts II through V provide the details of these interstate commerce charges: Marshall, Dowd, Kelly, and Abeles were individually accused of having crossed state lines on their December 1969 road trip from Ithaca to Seattle with intent to organize TDA—despite the fact that the trip occurred six weeks before Boston activists first proposed the idea of national TDA protests. In addition, Joe Kelly did not join that December trip, being tied up with court appearances in Chicago.

Count VI charges the same against Lerner, not for travelling across state lines but for using "the facilities of interstate commerce, to-wit, the Pacific Northwest Bell Telephone Company, with intent to incite," etc. This refers to a single phone call Lerner made from Seattle to Rennie Davis, one of the Chicago 7 defendants, to ask how his trial was going. Stern, Lippman and Justesen, having lived in Seattle for years, were not charged under 18 U.S.C. 2101.

If the government's primary goal was to punish those involved in TDA demonstrations, it would have gone after leaders of similar demonstrations, some much larger and more violent, in over twenty other cities, including New York, Boston, and Washington, DC. Similarly, if the concern was over the safety of the Seattle courthouse, it would have made more sense to arrest the planners (whose plans were quite public) *before* any damage occurred. Clearly, Seattle's TDA demonstration was a fairly weak straw man as a conspiratorial event, but it apparently was the best approach the government could think of to stop SLF's growth.

Five of the eight, Michael Lerner, Susan Stern, Joe Kelly, Michael Abeles, and Jeff Dowd were arrested on April 16, the day the indictments were announced.

Lerner was arrested as he left his office on the UW campus. It was his first arrest. He got into his car with his dog, drove about twenty feet, and, he recalled:

All of a sudden there's a car in back of me and a car in front of me that suddenly slammed on their brakes. People jump out of the car and run over to me.

"'Get out of the car!'"

They're U.S. Marshals and they have guns. One of them jumps into my car and drives off with it, with my dog sitting in the back seat. And I'm put in the other one, handcuffed, and asked, "Why'd you do it?'"

And I said, "'Um, could you tell me what I'm supposed to have done here?'" I was tempted to say, 'Because I hated my mother.' But I didn't. That's how I learned that I was under indictment.[24]

Once in jail, Lerner petitioned for immediate release on personal recognizance. After all, he thought, he was an employed professor and the son of an East Coast judge. U.S. Attorney Pitkin was opposed to Lerner's release, "because he is a member of an organization [Weatherman] which has been unwilling to appear in court."[25] Never mind that Lerner loathed Weatherman and that he had gone to great pains in public speeches and articles to excoriate its strategies and tactics.

Susan Stern and Joe Kelly were busy supporting a student strike at Rainier Beach High School in south Seattle when they were caught. Stern had just returned the day before from New York, where she had gone to briefly try her hand at being an underground revolutionary. She didn't like it, and came back to Seattle. Driving to the high school, they got stoned. Happy to be home, she initially ignored Kelly's concerns at seeing police all over the high school property. But when Kelly insisted they leave, she agreed:

We stopped at a stop sign. From nowhere, five white cars surrounded us… twenty FBI agents with guns drawn were around the car; one muttered, "This must be Stern," and yanked me out, pulled my arms behind my back and I felt the tight cold click of handcuffs; they had me jammed up against the car. I saw them pull [Kelly] out, and handcuff him. I couldn't repress this awful urge to giggle; it all seemed so ludicrous…[In the car] one of the [agents] kept his hand on his gun inside his jacket the entire time. They all looked at me as if I would suddenly metamorphose into Superwoman, break the cuffs, slay them all with my cyanide fingernails, and fly away to Istanbul."[26]

Stern's descriptive language captures the serious yet giddy tone often found in participants' stories of the antiwar movement in the 1960s and early 1970s. Activists were serious about their cause, but they were also young, short-sighted, and optimistic enough to view it, occasionally, as a lark.

As Kelly, Stern, and Lerner were being processed, Michael Abeles arrived. He'd been stopped for speeding and taken to jail for not having a license. When police realized who he was, they rearrested him for conspiracy.

An hour or so later, Jeff Dowd was brought in. He'd heard about the indictments and wanted to warn Chip Marshall, who was returning to Seattle after giving a speech at Western Washington University in Bellingham, ninety miles to the north. Dowd waited on the freeway exit he thought Marshall would be using, and managed to flag him down. Dowd then went to remove guns and drugs from their house. It was poor timing, because the FBI had just arrived, search warrant in hand. Dowd was caught trying to escape through a bedroom window.[27] Among the items found in the house by the FBI were two twelve-gauge shotguns, some shells, and the *Department of Army Field Manual on Booby Traps*. Dowd's post-arrest phone call was to his attorney, whom he asked to notify his mother and his stepmother.

Susan Stern on April 16, 1970, the day of her arrest for conspiracy, standing in front of the Seattle federal courthouse after being booked. *Courtesy Paul Dorpat; Doyal Gudgel, photographer*

After the warning from Dowd, Marshall went into hiding for a couple of days before emerging to speak at an antiwar rally. He closed by announcing he would now retire to the Century Tavern on University Way to have a drink and be arrested. Which he was, by several FBI Special Agents and five Seattle police officers. Marshall recalls that being indicted wasn't really a surprise: "I think we were ready for it, because our view was that we were revolutionaries and this is what happens…I can't say we were happy about it, but on the other hand, I can't say we were sad either."[28]

Roger Lippman who, along with Michael Justesen and Susan Stern had the closest apparent relationship with Weatherman, was in California at the time the indictments were announced. He had gone to an anti-ROTC demonstration on the UC Berkeley campus with several others including Justesen:

> The demonstration looked like a trap to us. We decided to get out of there. We split up and met at Shakey's Pizza on Shattuck Ave. Based on previous experience, we were carrying lead pipes as defense against jocks and lead fishing weights in case we couldn't find any rocks. The cops burst into the restaurant, holsters unsnapped and jammed us up against the wall. Justesen escaped, but four of us were arrested. The others were bailed out but I was held when they learned about the Seattle indictments.[29]

Lippman was incarcerated in the Bay Area for about a month. He was then bailed out, and returned on his own to Seattle where he was arraigned at the end of May. Lippman, who had also been in California during TDA, thought he was included in the indictments because "they were trying to put together a panel of defendants who looked scary to the average jury, and I fit in pretty well with that."[30]

Seven in custody and much to be done: bail, attorneys, fund-raising, continuation of SLF organizing projects. But first, the seven captured conspirators had to meet and learn to work together, something conspirators should already be good at, but, since there hadn't been a conspiracy, that camaraderie didn't exist. Simply agreeing that racism, capitalism, and the war were bad things wasn't a strong enough foundation to coordinate an effective legal defense.

Where they existed, their relationships prior to the indictments were mostly peripheral, and not necessarily friendly. Marshall and Kelly were good friends from college, but that was about it. Lippman didn't meet Abeles until after the indictments when he was returned to Seattle. Lerner, Lippman, and Stern hadn't crossed paths much, and didn't always like or trust each other when they had. Dowd, Kelly, Marshall, and Lerner definitely disagreed with the politics and approaches of the Weatherman-leaning Lippman, Stern, and Justesen. Lerner didn't trust any of them, especially Abeles and Dowd, who were the adolescent wild cards. Susan Stern, with her militancy and drug use, and perhaps partly because she was a woman, was considered somewhat unpredictable by them all.

This rally to support Black Panther Bobby Seale was held on the Seattle federal courthouse lawn just two days after the Seattle 7 arrests for conspiracy and intent to riot. *Courtesy Paul Dorpat; Doyal Gudgel, photographer*

6

Spring into Summer

We were on a merry-go-round from the time of our arrest until the time we finally went to prison. It never stopped once.
—Susan Stern, Seattle 7 defendant

The spring and summer of 1970 saw typical Seattle weather as April's showers extended into May and June, tapered off to a dry August, and temperatures crawled from the mid-fifties to the low seventies. At least it was better than the beginning of the year when Michael Lerner, perhaps changing his mind about Seattle's revolutionary potential, worried that the city was too rainy for mass meetings outside and had too few options for large indoor rallies.

An SLF flyer with the heading "What's Going On Here?" appeared stapled to telephone poles around town: "It's been another grim week in Seattle. Monday, Boeing announced 13,000 more layoffs and the people suffered through another stacked I-90 hearing. Tuesday, the city prosecutor refused to take Larry Ward's murderer to court,[1] and Wednesday, seven Seattle Liberation Front members were arrested on phony charges of destroying federal property. What's the connection between these events?"[2]

The answer, the flyer explained, was that the war, racism, and capitalism together are the root cause of all these problems. The flyer also asked that donations for a Seattle 8 defense fund be sent to the aptly named Box 1984.[3]

It was true that nobody east of the Rockies or south of the Columbia River was paying much attention to Seattle. One of the rare national media articles about the indictments, this one in the left-wing magazine *The Nation*, led with "in this Pacific Northwest city, far from the attention of the national press and television, the federal government seems determined to make examples of eight young defendants whose only crime, in the opinion of a local ACLU official, is 'that they are damn good organizers.'"[4]

Meanwhile, the Vietnam War was becoming increasingly ugly, and both local and national law enforcement agencies were responding to antiwar protests with stepped up arrests, more tear gas, and greater shows of force. A theatrical red and black cover splashed with the words "The Violent Left" was the design of choice for the May 1970 issue of *Seattle Magazine*. Part scare-tactic and part patronizing, the article documented Seattle's frequent bombings and demonstrations, and quoted liberally from speeches and interviews with Chip Marshall and Michael Lerner: "This is Germany, 1932. Fascism or revolution—that's the only choice," Marshall is quoted as saying as he poured himself another beer at the Century Tavern. More seriously, he adds, "This is the only place in the country that has a city-wide movement going on."

An SLF flyer distributed in the summer headed "DO IT!" listed collectives a person could call "if you believe that America needs changing." It revealed SLF's philosophical ties to third world liberation movements and to youth culture, and demonstrated the breadth of its organizing reach:

- Help with the Sky River Festival or set up rock concerts locally—call the Hydra Collective at LA 2-6744
- Help the GI movement—call Long Time Coming at LA 5-3203
- Work with people on welfare—call Zapata at EA 9-1251
- Work on a Free Store—call Tupamaros at CH 4-2442
- Take or set up classes on the war, racism, legal aid, medical, self-defense, etc.—call the Liberation School at EA 2-8152
- Want to help setup a theatre group—call the Grodes at EA 5-1546
- Work on Women's Liberation—call Stonerage at SU 4-9164 or the Liberation School at EA 2-8152
- Circulate the SLF anti-war, anti-tax initiative—call ME 4-2927
- Take classes on imperialism—call ME 4-2927.[5]

The 1970 May Day antiwar rallies around the country received a significant attendance boost in reaction to President Nixon's announcement on April 30 that he had escalated the war into Cambodia with a major ground invasion. (The massive carpet bombing of Cambodia, begun a year earlier under Nixon's orders, had been kept secret.)

Seattle's May Day rally occurred under unusually sunny skies and, despite the news of the expanded war, generally good spirits. The *Post-Intelligencer* reported that it was "almost a love-in…U.S. Marshal Charles Robinson moved easily through the crowd, with the air of a host who was glad everybody had come and wanted them to feel at home." Chip Marshall, one of the speakers, cautioned the crowd, "I wouldn't despair. There is a tendency in people to look at things as a half-hour TV show and think that everything should all be wound up quickly with a shoot-out."

The rally grew slightly more contentious when it moved toward downtown Boeing offices, where police used their clubs to protect the airplane company from demonstrators entering their building. Nine people were arrested and several newsmen were roughed up. The *P-I* reported: "When one newsman asked if an arrested person was to be jailed, a police officer said brusquely: 'I don't think the *Post-Intelligencer* needs to know that.'"[6]

However, as news of the war's expansion revealed gruesome stories of more villages torched, more crops destroyed, and more civilians killed, an estimated four million students on at about four hundred fifty campuses

Boeing was a major target for SLF because of its massive military defense contracts. This demonstration was held in front of their Seattle office on Second Avenue in May 1970. *MOHAI, Seattle Post-Intelligencer Collection, 1986.5.52186.6*

nationwide held strikes that closed down over half of them.[7] On the UW campus, strike actions were endorsed by many faculty members. Whole departments as well as individual professors canceled classes. Strike demands included an end to ROTC on campus, support for the Black Student Union's demands to end relations with Brigham Young University, an end to the war, freedom for Bobby Seale, and more. Committees were set up for bail funds, legal aid, information, medical assistance, etc., all designed, not unlike the 1919 Seattle general strike, to cover functions needed for daily life under changed circumstances.

After three days of a similar strike at Kent State University, the governor of Ohio called in the National Guard to end it. Troops sprayed live ammunition into a rally of peacefully striking students on the campus lawn, killing four students (only two of whom had been participating in the rally) and wounding nine others.[8] Feelings of anger and helplessness around the country were redoubled, and brought frighteningly new meaning to the Weatherman phrase "bring the war home."

One young FBI agent working in the Seattle office recalls, "I will never forget Kent State—I remember having a huge argument with my Seattle agent co-workers. Some of them thought it was the right thing. 'Are you out of your minds?' I said. 'They were *college kids*, not revolutionaries. What are you doing, live ammo on a college campus!'"[9]

Tuesday, May 5, one day after the Kent State killings, instead of the usual several thousand participants, almost ten thousand people turned up for an afternoon mass protest on the UW campus. The shock of the murders had galvanized many people to move off the sidelines into active dissent. The idea of taking over the I-5 freeway to march downtown spread spontaneously through the crowd. About seven thousand walked the few blocks to the 45th Street freeway entrance where they spilled onto all the southbound lanes and then spread over the northbound lanes. They talked with drivers about the war as they stopped all traffic, which backed up over thirty miles. There was no violence. Back on campus, the rally continued; UW President Charles Odegaard noted his concern over the Kent State deaths, but also called in 250 riot-geared Tactical Unit policemen to the campus.

The next day, three thousand people repeated the tactic of walking onto I-5, stopping all traffic. Like the day before, it began peacefully, but after moving almost a mile down the freeway, police used tear gas and clubs to re-open the freeway, lane by lane.

Protests against the war in Southeast Asia intensified when Ohio National Guardsmen killed four students at Kent State University. In Seattle, thousands of students took to the I-5 freeway for several days in a row, shutting it down. *University of Washington Libraries, Special Collections, Joseph Karpen, photographer, UW38751*

Freeway takeovers continued through the week, along with running confrontations on the UW campus. On Friday, May 8, Mayor Uhlman closed the express lanes on I-5 for students and also "reserved [some] for state troopers in case of any trouble."[10] President Odegaard cancelled classes in honor of the four dead Kent State students. Mayor Uhlman gave city employees the day off with pay, declaring a citywide day of mourning for the Kent State students. Uhlman and indicted federal conspirator Chip Marshall shared the podium that Friday afternoon as over ten thousand people rallied peacefully in a light rain in front of the federal courthouse. When the rally ended, officials closed the express lanes to cars and allowed demonstrators to walk back to campus.

Seven days later, on May 15, two students at Jackson State College in Mississippi were gunned down by police as they participated in a demonstration against racism, the expansion of the war, and the killings the week before at Kent State. UW rallies and strike committees centered on disrupting ROTC activity, blocking their graduation ceremonies, and occupying their buildings. Violent evening and night clashes occurred in the neighborhood surrounding the campus between "roving, chanting, rock-throwing bands of youth ranging up to 300 in number," police, and

This rainy May 8 rally in downtown Seattle was held in honor of the four Kent State students killed four days earlier. Mayor Wes Uhlman declared a day of mourning for the city, and shared the podium with Seattle 7 alleged-conspirator Chip Marshall. *University of Washington Libraries, Special Collections, Joseph Karpen, photographer, UW38752*

a "vigilante group [of] about 20 men, carrying clubs [who] roamed the University District and beat some protesters with nightsticks."[11] Some of these vigilantes were later identified as off-duty policemen.

President Odegaard, fearing escalating protests and strikes on his campus, implored President Nixon to explain his Vietnam War policy in a way people could understand.[12] Presciently, that same week, and still two years before the Watergate break-in, a small article appeared in the *Seattle Times* headed "Nixon Impeachment Studied."[13] The nation was getting tired of the war and tired of government lies about the war.

◆

A major item on SLF's revised to-do list that summer was the work of the defense collective, which would raise money, manage publicity, and help the attorneys and defendants gear up for their trial. Jane Smith was a key player because of her legal aid experience and her longstanding friendship with the Ithaca transplants. Most other members of the defense collective were women as well. Joe Kelly (who later married one of its members) recalls that the women "were used and abused by a lot of the defendants. People would roar into their house and eat all their food and disappear."[14]

One day as the defense attorneys, the defendants, and the defense collective gathered to discuss strategy, Kelly, in some ways the most thoughtful and careful of the defendants, noticed a man among them whom he did not know. Kelly had just arrived from Chicago, where he'd completed a three month sentence for aggravated battery from an antiwar action there. This was his first meeting with the attorneys and the defense collective.

"Who is this guy?" Kelly asked when he saw a stranger join the group. "I don't like the way he looks. Why is he here?" When no one could provide a good answer, he told the man, whose name was David Sannes, to leave.

David Sannes was an FBI informer and provocateur who had been hanging around SLF for a while. He had a code name, TJ, and a post office box issued to him by the Seattle FBI and Stan Pitkin.[15] He later told his story of spying and dirty tricks to Public Broadcasting reporter Paul Jacobs for a television series called *The Great American Dream Machine*.[16]

Paul Jacobs interviewed several other men in addition to Sannes, including Jeff Desmond and Horace "Red" Parker, both of Seattle, who offered up similar stories of FBI-financed anti-SLF chicanery. Parker was to become the key prosecution witness in the Seattle 7 trial; Chip Marshall's cross-examination of him was a courtroom highlight.

The Great American Dream Machine was produced by National Educational Television (NET). NET sought comment from the FBI agents and policemen named by Sannes and the others as their handlers and bankers. In major stonewalling mode to protect his illegal and still secret COINTELPRO provocateur and harassment activities, J. Edgar Hoover strongly denied everything and threatened to sue NET. Seattle police similarly denied everything, and forwarded their objections to Attorney General John Mitchell and the Federal Communications Commission.[17]

Cowed, PBS cancelled the segment. Executive producer Al Perlmutter called the PBS action to pull the show "a terribly sad and unfortunate decision…it's censorship, I believe, without question."[18] A few weeks later, PBS recovered its sense of journalistic responsibility and showed the segment, with the addition of a panel discussion moderated by respected newsman Jim Lehrer. A table full of PBS news people and executives discussed how PBS had handled or mishandled the situation. Reporter Paul Jacobs was grilled on how he had verified his sources and their stories. As Lehrer noted, it was a news story about the news.

Sannes' story was this: a returning Vietnam veteran and manager of a tavern near the UW, he'd volunteered to be an undercover agent for the FBI in Seattle. His contacts in the agency were Burt Carter and Louis Harris, the latter of whom was omnipresent in the Seattle 7 courtroom as the prosecution's primary FBI case agent. Sannes said that Harris instructed him to "find people interested in bombing. These were people that I sought out for the FBI that I convinced to actually bomb [something]."[19]

The particular something he urged them to bomb was state highway 520's heavily used bridge that spans Lake Washington between Seattle and its bedroom suburbs to the east. "I was instructed to infiltrate bombing groups to gain credibility as a bomber by actually doing bombings." Sannes noted that it took "many weeks of persuasion" to convince his targets to agree to blow up the bridge. Even then, "none of these individuals had any knowledge of explosives themselves. It was necessary for them to have outside explosive help and that was me." Sannes, however, scuttled the plan when his FBI handlers told him that one or more of the bombers "had to die in a booby-trap explosion."[20]

While attending the Seattle 7 defense collective meetings before Kelly arrived, Sannes had put forward "a never ending flow of suggestions and ideas," including bomb threats associated with the trial, using "various recipes for homemade explosives, nerve gases, etc. His favorite appeared to be a mixture of nitric acid and iodine which he claimed was many times more explosive than nitroglycerin and excellent for making land mines on public officials' front yards, etc.…These kinds of conversations only reinforced our opinion that he was eccentric," said one SLF member.[21]

Sannes' most disturbing plan involved a fake kidnapping and threatened execution of one of the Seattle 7 defendants, including a warning note from an invented vigilante group named the Committee for Public Safety. "I personally didn't like it for obvious reasons of illegality and even more so its manipulative nature and effect on our friends," testified an SLF member in a later deposition.[22]

Another of the PBS show's trio of interviewees did carry out a Seattle bombing. Unlike Sannes, Jeff Desmond didn't volunteer to be an agent provocateur. Seattle FBI agent Louis Harris came to Desmond's home to offer him money "to work undercover in bombing activities for the FBI."[23] Desmond was on the fringes of the antiwar movement in Seattle, had explosives experience from his employment at DuPont Chemical, and was a heroin addict. In a signed deposition in 1971, Desmond recounted several meetings with Harris and the money he received from Harris to purchase bomb-making material. He named the people that he recruited and described the bombs that he built.

After an initial bombing of a construction site near the UW campus, Harris instructed Desmond "to alert him about future bombings [for entrapment purposes]."[24] Subsequently the Seattle police were brought in, so Desmond was taking orders from and reporting to both the FBI and the Seattle police. Federal and local law enforcement apparently had to create a bombing in order to catch a bomber.

Like many agent provocateurs, Desmond's cover was blown when he was not charged after being arrested during a bomb placement. In March 1970, he warned both the Seattle police and the FBI that he was leading several activists to plant a bomb at the U.S. Post Office near the UW campus on a certain day and time. Caught in the act were Desmond and two men who subsequently became unindicted co-conspirators in the Seattle 8 indictments.

Desmond testified about his arrest: "After being put in a questioning room separate from the others arrested, I was congratulated by Lt. Richard Schoener of the Seattle Police. I told him that I hurt badly from having been beaten on the way to jail—Lt. Schoener then went out, got me a quarter spoon of heroin and apparatus. He gave me the heroin and material to shoot it with and left the room and locked the door. I shot up the heroin then—in Lt. Schoener's office in the downtown Seattle precinct. I was told I'd have to spend the night in jail to make the bombing arrest look good. The next morning I was released on my personal recognizance while the others were held on $25,000 bond…[after that] it was impossible for me to work undercover for either the Seattle Police or the Seattle office of the FBI."[25]

As late as 1972, the FBI was still boiling mad over the Sannes and Desmond TV stories. They wanted to pursue legal action against them, but Hoover's office said no, because their depositions "possess a scintilla of truth, it can be expected that defense attorneys…will exploit these instances to the Bureau's disadvantage. Additionally it is recognized that such proceedings could result in the undesirable practice of bringing Bureau records and operations into open hearings."[26]

In a still unsolved case, Desmond was shot to death in his Seattle apartment in 1975.

In early July as pretrial planning continued, the Seattle FBI office sent its regular status memo "Subject; COINTELPRO—NEW LEFT" to Director Hoover. It appears to be proposing a solution to the problem of the still missing alleged conspirator Michael Justesen: "In the event federal process against (REDACTED) is dismissed prior to the trial of the 'Seattle 8'…consideration will be given to planting a story that (REDACTED) was an informant in the case."[27] Best guess is that this proposes that the FBI start rumors that Justesen himself was an informer, thus making it more difficult for him to find safety underground, perhaps driving him into the open, and then to arrest.

Being female was complicated in the spring and summer of 1970. The growing women's movement gave Susan Stern the chance to find the language and a context for thinking and speaking about being a woman. She started to think and talk about women's rights, and how they didn't have many. Men, it seemed, were in charge of everything, including women. Why hadn't she noticed that before? It was a question that women all over the country were asking more frequently.

In 1969, Stern had hosted what may have been the city's first women's liberation discussion group in her basement. Both young and middle-aged women came to talk about their lives; some were new to political involvement, and others had been active in old left groups from the 1930s and 40s. Conversations like these, where women talked, often for the first time, about their personal experiences as second-class citizens, were called consciousness-raising groups. They were this generation of American women's tentative steps toward realizing that gender inequity wasn't their personal failing, but was anchored deeply into the bedrock of their culture.

One married UW graduate student and antiwar activist who helped organize Stern's basement meetings told her story to the group. She had gone to a surgeon's office because she'd felt a lump in her breast. Her husband, also a graduate student and also active in campus antiwar activity, had accompanied her.

The surgeon recommended a biopsy under anesthesia. He explained that the standard practice of the day was to keep the woman sedated while the lab examines the tissue. If it's cancerous, the breast would be removed without waking the patient, thus leaving her no opportunity to consider other options. After the surgeon described the procedure, he passed the consent form to her husband for his signature—it was he, not the woman with the lump, who had authority over the breast.

As the consciousness raising discussions continued, Susan Stern felt the ground firm up, a little, under her feet. She felt as if maybe, finally, she was becoming a real person, with things to say and a right to say them. "Now, for the first time in my life I had something to talk about, and people listened to me, especially women…I talked incessantly. And as I talked, I grew. And as I grew, I thought more. And as I thought more, I read more widely. As I read more widely, I felt more secure in my knowledge… and I developed my Style…people looked at me, and God damn it, when I talked they listened, finally they listened."[28]

Susan Stern wasn't the only SLF woman who worked hard to get people to listen to her, to take her seriously. One day in late May 1970, SLF member Pat Sullivan and several of the Seattle 7 alleged conspirators were drinking beer in the Hideout Tavern in a rundown neighborhood on the waterfront. Looking up from the bar, Sullivan and her indicted comrades noticed a sign reading "Women's Liberation Front" surrounded by seventeen brassieres nailed to the wall. After a failed attempt to convince the bartender to take them down, the SLF contingent walked out. Returning three days later with thirty women and a few more men, they bypassed the bartender and began ripping the bras off the wall, throwing them in trash cans and setting them on fire. Bras and other underwear appeared and disappeared on the Hideout's walls over the following week as the battle raged on, each side declaring temporary victory, but leaving the wider war unwon.[29]

Despite articles and lip service about women as equal comrades in the struggle, it didn't parse out that way in real life. Women tended to do the cooking, the cleaning, and the secretarial work during the day, and to provide the sex at night. Stern was not the only woman to complain that it was usually the women in the collectives who worked the paying jobs to bring in rent and grocery money.

Some of the women in SLF had an epiphany about their situation after an August outdoor rock concert when several women complained to each other that they'd been sexually harassed and raped at the concert. The more they talked, the more the blame centered on the macho atmosphere created by the SLF leadership, in particular by those men now under federal indictment and facing a decade in prison.

The women agonized over how to respond: should they call the men out, tell the world that some of their revolutionary heroes were sexist pigs? Hit a man when he's down? Or take it quietly for the greater cause of ending the war, smashing racism, and toppling capitalism?

Some, but not all, of the Seattle women chose to speak up. They moved into their own collective house and wrote a scathing document, printed with the title "Gang Rape in Seattle" that named all of the male Seattle 7 defendants (with the exception of Roger Lippman, who is not named at all) as male chauvinists and worse.[30] It later became known as the Fanshen Statement,[31] and was more about being a woman in the antiwar movement than about rape at a rock festival. In fact, there is no mention of gang rape, nor are any of the named men directly accused of any rape at all. But they are accused of uniformly ignoring the contributions of women in the movement, of generally belittling women, and of "creating an atmosphere in which rape could occur and be condoned."[32]

The document begins forcefully:

> The Seattle Liberation Front sponsored the [1970] Sky River Rock Festival.[33] Three women were raped. One woman was stabbed attempting to escape. A fourth rape was prevented by a female "chauvin patrol."
>
> Two days after Sky River, women from the women's liberation movement intruded upon an SLF general meeting. We denounced seven men who had fucked us over, used and destroyed people, and created a white, male supremacist movement in Seattle.
>
> The movement in Seattle is, in many ways, a microcosm of the Movement across the country. The men we denounced are not unusually evil, brilliantly manipulative, or exceptional leaders in any sense. All over the country men have defined the Revolution. People who want to act have had to exist in the context these men set up. We feel a responsibility to sisters across the country to explain our action and the history behind it.[34]

The five-page, typed, single-spaced document describes the frenetic pace of collective life and how it "brought into being a way of life designed to keep us from anger, from love, from strength, from freedom, from all but the illusions of these things." The women concluded that their "oppression and liberation was peripheral to the things our 'brothers' talked about and did. The reality of our lives was peripheral to their revolution."[35] Whenever women in the movement tried to describe how the world looked from their perspective, they were generally told that the problems of white women had to take a back seat to the struggles of black and third world peoples, especially the beleaguered Vietnamese.

"You're not oppressed," Jeff Dowd was quoted by one SLF woman as saying, "Men are oppressed. We're the ones that are dying in Vietnam and rotting in the jails."[36] One of the defendants' friends who had come to Seattle from Ithaca recalled, "Everything we did in those days was evaluated on potential jail time" and "our friendships had been forged against threats much more vituperative than the women's strongly-felt internal criticisms."[37]

Despite this history, when this group of SLF women had finished writing, they tentatively passed their document around town and presented it to at least one SLF meeting. The discussions didn't go well. The men had louder voices. They didn't get the point. Abeles, bewildered, didn't see how he could oppress a woman when he was "socking it to them." One woman noted later that "the outcome of the Fanshen meeting turned simmering anger to a raging boil."[38] Others thought the statement was just sour grapes whining, but all the reported recollections of this part of SLF's history by both men and women included the word "painful."

Some of the women, particularly those working most directly with the trial defense, felt strongly that the statement misrepresented the sexual experiences of most SLF women, who often were enjoying their freedom as much as the men.[39] The sexual revolution was part of the culture and politics of the times. As one of the Fanshen authors described it later, "the paper itself was not a mere angry reaction to the reports of those [rape] events, but a deeper examination of sexism—and its swaggering adolescent cousin, machismo—in our immediate lives, and the need to get beyond it in order to build new political human beings."[40]

When some of the Seattle women mailed the Fanshen Statement to a few underground newspapers, it wasn't published. The San Francisco-based radical journal *Socialist Revolution* chose to support the Seattle defendants by not printing the women's statement. After the trial was over, they apologized to the women, and did print it, although they edited out the men's names.

The Seattle-based women's paper *Ain't I a Woman* printed the original version including the names in early October, with a short preface thanking the writers "for refusing to shut up and 'wait until after the Revolution,' for reminding us again that any male-dominated revolution would simply reinstitute oppression under another name."[41]

A left-leaning Seattle radio station, KRAB, hosted most of the indicted SLF leaders, including Susan Stern, just a few days before their trial began in late November. The participants sound exhausted, not only from a busy summer, but from the fact that the discussion was being taped at two in the morning, after most of them had been drinking at the Century Tavern and then attending a screening of *Woodstock*. Susan Stern brought up the Fanshen issue.

The men interrupted her, and each other, in an awkward conversation where they admitted that many of the women's charges were indeed true, and that the movement indeed was "almost entirely male-led."[42] They allowed that women's liberation groups "were among the most organized in the country."[43] But they justified their behavior by saying that they were too busy with external issues (ending the war, ending racism) to concentrate on dealing with their internal issues. Lerner noted that this came at a very bad time, that it was "hard to struggle with ourselves when the state is coming down on us" and went on to complain about the lack of national support their money-strapped defense team had received, and how everyone knew about the Chicago 7 but nobody had heard of the Seattle 7.[44]

Stern had lapsed into silence, but made another attempt. She was hesitant and uneasy. "You talk about support in terms of money. That's not support…you can't possibly understand how little you know about women's issues…Nobody's talking about their lives. Men talk in terms of ideas, not about their lives."[45] Lerner jumped in to defend the importance of ideas, saying that in many ways, his identity was his ideas. Stern struggled on, occasionally losing her point, admitting she was "loaded" on drugs or alcohol, but told Lerner that "ideas come into being somehow to individuals living human lives…I can't get the reality of other people's lives—babies burned in Vietnam, tired moms in welfare offices, people getting shot in their beds, the bitter reality of their daily lives—out of my mind."[46]

———————◆———————

The Fanshen Statement may have been written to try to save an already-fraying SLF by pointing out ways male members could recognize women's contributions and thus make the organization stronger and more effective. Unfortunately, it had the opposite effect. In retrospect, several SLF women mark the fallout from the statement as the beginning of the end of SLF as a functioning organization. After the meeting, the defense collective found their job of rallying support for the defendants suddenly much more difficult. Susan Stern, as she drafted her book from her post-trial cell at the Washington Corrections Center for Women, marked Fanshen as the end of SLF, at least the end of the parties. She didn't disagree so much with the content of the statement, but, like the editors of *Socialist Revolution* she was uncomfortable with the timing: "Singling out the Seattle 7 men did nothing but take the pressure off other men who were just as guilty of using politics as a sexual bait. It also made it impossible for the conspiracy men to function at a time when their lives depended upon it."[47]

7

Gearing Up for Trial

It is the spirit and not the form of law that keeps justice alive.
—EARL WARREN, CHIEF JUSTICE OF THE SUPREME COURT, 1953-1969

Even activists with many arrests on their records may never have experienced a jury trial in federal court where the customs are Byzantine and the language is anything but transparent. This was definitely the case with the Seattle 7. They were on a steep learning curve—sometimes they did their homework and sometimes they didn't. Sometimes they listened to their attorneys' advice and sometimes they didn't. In the decades since their trial, the seven have repeatedly pondered over their week and a half crash course in American justice. Could they have played it differently? Should they have? Would it have led to a different outcome?

The prosecution, it would become clear, had its own weaknesses and blind spots, and its own second thoughts. After U.S. Attorney Stan Pitkin assembled his witnesses and matched their testimony to Guy Goodwin's grand jury indictments, the lean and unsmiling lead prosecutor likely began to worry that he had been given a case that didn't hold much water. But with one good witness, a sympathetic jury, and if the defendants would cooperate by exhibiting bad behavior, perhaps he could pull it off. Besides, there wasn't much he could do about it. One local attorney told me that it is very difficult for U.S. Attorneys to stand up to the Department of Justice. The FBI in 1970, he added, was entirely unequipped to successfully handle antiwar protest trials because they treated them as political cases, not criminal ones. The FBI instructed their agents to collect political pamphlets and listen to speeches by radical leaders—"all this political mumbo jumbo stuff"—instead of arresting people in the act of committing a crime.[1]

A retired local FBI agent agreed: "What a stupid case to bring; you indict them for conspiracy and not one was caught with a brick in his or her hand. That's totally crazy. What a waste of resources and money."[2] This agent was fresh out of law school in 1968, and had joined the FBI to avoid the draft. He continued:

The Bureau didn't understand what was going on. They saw the Weather Underground as a serious threat to national security. And it wasn't. They didn't have the organizational skills, they were feeding off the antiwar movement, the drug culture…I was trying to educate the Bureau—these old guys were very conservative. They would see ten thousand people demonstrating as ten thousand revolutionaries. I mingled with these demonstrators and yes, there were some radical types, but most were college kids or their parents. And because someone has long hair and a beard, it doesn't mean they are revolutionaries. I was educating [my fellow FBI agents] that you don't judge a book by its cover.[3]

Defense attorney Michael Tigar believed that Pitkin "appeared to have swallowed whole the Goodwin/FBI theory that my clients were dangerous revolutionaries. In the end, this delusion was the government's undoing. Pitkin had lost that essential skeptical detachment from the evidence."[4]

Supporting U.S. Attorney Pitkin on the Seattle 7 case were William Erxleben and Charles Billinghurst, both local Assistant U.S. Attorneys. Neither was particularly active in the courtroom itself, although they participated in pretrial preparations and out-of-courtroom assignments.

The Seattle prosecution's inadequacies were not tied to their courtroom errors as much as they reflected the weaknesses of the indictments themselves, which in turn were driven by the misunderstandings and paranoia of President Nixon, Attorney General Mitchell, and FBI Director Hoover. In many ways, the government was fighting their last war against the old left Communist Party, using tactics and approaches that were no longer effective against dissent from these Seattle representatives of the New Left.

As they assembled their legal team and became acquainted with each other, the defendants stayed true to their own individual predilections and personalities, which brought them both good luck and disaster over the course of the trial and its aftermath. They had to function in two milieus at the same time—the alien world of the federal justice system and their accustomed world of antiwar and community organizing. Guy Goodwin's strategy of intimidation and distraction was designed to make them stumble in both environments, and they did.

The Seattle 7 defense attorneys were as disparate a mix of individuals as the defendants themselves. The out-of-town hotshot was Michael Tigar, an eager junior helper on the Chicago 7 defense team, and already an attorney with a record of fiercely defending the free speech of political activists of any stripe. A large man with many interests, a prodigious memory, and huge grasp of detail, Tigar could reel off complicated French recipes as easily as obscure but entirely relevant legal citations from 150 years past.

Called "one of the most theatrical defense attorneys in the country" by *New Yorker* legal affairs columnist Jeffrey Toobin, Tigar today still likes to defend people on the left and the right who are being crushed "by the oppressive hand of the state." In his book *Law and the Rise of Capitalism,* Tigar calls for "a new jurisprudence of insurgency."[5] Tigar is also a playwright, penning scripts from great legal battles of the past, including the 1886 rigged trial and executions of the Haymarket anarchists in Chicago.[6]

The attorney with the most criminal courtroom experience, and the one who was most certain the defense could win, was a mild-mannered intercollegiate boxing champion from eastern Washington named Carl Maxey. Years later, Michael Lerner said Maxey "was the only adult in the trial except me. And I wasn't much of an adult."[7]

Maxey started life by being abandoned twice, once by his mother who gave him away, and then two years later in Spokane, Washington, when his adoptive parents died. Maxey was then sent to an orphanage, one of only two black children housed there. Maxey was the bigger of the two, and discovered he had a penchant for protecting the weak, as his smaller black friend was frequently bullied. When the managers of the orphanage were convicted of sexually assaulting some of the white boys, the institution did some housecleaning, which included sweeping away the two black kids. Maxey was sent to juvenile detention. "They threw us out," Maxey later said, "And the incident that precipitated it was sexual misconduct, all involving white people. So if you wonder where some of my fire comes from, it comes from a memory that includes this event."[8]

Maxey was taken in by a Jesuit-run Native American orphanage in Idaho, where his intelligence and athleticism were recognized and encouraged. He graduated from college and law school at Gonzaga University in Spokane, along the way becoming 1950 intercollegiate light heavyweight boxing champion. He was known as a "scrappy civil rights lawyer credited with virtually singlehandedly desegregating much of the inland Northwest."[9] Despite his many successes, Maxey shot himself in his bedroom in 1997. He was 73 years old.

The third attorney for the defense was Lee Holley, a stocky Korean War veteran who sometimes wore overalls in court. He had been arrested at the 1968 Chicago Democratic Convention and had recently moved to Seattle after defending alleged communists in New York. Arriving in Seattle, he worked with draft resisters, and later for prisoner rights organizations. Of the Seattle defendants he later said, "It's important for attorneys to keep a sense of humor—I learned that from the Seattle 7. It's an important lesson. Juries love it when you make fun of yourself. You win cases that way. Our side had a good sense of humor."[10] Holley was quite taken with the defendants' freewheeling focus on drugs and sex, partaking of both during many parties before and during the trial. One SLF activist suggested that he'd come out west to find "something more meaningful than what his life had been."[11] Holley thought Tigar was the best attorney he'd ever met and said Maxey was a joy to work with.[12]

Finally there was Jeff Steinborn, a young local attorney who remembers being the first attorney recruited to the case. Joe Kelly, educated by earlier legal entanglements, had realized that they were going to need good representation, even before the indictments came down. Through Jane Smith, who had returned to Seattle to work as a legal aide in an office near Steinborn's, Kelly made an appointment with Steinborn and his colleagues. The attorneys couldn't understand why he was there, as no one had been arrested yet.

"Well, it's just a matter of time," Kelly responded. Steinborn believed him, and started hanging out with Kelly and his friends. Steinborn recalled:

> I went out to the Blue Moon [Tavern] and hustled the business. I knew I wanted the case. I'd been a lawyer long enough to realize you could get any case you wanted if you were willing to do it for free. So I went out and met the defendants and I was the first lawyer hired, even though I was right out of law school and didn't have a clue what I was doing.
>
> Then I helped them to hire some really good lawyers like Carl Maxey and Mike Tigar, both friends of mine. I was the junior lawyer in the midst of seriously excellent lawyers. Carl was the king of Spokane and a master trial lawyer.[13]

If you're interested in the law as an instrument of social justice, it was the best train in town, the most interesting case; the most likely to have an impact, the most likely to make a big splash. And I was the age of the defendants and their lifestyle and politics were very attractive, although I never became a radical myself. I've always just been kind of a generic ACLU [American Civil Liberties Union] member. That's what ACLU liberals do—they defend radicals. And it was fun, a good time. We partied. Lots of pot, lots of sex, lots of everything. So it was attractive to me in a lot of ways. Very free and good people.[14]

Chip Marshall and Michael Lerner chose to defend themselves, called acting *pro se*. The four defense attorneys agreed to this, appreciating their verbal skills and noting that *pro se* defendants are often allowed more speaking latitude than professional attorneys.

If the case was handled properly, the defense attorneys thought they had at least a fighting chance of squeezing out a win. What they didn't know was that proper handling was entirely out of their control.

Defense attorneys and the SLF defense collective operated from an office in the Smith Tower (once the tallest building west of Chicago) in Seattle's Pioneer Square. From here fundraising efforts, speaking engagements, press relations, and volunteer help were coordinated, as well as attorney interviews and attorney–defendant meetings. It was also where the FBI had planted David Sannes, until he was outed by Kelly.

A group of UW professors also established a defense committee to raise awareness of the free speech aspects of the charges and to raise money to help defray attorney fees. (This committee had a large sponsorship list including several of the Chicago 7 defendants and attorneys, and nationally known intellectuals and antiwar activists such as Howard Zinn, Noam Chomsky, I. F. Stone, and Jane Spock.) They called their group "Conspirare," Latin for "to breathe together," and emphasized the fact that the defendants were all charged with activities protected by the First Amendment.

One of the issues the SLF defense collective faced, beyond keeping their leadership out of prison, was how best to play the trial for the good of the entire movement. Should they do whatever was needed to keep them out of prison, even if it meant compromising their political principles, or should they use the trial as a platform for political education?

Should large demonstrations be planned outside the courtroom? How militant should they be?

Although the trial date was delayed several times, allowing more time to plan, the defense collective and the defendants never came to clear or unified decisions on these questions. In October, as the trial date seemed imminent, they called an open meeting to discuss these strategic difficulties: "It was the first time that the long-term political strategy behind the trial was discussed, [particularly] the effectiveness of militant disruption outside the courtroom. People also argued about the conflicting goals of getting acquitted and of using the trial as a focus for political action."[15]

In the end, they still could not settle on any clear direction. This lack of an agreed-upon strategy meant that their actions in the courtroom were occasionally scattershot, off-the-cuff, and dysfunctional. The defendants and their supporters had a tendency to ricochet between being overly defensive or provocatively confrontational.

The Seattle 7 case was scheduled on U.S. District Court Judge George H. Boldt's docket. Boldt had cut his judicial teeth on organized crime and labor racketeering cases. Sometimes called "lightning Boldt" because of his no-nonsense, no-delay approach to running his courtroom, he was considerably challenged by the unorganized behavior of the Seattle 7 defendants.[16]

Boldt's daughter described her father as a very patriotic person and a conservative in most ways. He loved his job, believed in being prepared, and "didn't like histrionics at all." She recalled that the Seattle 7 trial was "more or less a nightmare for my dad."[17] Robby Stern (Susan and Robby had divorced by this time) attended several days of the trial. He described Boldt as having "not an ounce of informality about him…he was constantly banging his gavel…it must have been a nightmare for him."[18] Boldt was sixty-six years old at the time of the Seattle 7 trial.

The opening date of the trial was like a mirage disappearing in front of a speeding car on the hot blacktop of a desert road—set and re-set over the summer and fall of 1970 almost to Thanksgiving, sometimes delayed by the government and sometimes by the defendants. At one point, the defense decided that they couldn't get a fair trial in Seattle and so it was moved to Tacoma, a wood and pulp mill town thirty-five miles south of Seattle along Interstate 5. Then the defense decided that was a mistake—too difficult to get SLF supporters there every day and a much more conservative catchment area for jury selection. Judge Boldt refused to return the venue to Seattle. The defense appealed. The Ninth Circuit Court denied the appeal.

Michael Abeles, eternal optimist and trickster, visited the Tacoma City Council to ask the mayor and council for a "courtroom large enough to hold all the spectators who want to attend; for parking, parade and demonstration permits; free food, clothing and housing for persons attending the trial; approval for high school and community college students to attend the trial during classroom hours; and approval for the defendants to speak at high schools." He added that he also was requesting "release of all nonwhites from prisons and release of all prisoners held on narcotics charges."[19]

The defendants also asked Judge Boldt to disqualify himself in favor of a judge from a "neutral" country, and if that didn't fly, to disqualify himself because he belonged to "racist and sexist" civic organizations. They also asked for lists of any stocks he owned in "war-profiteering corporations."[20] Lerner petitioned Boldt to disqualify himself on grounds that Boldt had previously not treated other *pro se* defendants fairly. Boldt refused them all.

The defense also asked that the charges be dismissed because the indictments read more like a catalogue of constitutional rights than a list of criminal acts. The defense asked to examine the grand jury minutes and a host of other pretrial motions; all denied.

As the pretrial jockeying continued, defense attorney Tigar reflected on his current caseload to a group of fellow litigators: "No, I do not think, and I have not thought, that our courtrooms should be instruments of revolution, but I warn the profession, including those of its members who are prosecutors and judges, that if our courtrooms begin by being instruments of intolerable repression, then they may well turn into instruments of revolution, just as Boston courts were in 1761, and that gentlemen, is the challenge to the profession."[21]

PART TWO

Trial

Front of four-page flyer calling for support of the Seattle 8
Conspiracy Defense Collective. *Author's collection.*

8

Let the Circus Begin

JUDGE BOLDT: If you speak again you will be ejected from the room.

SPECTATOR: People aren't allowed to speak?

JUDGE BOLDT: Of course not.

—SEATTLE 7 TRIAL TRANSCRIPT, NOVEMBER 24, 1970

Because trials are often covered by news media in more detail than their precipitating events, political defendants like the Seattle 7 can use their trial to explain their cause to a broader audience. Defendants can put on nice clothes, cut their hair, look respectable for the cameras. If they choose to defend themselves *pro se*, they might be able to squeeze in a rallying speech or two. The trial itself thus becomes an organizing tool.

But trials are also highly stressful events for defendants. Much is at risk—the Seattle 7 faced up to ten years in federal prison. They were unfamiliar with legal language and procedures. The stage, as it were, was owned by the opposition. They were still getting to know their own attorneys, not to mention each other. Uncertainty, anxiety, and friction couldn't help but cloud their courtroom behavior. Missteps by all led to chaos and an end unforeseen by the judge, the prosecution, and the defendants.

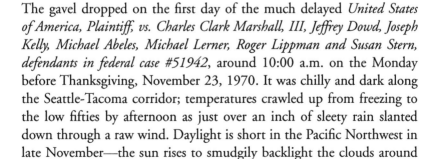

The gavel dropped on the first day of the much delayed *United States of America, Plaintiff, vs. Charles Clark Marshall, III, Jeffrey Dowd, Joseph Kelly, Michael Abeles, Michael Lerner, Roger Lippman and Susan Stern, defendants in federal case #51942*, around 10:00 a.m. on the Monday before Thanksgiving, November 23, 1970. It was chilly and dark along the Seattle-Tacoma corridor; temperatures crawled up from freezing to the low fifties by afternoon as just over an inch of sleety rain slanted down through a raw wind. Daylight is short in the Pacific Northwest in late November—the sun rises to smudgily backlight the clouds around 7:30 a.m. and is long gone by 4:30 p.m.

There were many facts American citizens didn't know about their government in the winter of 1970. Only a few people in the FBI and the Department of Justice knew that the FBI was regularly placing warrantless wiretaps, opening mail, following law-abiding citizens, writing fake letters to scare parents and create dissention within antiwar and civil rights organizations, placing slanderous "news" articles in city newspapers, and keeping files on millions of Americans who had never been accused of a crime. FBI agents in the late 1960s and early 1970s had busily recruited hundreds of college students to infiltrate and inform on student peace groups. Dozens, like David Sannes and Jeff Desmond, were told by their FBI handlers to promote increasingly more violent actions in the groups they infiltrated—their purpose being to set up arrests on ever more serious charges, thereby neutralizing (one of FBI Director Hoover's favorite terms) the groups' leaders and forcing the remaining members to focus on legal defenses rather than protesting the war.

On the international front, Americans did not yet know how spectacularly the U.S. war in Southeast Asia was failing to meet its military or geopolitical goals. Detailed in the leaked Pentagon Papers, a government analysis of American goals and progress there from 1945 to 1967, the report concluded that despite considerable long-term diplomatic and military American intervention in those countries' sovereign affairs, the United States government was not meeting any of its goals. It appeared that the primary reason for persisting was simply to postpone a humiliating defeat.

With President Nixon's blessing, White House staffers and former Seattleites John Ehrlichman and Egil Krogh retaliated against Daniel Ellsberg, the analyst who leaked the report to the press, by engineering a break-in and burglary at Ellsberg's psychiatrist's office in a failed attempt to find evidence that would discredit Ellsberg's sanity. After his stint in prison for conspiracy and obstruction of justice, Krogh, much reformed, later wrote, "As President Nixon himself said to David Frost during an interview six years later, 'When the president does it, that means it is not illegal.' To this day the implications of this statement are staggering."[1]

All that unconstitutional federal trickery, however, was to come to light after 1970, after the Seattle 7 trial. People who worked in protest movements in 1970 had a feeling those things were going on, but even the most paranoid of them had no idea of the extent of it, nor the fact that so much of it was planned, authorized by, and funded from President Nixon's Oval Office. And most people, like the citizens called to the jury panel in Tacoma on this Thanksgiving week, were busy with their own lives, and spent little time thinking at all about what their government was doing.

Judge Boldt's courtroom occupied the third floor of a four-story Beaux Arts style building completed in 1910. Built of steel and Indiana limestone, with tall windows and dark carved woodwork, it still sprawls across the block along A Street between South 11th and 12th Streets in downtown Tacoma. It was the pride of the city, and is today a historical landmark.

Building preparations for the trial by the careful U.S. Marshal Robinson set the stage for a narrative that many expected and some feared. The windows were taped and covered in plywood. All the entrances except one were sealed off and that single entry was barricaded with chain link and plywood to cordon it off from the rest of the building. Plywood fronts had also been installed across windows of a Weyerhaeuser building kitty-corner from the courthouse. Fearing that Robinson's preparations might encourage the very outcomes he was trying to prevent, defense attorney Maxey argued that the security measures were likely to give prospective jurors the impression that "they should be fearful of the defendants...that they are dangerous."[2] Maxey asked that they be removed or at least reduced. Judge Boldt denied his request.

Spectators admitted to the building were given a date-stamped entrance ticket, as were the defendants. Later on, spectators were accused of forging tickets and were denied entry. Stairways were blocked and entrants had to file past armed guards to reach the one small elevator to the third floor courtroom. Also on the third floor were the judge's chambers, a waiting room for witnesses, a small jail cell, space for U.S. Marshals, a small library, the jury room, and conference rooms for the defense, the prosecution, and the press. Judge Boldt had altered the interior of his courtroom, moving his raised desk from the middle front to an angled position in the front left corner. He thought he had a better view of the defendants, the attorneys, and the spectators from that viewpoint. A private door to his chambers was directly behind his desk, a design he would come to be grateful for when the going got rough.

The court was jammed with the 130 prospective jurors (called the jury panel, from which the final jury of twelve regulars and six alternates would be chosen), about fifty supporters of the defendants (described as "predominantly long-haired" by the local press),[3] twenty-eight news media, the defendants and their attorneys, and three government attorneys plus FBI case agent Louis Harris. Marshal Robinson was also omnipresent, along with his armed and uniformed officers. Robinson's presence became an issue for the defense because he was also listed as a prosecution witness, presumably to describe the events of TDA, at which he had been a major player. The courtroom normally seats 120; extra chairs were brought in, but some still had to stand.

Judge Boldt's first order of business was to select the men and women who would decide whether the federal government's allegations were true beyond a reasonable doubt. Did the defendants conspire "together with each other, each with the other, and with diverse other persons… to commit the following offenses against the United States, to willfully

November 23, 1970, Day One of the Seattle 7 federal conspiracy trial. Michael Lerner, in raincoat and scarf, is speaking; Joe Kelly is to the left with his arms crossed; to the left of Kelly is defense attorney Michael Tigar. *MOHAI, Seattle Post-Intelligencer Collection, 1986.5.53302.28*

A defendant, Michael Abeles, slumped across chairs during jury questioning.

Defendant Michael Abeles, caught by a newspaper sketch artist, slumping across chairs during the second day of jury selection. Prospective jurors were questioned up to one hour each. *By permission, Dick Miller/The Seattle Times; image courtesy Seattle Public Library*

and unlawfully injure and aid, abet, counsel and procure others to willfully and unlawfully injure the property of the United States, that is, the United States Courthouse at 5th Avenue and Spring Street?" In addition, did Marshall, Dowd, Kelly, and Abeles cross state lines "with the intent to incite, organize, promote and encourage a riot" and did Lerner use an instrument of "interstate commerce, to-wit, the Pacific Northwest Bell Telephone Company, with intent to incite, organize, promote and encourage a riot?"

Attorneys for both sides optimistically expected to complete jury selection on this first day.

There are many strategies for winnowing the final jury members from the larger jury panel. In the 1970s, both defending and prosecuting attorneys were learning to construct psychological and life experience questions to tease out a potential juror's personal biases for or against defendants and the nature of their alleged crimes. The goal of successful jury selection is to seat only those jurors who emotionally lean to one's own side, independent of the legal evidence. For the Seattle 7 prosecution, that meant keeping off the jury males in their 20s or 30s with hair below their ears who may indicate doubts about U.S. action in Vietnam.

The so-called right to a jury of one's peers derives from the Sixth Amendment of the U.S. Constitution, although the phrase "jury of one's peers" does not appear. The full Sixth Amendment reads: "In all criminal prosecutions, the accused shall enjoy the right to a speedy and public trial, by an impartial jury of the state and district wherein the crime shall have been committed, which district shall have been previously ascertained by law, and to be informed of the nature and cause of the accusation; to be confronted with the witnesses against him; to have compulsory process for obtaining witnesses in his favor, and to have the assistance of counsel for his defense."

The Constitutional phrase "impartial jury," however, has been part of English common law ever since the Magna Carta. The great English jurist William Blackstone wrote in the eighteenth century that conviction must "be confirmed by the unanimous suffrage of twelve of [the accused's] equals and neighbors indifferently chosen and superior to all suspicion."[4]

The jury selection process, then, is essentially a trial within the trial and it can be lengthy and complex. Identifying twelve "equals and neighbors" to pass judgment on the Seattle 7 proved to be both elusive and contentious. In Judge Boldt's courtroom on this Thanksgiving week it was unexpectedly so—three full days of anger and confusion spread over 634 pages of transcript.

As he entered his courtroom for the first time, Judge Boldt was greeted by spectators stomping and singing "Poison Ivy," a song recorded by the Coasters in 1959 and later covered by the Rolling Stones. Chip Marshall started the day by circulating around the courtroom, handing out Air Force recruiting pamphlets in an impromptu guerrilla theater act. A deputy marshal complained about finding stickers saying "Free the Seattle 8" stuck on walls and furniture around the courtroom. He said he caught defendant Jeff Dowd sticking one on a wall and when asked to take it off, the marshal complained, "he gave me the finger," and added, "They don't come off when they dry."[5]

The first line caught by the transcriptionist in the courtroom was spoken by a defendant: "Please stand for a moment of silence, your Honor, in honor of those people killed by United States bombs in North Vietnam."[6] About fifty spectators rose to their feet and cheered, fists raised.

Judge Boldt immediately told the marshals to eject two of the noisiest spectators. Using the tools they were familiar with, the defendants' courtroom behavior was much appreciated by their supporters, but it frequently dismayed their attorneys and alternately frightened or angered the judge.

With these opening salvos, the defendants and their supporters signaled loudly that they viewed the charges against them as blatantly political and spurious. Michael Lerner recalled thinking:

> How do we use this trial to help educate people about what's wrong with the war? That was the main thing we could do. Because we knew we were innocent of the charges. We couldn't imagine there would be a jury that, once they heard us, would actually convict us of these crimes that were totally bogus. There had been no conspiracy to destroy federal property, and there had been no using the facilities of interstate commerce with the intent of inciting to riot. They were both totally phony. So it didn't occur to us that we could get convicted. Not really. At least not until the trial started.[7]

Defendants and their supporters continued to interrupt the expected flow of an organized courtroom. SLF members on the chilly and damp sidewalk outside did the same,

Michael Lerner began to read his opening statement with a red telephone hung around his neck.— Staff sketches by Dick Miller.

Michael Lerner standing in a suit and tie, wearing a desk telephone slung around his neck, emphasizing that his charge of crossing state lines was not, like the Ithaca crowd, driving a car but using a telephone to call a Chicago 7 defendant to ask him how their case was going. Judge Boldt made him take it off. *By permission, Dick Miller/The Seattle Times; image courtesy Seattle Public Library* chanting antiwar slogans as they marched around the building, hemmed in by Tacoma city policemen carrying gas masks. Over the course of the twelve-day trial, a number of these stalwart SLF supporters were cited for carrying red or black flags, which was illegal in Tacoma under a 1914 law aimed at suppressing IWW marches.

Lerner stood up in the early moments of the jury selection process to introduce Chicago 7 defendant David Dellinger, who was among the seated spectators.[8] Boldt told Lerner that he couldn't do that; Marshall spoke up to announce that Dellinger knew more about this kind of trial than anyone in the courtroom, and that "his questions to the jurors would help us get a fair trial."[9]

Motion denied.

Despite the defendants' experience-based lack of trust in the ways of the FBI and local police (Abeles, Kelly, and Dowd, in fact, had been arrested again, just two days before the trial opened, when police broke up a party intended to raise money for their defense), they initially believed that they would be tried by an impartial jury representing a cross-section of Americans. To them, that meant including people in their twenties and people who opposed the Vietnam War. By May 1970 only 36 percent of Americans felt that the United States was right to send troops to Vietnam. In addition, in 1970 over half said the U.S. intervention was a mistake.[10] Surely that ratio should be reflected in the jury pool. At the very least, the defendants hoped for jurors with whom they could create a human connection. In retrospect, though, Susan Stern wasn't so sure; she remembered thinking as she smiled at the potential jurors, "we didn't have a hope in hell of convincing those people how nice, lovable and framed we were."[11]

In these first days as his own attorney, Chip Marshall worked hard to build a sympathetic bridge between the defendants and the jurors. He made humorous analogies and took an "aw shucks" approach, as if he were saying, "gosh, none of us is used to this courtroom talk; let's just settle this like the rational human beings we all are." When potential juror Mrs. Tucker admitted she had negative feelings about what she'd read about SDS, Marshall responded: "All we are asking is that people have an open mind...we are not asking for ostriches and people who never heard of SDS."[12] He sympathized with the potential difficulties of voicing an independent opinion during jury deliberations. It's hard, he said, to speak up when you don't agree with what everyone else is saying, to be an isolated one against eleven.

Michael Lerner, also defending himself, voiced concern that jurors might believe that the defendants were innocent of the stated charges, but guilty of other things that the jurors didn't like, such as having long hair or listening to rock and roll, and so would vote for conviction anyway.[13]

Racism was another cultural divide splitting the landscape. Seattle Liberation Front, Students for a Democratic Society, and Weatherman were all vocal supporters of the Black Panthers, a group viewed by many Americans as terrorists and a major threat to national security. The prosecution wasted no time in connecting these dots. However racist the nearly all-white jury panel (the final jury was all white) may have been, most of them knew to avoid sounding blatantly racist in public. Both Lerner and Marshall sympathetically noted that jurors might feel defensive and uncomfortable when questioned in such a way that might force them to admit racial prejudice. In fact, one prospective juror did disqualify herself when she said that her ability to judge fairly would be negatively affected by the fact that defense attorney Maxey was black.[14]

The first day of jury selection ended with no juror seated.

———————◆———————

On Tuesday, the second day of jury selection, Lerner asked "Your Honor, first I would like to request that the jury be provided with water. I notice that we [have some for us] whenever we are thirsty."[15] Marshall also continued to indicate his concern for the well-being of the jury panel, saying, "Your Honor, I guess that you had planned to have a court session on Friday, but we would like to ask that since it is Thanksgiving, it would be nice to have…off this Friday—I think it would be nice for everybody."[16]

On this Tuesday morning, Judge Boldt made the first of his many misidentifications among the defendants. This exchange about the unfairness of each defendant being allotted only two peremptory challenges (which allows attorneys to excuse a potential juror without having to give a reason) is typical:

LERNER: They [the two peremptory challenges] will be exercised independently of each other.

BOLDT: That is entirely up to you, Mr. Marshall, and your colleagues.

LERNER: I am Mr. Lerner.

KELLY: I am Kelly.

BOLDT: I beg your pardon, I know, but I misspoke myself. You did not take offense to that?

LERNER: No, but I take offense to getting only two peremptory challenges.

BOLDT: I understand that, Mr. Marshall.

MARSHALL: He is mixed up again.

STERN: Mr. Lerner.

BOLDT: Please don't shout, Mrs. Stern. This is not conducive to any rational consideration of the matters under consideration now.

LERNER: A rose is just as sweet under any name; but the challenges are only two and that seems to me to be an abuse of discretion…

BOLDT: Your objection is noted for the record, Mr. Marshall.

MARSHALL: Marshall?

BOLDT: Mr. Lerner, excuse me. And, denied.[17]

The other way to excuse a potential juror is a "challenge for cause" where the attorney must explain the reason. Again, the whole idea is for each side to construct a jury emotionally sympathetic to their side, but to do it in a way that looks fair.

Defense attorney Tigar argued that the prosecution could not legally exercise peremptory challenges on Sixth Amendment grounds: "I think you will take judicial notice that Mr. Gilich [a prospective juror who had been peremptorily challenged by the prosecution] was the youngest or second youngest member of the jury panel. The impact of Mr. Pitkin's peremptory challenge was to distort the character of the jury panel and go farther and farther away from the Constitutional idea of a cross section of the community."[18] Michael Abeles spoke up, saying the jury pool members are "not only not our peer group in age or similar life style or ideas, but they are not even a cross-segment of American society. Out of 115 people being selected for this thing, there [are] one or two black people."[19]

Judge Boldt was unmoved. He denied this entire line of thinking.

The Orwellian doublespeak of the conspiracy and intent-to-riot statutes under which the defendants were indicted was difficult for anyone to understand. The potential jurors were no exception. For instance, Judge Boldt explained to potential juror Dean McNee, "Now, of course, this case…charges that there was incitement of a riot, and the inflicting of damage on the United States Courthouse at Seattle." Defendant Marshall broke in to say, "I think you are reading the Indictment wrong, we are not charged with inciting a riot, we are [charged] with intent and conspiracy, it says nothing about us doing any violence at all."[20]

Tigar continued to point out the discrepancies between the language of the indictment and the words used by the judge and the prosecution to describe the defendants' alleged crimes. The federal conspiracy and anti-riot bill language is complex; it outlaws "conspiring to injure" federal property and crossing state lines with "intent to incite" a riot. The police had not arrested any of the Seattle 8 for damaging property or rioting at TDA, because they never saw them doing so. Yet, because it's easier to understand, the prosecution and the judge frequently talked about the broken windows and splattered paint at TDA as if that's what the trial was about.

Lerner added an argument familiar in many antiwar teach-ins of the time: the U.S. government was intending, inciting, and committing far more violence than anything any antiwar demonstrator had ever dreamed of doing.

> LERNER: As your Honor probably knows, without declaration of war by the Congress of the United States, the government is pursuing a policy of military aggression in Vietnam.
>
> BOLDT: Well, excuse me, Mr. Lerner, I cannot undertake to have you make a statement of that kind. I know there is a conflict going on in Vietnam, and if you will limit it to that—
>
> LERNER: There is a conflict in which the United States is using violence.
>
> BOLDT: Using force.[21]

As this conversation wound down, yet another potential juror answered, "No, I do not" to the question, "Do you have any opinion about the merits or demerits of the war in Vietnam?"[22]

9

A Peerless Jury is Seated

The judicial system has to be aware that justice and obedience are not the same thing.

—Chip Marshall, Seattle 7 defendant

Underestimating the power, flexibility, and tenacity of the U.S. government was a common error among many dissidents of the 1960s and 70s. The lengthy and argumentative Seattle 7 jury selection process was an eye-opener for the defendants and their supporters. Far more than their previous scuffles with the law, including Kelly and Lippman's previous months in Chicago and California courtrooms and jails, these first three days of the trial made it icily clear that the legal world was a cold and unfriendly environment. Everything they had learned in school about the rule of law and judicial fairness was being contradicted by the reality in front of them. They knew that black people were frequently convicted unfairly, but even with the Chicago 7 case fresh in their minds, they just didn't expect it to happen to them. They still thought they could debate, organize, and win an acquittal on the basis of the righteousness of their cause and the flimsiness of the charges against them.

That hope disappeared as their procedural objections were routinely denied and as members of the jury pool repeatedly stated under oath that they had no strong feelings one way or the other about their country's war in Vietnam. The defendants, whose daily lives for several years had been completely devoted to ending the war, couldn't believe that such people existed.

One of the few members of the jury panel who was in his twenties was Dean McNee, a middle school teacher from the small fishing and logging town of Hoquiam on Washington's Olympic Peninsula. McNee recalled his fellow prospective jurists: "There weren't a lot of people with facial hair or long hair. I think I was wearing muttonchops and hair down to my shoulders at that time. My hair was actually combed and I kept it combed. So I never really passed myself off as any kind of a hippie sort of character. I thought I was dressing stylishly, and grooming stylishly."[1]

Profiling, or assuming a person's political or cultural preferences could be identified by simply looking at his or her physical appearance, was alive and well in the 1960s, even if the term was not yet in vogue. Then, the length of a young man's hair was widely believed to accurately reflect his politics. Long hair meant a person was irresponsible, dangerously anti-American, and clearly not in the military. Long hair symbolized subversion, sex, drugs, and rock and roll.

It is hard, today, to understand the antagonism that long hair created in the late 1960s and early 1970s. Male high school students were expelled from school for "failing to cut [their] long 'Beatle-type' hair."[2] At the same time, the defendants' long hair sometimes led to joking and wishful comments from the older men in the Seattle 7 courtroom. After the trial, when the Seattle 7 had been sent to federal prisons, the intake process invariably began with shaving their heads.

Prosecutor Pitkin decided to press the long-haired McNee about circumstances in which he (McNee) thought violence might be appropriate. McNee responded that self-defense was one such example. Pitkin then asked whether or not McNee "knows the difference between Revolutionary Youth Movement 1 and Revolutionary Youth Movement 2."[3] The difference between these two splinter groups within SDS was fairly arcane knowledge about factional infighting, and was of no relevance to the charges against the defendants. McNee had already testified that he was never a member of SDS and he now stated he had never heard those terms. Nevertheless, Pitkin exercised one of his peremptory challenges to excuse McNee.

Spectators exploded with noisy anger as McNee was escorted out of the courtroom.[4] Abeles, Stern, and Lerner all loudly objected to the dismissal of this man whom, Abeles noted, "speaks for over 55 percent of the population, he is under 25 years of age…the government is doing that specifically to keep young people from the jury."[5] The twenty-seven-year-old Lerner attempted to summarize, "Your Honor, the previous exchange in front of the jury ought to be clarified in one respect, and that is this, we have nothing against people over 25 years of age, and we think that many of those people will attempt to give a fair verdict, but the government has systematically attempted to make it impossible for you to have anybody who comes from an even vaguely similar group to our background...Obviously he [U.S. Attorney Pitkin] doesn't want a fair trial."[6]

McNee, hustled out of the courtroom, wasn't sure what to think:

> I was a little disappointed that I didn't get to serve...I moved out of the jury box and a bailiff met me at the end of the little railing and we walked together down the stairs and out the front door. Some windows in the stairwell had been plywooded over. And some chain link had been erected in the stairwells to make them narrow, so that you could only go through a small door in the chain link...There was a lot of commotion outside, and I was thinking, what's going to happen here...I remember a couple people, I don't remember if they reached their hand out toward me, saying "Thank you" or "Congratulations'" or "Brother" or something like that, but it didn't seem like these people...were scary.[7]

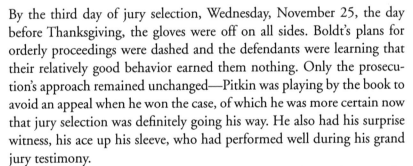

By the third day of jury selection, Wednesday, November 25, the day before Thanksgiving, the gloves were off on all sides. Boldt's plans for orderly proceedings were dashed and the defendants were learning that their relatively good behavior earned them nothing. Only the prosecution's approach remained unchanged—Pitkin was playing by the book to avoid an appeal when he won the case, of which he was more certain now that jury selection was definitely going his way. He also had his surprise witness, his ace up his sleeve, who had performed well during his grand jury testimony.

Wednesday, the *Seattle Times* noted, "was the most hectic day since the trial opened...four spectators—among about 50 supporters of the defendants—were ejected by deputy marshals," and "six of the defendants [all except Susan Stern] were given a final warning about contempt."[8]

One potential juror, Roy Magnussen, testified that he had read about the February 17 demonstration at the Seattle federal courthouse. His comments underlined the conceptual difficulties that stymied the potential jurors about the accusations against the defendants:

> BOLDT: And what, if anything have you learned since then concerning it [the charges against the defendants] from any source whatever?
>
> JUROR MAGNUSSEN: Well, that they are accusing eight people of damaging the building, that one of them was still at large, one of them is a female. That is about the extent of it."[9]

Chip Marshall jumped right in:

> MARSHALL: Excuse me, he said they were accusing people of damaging property. Does he understand there is a charge of conspiracy?
>
> BOLDT: Let's not get involved with that, Mr. Marshall.[10]

Then, Magnussen mentioned a newspaper photograph he'd seen:

> BOLDT: Was there anything about the picture or your reaction to it that gave you some aversion to the persons you saw in the picture?
>
> JUROR MAGNUSSEN: Nothing except that some of them needed haircuts.
>
> *(Spectators booed.)*[11]

Several prospective jurors were asked if they had a daughter, and if so, would they care if she wanted to marry one of the defendants. One juror noted that he wouldn't care, except "not the lady," referring to Susan Stern. This occasioned much laughter in the courtroom; gay rights and marriage equality had not made many inroads into public conversations in 1970.

In an afternoon interchange about men with long hair, Judge Boldt attempted some humor. He asked one prospective juror about his attitude toward "young people with long hair, beards, or dress commonly referred to as the hippie or New Left." The juror responded that his "daughter and her husband are on the fringe of that." Judge Boldt then commented, "Well, there are those of us who have just a little fringe on top; you are not speaking of that kind of fringe, I take it."[12]

One potential juror, a Robert Owen, who had hair similar to McNee's, was asked if he had ever participated in a protest demonstration:

> JUROR OWEN: Well, I personally have never engaged in any public demonstrations. I feel that to be able to talk, to speak, to demonstrate should be a privilege that everyone should enjoy regardless of race, creed or color. I personally have never done so, I don't wish to do so. If I were to do so, I would want to do so in a peaceful manner. I am not a fighter, I am a lover."
>
> *(Whereupon, spectators applauded.)*
>
> BOLDT: That is the trouble with you fellows that have got so much hair.[13]

Owen was then excused by the prosecution.

Women's rights also bubbled up. Lerner objected when many of the women in the jury panel were excused because they said they had childcare responsibilities; Lerner told the court that it should provide babysitters so the women could participate in jury duty as freely as men.[14] Prospective juror Martin E. Solomon was asked whether or not anything he had read or heard affected his attitude toward any of the defendants. His response:

> JUROR SOLOMON: Well, only one possibility, yesterday I heard the question being asked about women's liberation.
>
> BOLDT: Yes?
>
> JUROR SOLOMON: Well, if this was to come up, it lowers my opinion of anybody that belongs to it.
>
> MARSHALL: We object for cause.[15]

After the lunch break, the spectators opened the afternoon session by singing "Hey, Mr. Robinson" to the tune of Simon and Garfunkel's song "Mrs. Robinson," directed, of course, to U.S. Marshal Charles Robinson. Then, "when Judge Boldt finally entered the courtroom, supporters of the defendants rose, raised clenched fists and were led in a 'Power to the People' cheer by defendant Michael Abeles. Judge Boldt, his lips pursed and face flushed, looked sternly at the spectators but made no admonishment."[16]

Moving right along, prospective juror J. P. Cawdrey said in response to questions about his political opinions: "In regard to the war in Vietnam, I am opposed to it. I would like to see the United States get out as rapidly as possible. In regard to dealing with young people, I am involved in the Narcotics Center and I am involved with young people and have staff members with long hair."[17]

Attorney Pitkin then got to work, telling Cawdrey to contemplate the idea that if the defendants were found guilty by a jury of which he was a member, his effectiveness with his clients at the Narcotics Center might suffer, and therefore Cawdrey might lose his job. Pitkin framed this issue to suggest that, because of the job loss possibility, Cawdrey might be biased toward a "not guilty" verdict and therefore should not be on this jury. (However, the prosecution had no problem approving an earlier prospective juror who was employed on military contracts and who admitted that if the war ended, he might lose his job. Pitkin let this response slide right through without challenge.)

Cawdrey replied that although Pitkin's hypothetical situation is "conceivable," it is "difficult to visualize that kind of circumstance."[18]

Judge Boldt then asked Cawdrey's opinion of "public demonstrations and protests."

> Juror Cawdrey: I'm very much in favor of them. I think that one of the ways that a confrontation can be arranged with the establishment and with the government as it exists is through public assembly.
>
> Boldt: And what are your views or thinking concerning people who express opposition to the war in Vietnam?
>
> Juror Cawdrey: I'm with them, I'm favorable to them.[19]

Pitkin had heard enough. He exercised his peremptory challenge against Cawdrey. The defendants and spectators again erupted with frustration and anger, shouting that it was impossible for them to get a representative jury or a fair trial. As the *Seattle Times* reported:

> Defendants rose to their feet, shouting objections. Their supporters began stamping their feet and shouting. Judge Boldt stood and said: "Please be seated. Be silent. Remove these spectators." Defendant Jeffrey Dowd shouted, "Make them drag you out."
>
> Judge Boldt told the defendants, "Your conduct has been a contempt of this court." He told them: "You have been disruptive of this trial." Susan Stern, the only woman defendant, shouted: "This trial has been disruptive of our lives."
>
> Abeles stood and shouted: "I charge Stan Pitkin with outrageous prejudice." He later added: "If I had not said what I said, I would be in contempt of myself instead of this court."
>
> Some spectators shouted at the judge: "You are the real criminal."
>
> When the situation cooled down…[Chip] Marshall…told Judge Boldt he held no personal grudge against him. Marshall told the judge "you have bent over backwards structurally" for the defendants, but the structure is outmoded.[20]

Boldt ordered the marshals to eject several spectators from the courtroom, which they did, threatening them with blackjacks, and ordered the jurors to "retire from the courtroom immediately."[21] The defendants all objected, Dowd shouting, "This is not Germany." The judge responded:

BOLDT: Your conduct—Mr. Abeles, Mr. Dowd, Mr. Marshall, Mr. Lippman, Mr. Kelly, your conduct has been a contempt of this court. Your actions—

MARSHALL: Your Honor—

BOLDT: Will you please be quiet long enough for me to say what I have to say. Your actions have been extremely disruptive of this trial.

(A Woman's Voice from the Audience: This trial has been extremely disruptive of our life.)

BOLDT: Remove this person immediately. Remove her, please.

KELLY: I find this contempt of any kind of fair trial.

BOLDT: Remove this person immediately.

STEINBORN: I would like the record to show that the marshal has a blackjack in his hand, and is threatening the defendant with it.[22]

A minute or so later, Tigar added: "If your Honor please, there are standing in the courtroom now one, two, three, four, five, six, seven United States marshals who are armed—excuse me, and there is one seated and there is an agent of the Federal Bureau of Investigation and there are a number of other officers who act under your Honor's direction…what Mr. Pitkin has done here today utterly belies any statement that he has made on the record about his desire to have this case tried fairly."[23]

Many years later, Juror Audrey Waldorf recalled "I think every marshal in the country was in the courtroom." She also remembered her distaste of the defendants' behavior. "I don't think it had an effect on me as far as being a juror. But the language was very, very disrespectful…very disrespectful of the flag. And what they said to Judge Boldt, I was just horrified by. It was really all very, very disrespectful of the courtroom."[24]

Judge Boldt continued to try to regain control with threats of contempt charges:

BOLDT: Now, those young men whom I named a few moments ago, you were shouting, you were making violent gestures.

MARSHALL: We were talking about peace in Vietnam.

ABELES: Violent gestures? Judge, what is a violent gesture?

BOLDT: And even while I'm speaking you are interrupting and preventing me from saying what I have to say. This conduct has been just beyond any possible justification, and in my opinion would constitute contempt. But I do not propose to make that of it on this occasion, but I caution you now, and I want you to understand that if any one of you participates in any such action again I will cite you for contempt.[25]

This brought on more shouts from the spectators, and another one was ejected, bringing the total to eight for the day.

BOLDT: Now, I regret that we have gotten to this point very much, but it has arrived, and we will have to deal with it, and I am admonishing you now, each of you—I think one of the defendants has left the room.

MARSHALL: No, we all look alike.

BOLDT: Where is he?

MARSHALL: We're all here.

LERNER: We're all here.

TIGAR: Your Honor, two of the counsel [Attorneys Holley and Steinborn] have left the room momentarily. May the record reflect that they walked out with the spectator who you ejected.[26]

Attorney Holley, when he returned, said to the judge "Throughout history people have sat silent when silence was a crime. Six million Jewish people marched to the gas chamber in silence and a million and a half Vietnamese people have been killed while the American people have been silent, and some people feel that silence is not justice."[27]

Lerner continued, "Now, what we have seen here, your Honor, is a systematic attempt to uproot any possibility of a fair trial by taking away any young person or any person even not so young who holds opinions vaguely close to the opinion of the participants in this trial…we have a pattern of discrimination…Now you cannot simply pretend that this is not happening."[28]

Lerner was applauded by the spectators; Abeles continued on in this vein and was also applauded. Judge Boldt was far from controlling his courtroom, and the trial itself had not yet begun.

Defense attorney Steinborn bore down on the blackjack-wielding marshals:

STEINBORN: I think this comment should go on the record, I turned around and saw the United States Marshal with a blackjack in his hand about to strike a young lady with it and he had a look in his eyes like a wild animal.

BOLDT: Well—

STEINBORN: (interposing) Just a minute. I might say if he were not restrained I would have restrained him with a chair, perhaps.[29]

Abeles spoke up:

This case is about freedom of speech…and if people have to risk contempt for that, then it is better to take contempt, your Honor, than to go on being silent…It is like a man going out of a burning house and yelling an obscenity and then arresting him for breaking the peace rather than arresting the people who set the fire in the first place, like Mr. Pitkin.

(Spectators applauded.)[30]

Judge Boldt finally called a recess, and when court reconvened half an hour later, much of the energy had been spent. The attorneys agreed that they would all cooperate to complete jury selection before the end of the day.

Tigar then brought up another issue that continued throughout the trial: Judge Boldt's decision not to allow entry to waiting spectators when seats were available because, Boldt said, the spectators are all "adherents of the defendants," and he and Mr. Pitkin were concerned that "they will mingle with the jurors."[31]

The final ten minutes of the session were devoted to deciding to take the Friday after Thanksgiving off, and to reconvene on Monday morning, November 30, at 8:45 a.m.

The chosen jurors included four women and eight men. Two were under thirty and six were over forty. Defense attorney Lee Holley handwrote a list of the jurors including their names, birthdates, highest school grade they completed, and their astrological signs. Only three had attended any college. Eighteen potential jurors had disqualified themselves, saying they had biases against the defendant's dress, hair, and participation in demonstrations.

The final twelve jurors and six alternates all declared under oath that they had no, and had never had any, opinion about the Vietnam War, which had been going on for close to ten years, and was, by the end of 1970, responsible for the deaths of 54,909 American soldiers.[32] Defense attorney Carl Maxey later said that the defendants felt "that anybody that didn't have an opinion on the war was not abreast of the democratic demands of our times."[33]

Decades later, defendant Lippman recalled the jurors: "It's just amazing how blank a face can be…I would say I have never had any impression of them…I was 20 or 22, they were 50 or 60. I couldn't really understand them anyway. But they were rural southwest Washington kind of people. I had no idea."[34]

Chip Marshall wrote later from jail that Pitkin had thrown out "any prospective juror whose sideburns extended past the top of his ears or whose opinions extended beyond the Green Bay Packers."[35]

Judge Boldt remained challenged by the defendants and their supporters as they continually chipped away at his usual courtroom management techniques. The defense attorneys had to scramble hard to defend their clients from the prosecutors, the judge, the legal process, and from each other. The prosecutors, however, were smiling like Cheshire cats; they thought they were on a fast track—they'd empaneled a good, law-abiding jury and in the wings they had their surprise witness who would dramatically confirm the defendants' conspiratorial guilt.

10

Jail Them, Not Us

We were a whole bunch of actors and no director.
—JOE KELLY, SEATTLE 7 DEFENDANT

The defendants and their attorneys continued to have differing ideas about courtroom strategy. Was their goal to stay out of prison or end the war or fix the inequities in the American judicial system? Without a clear goal, there was no defined strategy, and without a strategy, there could be no organized tactics, either inside or outside the courtroom. Time was short, much was at stake, and feelings ran high.

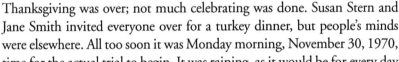

Thanksgiving was over; not much celebrating was done. Susan Stern and Jane Smith invited everyone over for a turkey dinner, but people's minds were elsewhere. All too soon it was Monday morning, November 30, 1970, time for the actual trial to begin. It was raining, as it would be for every day of the proceedings. FBI cameras were trained on the courthouse, taking pictures of chilled and damp SLF supporters on the sidewalk as they waited to be admitted. Police on foot, on motorcycles, and in cars routinely circled the building with its grimly taped and covered windows.

Robinson had brought in extra marshals from Los Angeles to supplement his crew. Trial participants reported that the Californians were responsible for most of the physical attacks on spectators and defendants that were to occur over the following days of the trial. Everyone was keyed up. Early on this first day, one of the marshals was allegedly seen in the men's rest room stirring up trouble by writing provocative radical graffiti on the walls.

The jury was present and accounted for, having arrived "through the alley...[the building] was boarded up, but you eventually got into a back entrance...marshals all around there," one juror recalled. "I wasn't afraid I would be hurt. I was just nervous...just the tension in the courtroom, and then knowing what it was about...My son played soccer with somebody whose father was an FBI agent, and so he was in the courtroom."[1]

One SLF defense collective member had assigned himself the job of rousting the defendants off their mattresses every morning and driving them the thirty-five miles south down I-5 to Tacoma in a green Chevy van. This was a thankless task, as the defendants, particularly Dowd, Abeles, and Stern, were not morning people, and had usually been partying long into the night. The parties did double duty—they let off steam after a long and frustrating day in court and they raised funds for the defense. These events tended to attract large and noisy crowds, which in turn attracted police hassles and occasional arrests.

It was not unusual for the defendants to smoke marijuana in the back of the van on the way to the courthouse. There were rumors as well that the water jugs in the defense conference room were filled not with water, but with vodka. One supporter said that the defendants got permission to have grape Kool-Aid at the defense table, which of course was really wine. One day the press, who had a room adjacent to the defense room, complained that the smell of marijuana smoke was drifting into their room. Defense attorney Steinborn's response was to say maybe they should invite the press in for a joint.[2]

Many of the defendants' supporters didn't have cars, so it was difficult for them to get to Tacoma. Those who arrived were often denied admission and spent the day walking up and down on the sidewalk chanting encouraging messages in the direction of the third floor courtroom windows. The issue of better access for the public was a continuing thread throughout the trial, with the defendants and their attorneys frequently asking Boldt and U.S. Marshal Robinson to allow more public access to the proceedings, along with quicker admittance frisk and search procedures. It was unusual in 1970 to have any search measures at all.

The supporters who did make it inside were often appalled at their close-up look at American justice. They responded by insisting on becoming active members of the trial process—jeering, laughing, singing, fist-pumping, and chanting antiwar slogans. They knew the trial was about more than these particular indictments and these particular defendants. Shoving matches, orders to leave, and threats of contempt occurred every day. Spectators took to staying in the courtroom during recesses and lounging around in the jurors' box. For Judge Boldt, it was like herding unruly hissing cats, a losing battle. For the spectator-participants, it was the civics lesson they should have received in school.

As the *UW Daily* pointed out,

> This trial is not a specific attack on the Seattle Eight, as much as it is an attempt by the government to establish a legal precedent by which all demonstrators in the future can be prosecuted….No such precedent… was set by the Chicago conspiracy trial, and if this relatively little-known case results in convictions, the whole anti-war movement is threatened… This is not a question of individual politics. This is an attempt to destroy the foundation of all mass movements.[3]

U.S. Attorney Stan Pitkin opened the trial well aware that his prosecution needed to prove that the defendants had engaged in more than constitutionally protected free speech. To do that, he must paint the defendants as violent protesters at the TDA demonstration, despite the fact that none of them were arrested that day (and cases had been subsequently dismissed on most of those who had been arrested). His opening statement to the jury lasted more than two hours, and included this about TDA: "The defendant Lippman at this time is observed throwing rocks at the police officers."[4] He apparently did not yet know that Lippman was in California at the time.

Pitkin, though, must have had some inkling that he was on alien territory. A few weeks before the trial began, he had called defense attorney Tigar, asking him to come immediately to his office because he'd found a new piece of evidence that might require him to bring more serious charges against his clients. Tigar tells the story:

> I rounded up two of the defendants, Michael Abeles and Jeff Dowd, and we went along to the federal building. Pitkin was in his office with the FBI case agent. In hushed tones…they led us into a room. The FBI agent carefully opened a wooden box. "This," he intoned, "was found at the scene of the demonstration."
>
> This was a World War II hand grenade body, the classic pineapple shape. It was empty of any explosives, no doubt having come from a war surplus store. It was painted baby blue. An alligator clip, such as electricians use, was soldered to the top of it.
>
> Abeles and Dowd began to giggle. "It's a roach clip," one of them finally sputtered.
>
> "What's a roach clip?" Pitkin asked, mystified.
>
> "Ask your teenagers," Dowd replied.[5]

These defendants were not like the cops-on-the-take that Pitkin had van-quished in the bribery and racketeering case he'd handled so well a few months earlier. These seven Seattle defendants were not motivated by personal greed, and didn't appear to have the instinct for self-preservation that leads most citizens to back down when confronted by overwhelming government power. The one exception was Lerner, who, unlike his fellow defendants, was facing his first experience in the clutches of the legal sys-tem. He was disturbed by his loss of personal control and he definitely did not want to go to prison. He had a real job and a concrete career plan. His courtroom strategy was to wear a jacket and tie every day, to not participate in the defendants' most raucous behaviors, and to argue with them for less confrontational tactics.

All the defendants, though, including Lerner, acted out of feelings of intense righteousness. After what they saw as the farce of jury selec-tion, they were now certain that their trial would be equally as rigged. They loosely agreed that they might as well use their courtroom time to continue to speak out against the war, which necessarily required being disruptive of the judicial process. No compromise, go out standing, fight the good fight to the end.

At the same time, as long as they were in a courtroom, they figured they might as well also try to reform its procedures. They took the time to spot procedural unfairness, and they didn't hesitate to point out what they saw. As American citizens, the least they could do was to demand that the court operate in line with U.S. Constitutional standards.

They also understood that despite the charges being the same, their sit-uation was quite different from the Chicago 7. They weren't national lead-ers, and wouldn't get nearly the level of media attention as did the Chicago defendants. They were also different from the Chicago 7, as Lerner put it, because "we were doing concrete organizing" as opposed to the Chicago 7 "who had little else to bind them together but the trial."[6] The Seattle 7 case, they were sure, was a government attempt to produce a greater repres-sive impact than the Chicago trial because the Seattle trial spoke directly to local activists in cities all over the country. Pitkin, however, continued to tell the press that there was no national significance to the case.

Continuing with his opening statement, Pitkin said he would call forty-five witnesses for the prosecution, and went to great pains to explain to the still-confused jury the opaque language of the federal conspiracy laws: "The prosecution will not have to show formal agreement on details of the alleged conspiracy [and] a person can be a member of a conspiracy without knowing all the details."[7]

In addition, he emphasized that the government had to prove the truth of only one of the eighteen overt acts listed in the indictment in order to bring in a guilty verdict. Pitkin also told the jury that an "overt act itself may be entirely lawful. It is the object of the conspiracy that must be unlawful."[8] Despite these legal lectures, one of the jurors' memories of the trial was that it was about bombs being planted in the federal courthouse. As a juror, what impressed her most was "how hard the court reporter was working" and that "there was a lot of speaking out of order."[9]

Pitkin took repeated pains to describe the defendants in serious, terrorist terms. One SLF supporter and good friend of the defendants said Pitkin "painted a portrait of these idiots as thugs. I couldn't believe that a grown up person like Pitkin could believe what he was saying... couldn't believe he could say these things with a straight face."[10]

———————◆———————

Carl Maxey opened for the defense. He introduced each defendant to the jury, had them stand up and look at the jury members individually. His subtext was that these are concerned young people: You know people just like them, perhaps your own children or grandchildren, your niece or nephew, your neighbor's children. He summarized, "The evidence will show the defendants are being charged not for what they did but for what they think. The evidence will show guilt by association, guilt by idea, guilt by drug culture, guilt for doing damage in the interests of ending the war."[11] He noted that although "there were thirty such [TDA] demonstrations throughout the United States, these are the only defendants out here in the obscure Northwest that have been charged."[12]

Maxey described the extreme preparedness of U.S. Marshal Robinson's Seattle courthouse security on the day of the TDA demonstration—emphasizing that the building was locked down on a regular work day, was packed with riot police who were backed up by many more officers across the street in the library. The date, time, and place of the protest was clearly public knowledge—posters and flyers were all over town. Not a very secret conspiracy, Maxey noted.

In conclusion, said Maxey, "We submit to you in finality that one of the reasons for this prosecution is to crush youth and put them on notice that no one can exercise these very things that they talk about—peace and freedom…But you must keep an open mind…there are two sides to each story and after you have heard it all I have an abiding faith that you will find there was no conspiracy and you won't be like the man who said, 'I don't have an opinion on the war.'"[13]

Michael Lerner's opening statement was next. He emphasized how little he and his co-defendants got along, "Most of us couldn't agree on anything…the SLF is the most undisciplined organization that ever existed. It is extremely difficult to get people together to know that there is a meeting, much less to work out some involved plot or planning."[14] He also emphasized that his own political view has been clear all along—moral outrage is not the way to create social change. That's why he was so opposed to Weatherman tactics. He then veered into an hour's lecture about racism, the violence of the war, and income inequality, and was repeatedly interrupted by Judge Boldt "to confine yourself to this particular matter."[15] He concluded with saying he didn't destroy any property and didn't use the telephone to incite to riot, "but I did try to explain to people why this society had to be transformed, and it seems to me that it would be a terrible shame if people felt they could no longer do that without going to jail for ten years."[16]

Chip Marshall was next to give his opening argument. It showcased his ability to approach complex ideas with humor and down-home analogies. When he talked to the jury about what a conspiracy was, he said maybe it was like a football team, where "eleven men conspire to do damage to other people."[17] With folksy good nature, he referred to U.S. Attorney Pitkin as "Stan."

Marshall sympathized with the ongoing confusion in the courtroom over identifying the defendants as individuals, and alluded to the public paranoia that assumed all long-haired antiwar activists were incipient if not actual Weatherman bombers. He made a joke about it, noting that "we all look alike…I guess, and that seems to be the problem with the government, that's why they mistake so many of us and have the wrong people."[18]

As with Lerner, Marshall was accustomed to having the podium and the judge had to ask him to speed it up several times. Marshall took pains to explain to the jurors that he trusted them to render a fair verdict, although he was a little worried that if they'd never been on the receiving end of a police baton or arrested for something they didn't do, perhaps they were inclined to give police undue credence. Stopped by the judge one last time, Marshall concluded, "Well, that's basically what I have to say. We didn't do it, and that's all. (*Laughter and applause.*)"[19]

The first trial day was over. After the jury was excused, the attorneys and the judge continued with technical discussions. Such conversations, either at Boldt's desk or in his office, were frequent and lengthy; they often were a platform for raising issues that the defense hoped would be of value in an appeal, if one were necessary. On this particular afternoon, Marshall accused Pitkin of falsely denying that there were FBI wiretaps in the defendants' conference room. Pitkin objected and Marshall called him a liar. Boldt said that Marshall's accusations were "serious misconduct and...disruptive of the proceedings."

"How can the truth be misconduct?" Marshall asked.

"It is disruptive of the proceedings, that is why."[20]

Boldt then asked Pitkin to write an affidavit on the matter. Pitkin equivocated, saying that he didn't actually know if there were FBI wiretaps in the defendants' room or not, so he wasn't sure what he could write.

The next day began with Boldt telling the spectators to be quiet and settle down, otherwise they would be ejected and not allowed to return. This did little to quell their penchant for ad lib participation. Boldt, at this relatively early stage, was still trying his best to appear less quixotic and doctrinaire than Julius Hoffman, his judicial counterpart in the Chicago 7 case. It wasn't to last.

Roger Lippman, as he did throughout the trial, then spoke up to ask for better management of search and seating procedures for spectators. Nothing was ever done about this ongoing issue, which remained a hot button for the defendants throughout the trial and was the unexpected trigger that brought down Boldt's judicial house of cards.

Up next, defense attorney Tigar's opening statement reminded the jury of the details of the charges, pointing out that the conspiracy law makes it a crime to *intend* to incite a riot, not to incite a riot itself. The law, Tigar says, "addresses itself to the content of men's minds. What did they think? That is the simple heart of this case."[21] He raised the specter of the 1968 Democratic Convention, which by this time had been officially declared a "police riot" by the National Commission on the Causes and Prevention of Violence.[22] After that public finding, who needed a conspiracy to encourage people to express their irritation over the fact that the Chicago 7 defendants, but not a single Chicago policeman, were in jail?

Judge Boldt then confused the two attorneys Maxey and Holley, the sort of error that led some observers to think that he was more than a little inattentive and even may have had some memory difficulties. Mixing up the names of the defendants was slightly more understandable as they were all white, young, and had long hair, but to confuse a well-known, well-dressed black attorney who had recently run in a statewide election with a younger white attorney in overalls was more difficult to brush off.

After excusing the jury for another technical discussion, Boldt asked if Pitkin was ready to begin. He was, and Boldt instructed the bailiff to call the first witness. The bailiff had to remind the judge that the jury was not present. It was a slow start. The first four prosecution witnesses were on the stand for short periods of time; they were landlords and utilities employees who substantiated Marshall, Dowd, Abeles, and Kelly's move from Ithaca to Seattle, and confirmed that Marshall, Dowd, and Kelly had rented a house in Seattle.

While this entirely uncontested evidence was discussed, Marshall interrupted to complain that spectators were being harassed and denied admittance, including Elizabeth Nucci, a co-founder of the Country Doctor clinic. She had intervened in a scuffle between U.S. Marshal Robinson and another woman spectator who, after mistakenly showing her entrance ticket for the previous day, was roughly shoved out. Nucci herself was then harassed and arrested for not saying she was sorry. Chip Marshall angrily said that "if he [Robinson] doesn't stop this kind of harassment, the next time he touches somebody, he is going to get decked, man." Boldt told him such threats constitute contempt of court. Michael Abeles said "So is Robinson's conduct."

Tigar spoke up to say that spectators were being videotaped while waiting to get in, which, he said, was unconstitutional search without probable cause. Boldt responded, "Your objection is noted and overruled" and then accused attorneys Steinborn and Holley of contributing to disturbances inside the courtroom.[23] Marshall piped up that he wanted a camera too, because "I've been in a number of controversies involving police officers" and that in his experience these altercations were generally decided by lying police covering for each other.[24]

The afternoon's witness was James Moore, a UW campus policeman, whose beat was student meetings at the HUB. He confused some dates and was unable to accurately describe what anyone was talking about at the SLF meetings. Although he recognized some of the defendants, he placed them mostly in hallways, not in the meetings themselves. He observed a karate session (one of the indictment's eighteen overt acts) on a grassy area on the UW campus, but Marshall, in his cross-examination got Moore to admit that the session was "a light-hearted affair, not well disciplined, with a lot of laughing and horseplay."[25] So far, the prosecution's formal case didn't sound very impressive.

The next morning, Wednesday, December 2, Lerner told the court, "My house was broken into last night and papers of the defense were taken. I reported this to the police and they asked me for a suspect, and I said… the only ones who could use them would be the Government."[26] When asked by Boldt if he would like the matter to be investigated by a federal agency, Lerner replied, "Well, your Honor, the only bureau of investigation that I know of available to you is precisely the chief suspect, so I don't see that there is any way of investigating it."[27]

These first two and a half days of the trial turned out to be a calm prelude to the main act—the surprise (to the defense team) appearance on the stand of Horace "Red" Parker, a paid FBI informant and provocateur who had infiltrated SLF.

11

The Rise and Fall of an FBI Provocateur

It was like a Twilight Zone episode, like a comic book, a piece of performance art.

—SLF SUPPORTER IN THE COURTROOM

Horace "Red" Parker took the stand Wednesday afternoon, December 2, under intense security. Parker had two armed U.S. marshals at his side, six more were stationed strategically throughout the room at all times during his testimony, and two additional men led him to and from the courtroom. Parker no longer looked like a wannabe Weatherman. The thirty-three-year-old was all spruced up in a suit and striped tie and button-down shirt. He was clean-shaven, his reddish hair was short and neatly parted on the right side. He wore glasses and spoke softly. He was a total surprise to the defense. One of the spectators quickly sketched a "Wanted Poster" of Parker and made plans to post copies all over town.

Pitkin guided his star witness through his history of hanging out with SLF members to uncover their Weatherman proclivities. Whenever possible, the prosecution brought the specter of Weatherman into the courtroom. If the government couldn't find one of those elusive Weathermen, it would invent one. Parker testified that his first move was to go to an SDS meeting on the UW campus where he was given leaflets about Karl Marx, Mao Tse-tung and other international communists:

PARKER: I took the literature to the FBI.

PITKIN: And what did you say to them?

PARKER: I told them there was a collective being formed on the University of Washington campus, and in my opinion these people were Communist revolutionaries…I had originally intended to join SDS and I was disappointed in what I saw. I found out that they were Communist revolutionaries rather than American revolutionaries.

PITKIN: Did [the FBI agent] ask you to do anything?

PARKER: He said "You have an opportunity to be of service to your country."

PITKIN: In what way?

PARKER: By infiltrating the SDS.[1]

The FBI then asked Parker to report to them any and all information about Weatherman. Parker explained to the court how his expenses were paid, and that he called the FBI with reports every day, sometimes twice a day, for over a year. He testified that the FBI paid for his apartment, all his expenses, and a monthly stipend, in cash. There was also a promise of relocation money if needed. The Seattle daily papers were particularly interested in these financial details; the city's economy remained in a deep dive and their readers were attracted to any stories about money.

Parker lived briefly in an SLF collective house known as The Fort, some of whose residents were known to be Weatherman-leaning. He named the people he thought were Seattle-based Weathermen, including defendant Roger Lippman: "In the Weathermen, Roger was the theorist.

Seattle Post-Intelligencer Thurs., Dec. 3, 1970 S★   B

—P.I. Sketches by Bob McCausland

HORACE L. PARKER, FBI INFORMER, TESTIFIED AT CONSPIRACY TRIAL
Former Weatherman told of the planning for Feb. 17 demonstrations here

Surprise witness, FBI informer, and provocateur Horace "Red" Parker takes the stand. *Seattle Post-Intelligencer sketch, December 3, 1970, Bob McCausland, seattlepi.com, image courtesy Seattle Public Library.*

He laid out the whole ideology and wrote the leaflets and if people didn't understand the Marxism very well, maybe the worship of Chairman Mao, they would go to Roger and he would answer questions or sit down and help. He is real well informed on those things."[2]

Despite this promising beginning, Parker turned out to be an imperfect prosecution witness. For one thing, he did not attend the TDA demonstration, and so could not comment on any of the defendants' presence or actions there. But more decisively, his eagerness to convict the defendants, his self-important role-playing as a covert operative, and his habit of mumbling undercut his testimony and irritated the judge and both teams of attorneys.

Parker frequently had to be reminded to speak up and when he did, he had a habit of drawing inferences and making assumptions about what other people were thinking. Personal guesses about other people's motivations and thoughts are not admissible, so the alert defense attorneys were constantly objecting to his testimony. Both the judge and Pitkin had to continually admonish Parker to stick to the facts, and Boldt then had to tell the jury to disregard whatever Parker had said about what he thought someone else was thinking. Ironically, that's what defines the crime of conspiracy—people assuming they know what other people are thinking.

Toward the end of the day, after yet another of Parker's statements was objected to and correctly stricken by the judge, Parker complained, "I don't understand." Pitkin, frustrated, responded "You don't have to," followed by laughter in the courtroom.[3] Although the defendants and their allies were still perturbed by the fact that they hadn't identified Parker as an FBI plant for over a year, and that parts of his testimony were potentially damaging, they also saw weaknesses in both his words and his actions. They spent the night contemplating their comeback when it was their turn to cross examine.

Day seven of the trial, Thursday, December 3, opened with everyone a little testy. Defendant Marshall moved to recess for the rest of the day as it was the first anniversary of the murders of Chicago Black Panthers Fred Hampton and Mark Clark by Chicago police and the FBI. Motion denied. After some squabbling over minor points about how the prosecution's exhibits were being entered into evidence, Pitkin began a review of the testimony from the day before, saying, "Now, a closer examination of the witness would indicate that he has seen this gal before…" Tigar immediately interrupted him, "Excuse me your Honor, I hate to interrupt, she is a woman."

As Pitkin looked puzzled, Stern jumped in, "From now on, please refer to a female as a woman, not a gal."[4] Boldt shot to his feet and angrily

—*P-I Sketch by Bob McCausland*

DEFENDANT JEFFREY DOWD BERATED FEDERAL JUDGE GEORGE H. BOLDT
Jurist had ejected another woman for remark made by one of defendants

Seattle 7 defendant Jeff Dowd berating Judge Boldt. Also visible in the sketch are defendants Roger Lippman (with glasses and headband), Susan Stern, Joe Kelly and Michael Abeles. *Seattle Post-Intelligencer sketch, December 4, 1970, Bob McCausland, seattlepi.com, image courtesy Seattle Public Library.*

ordered marshals to remove SLF defense collective member Jane Smith from the courtroom, thinking she, not Stern, had made the comment. Boldt repeatedly shouted "leave the room," and didn't sit down until he saw his orders obeyed.[5]

As Smith was being hustled out by armed marshals, shouts erupted that she hadn't said anything at all, that Boldt was mistaken and that it was Stern who had spoken. Stern confirmed it, and added, "We have something called women's liberation that men and women take very, very seriously and his reference to a woman as a gal would be the same thing as calling a Black man a nigger."[6] Jeff Dowd stood up and berated the judge, "you have a bad hearing and seeing problem...I will not be judged by somebody that can't hear and probably can't understand the testimony."[7]

The *Seattle Post-Intelligencer* agreed with the defendants, writing that Boldt had made an error and that the spectator had not spoken. Their headline was "Miscue Triggers More Trial Pandemonium" and included a large drawing of Jeff Dowd looming toward the judge, who looked uncertain as he tried to compose himself.[8] After the lunch break, Abeles presented Boldt with a pair of binoculars to aid his vision; the spectators duly applauded.[9] Spectators also cheered when they learned during the break that the U.S. Senate had refused to fund Boeing's military supersonic transport design-and-build project.

Tempers were clearly fraying on all sides. *Sabot*, a local underground newspaper, illustrated its article on this day in court with a drawing of Boldt in his signature bow tie, looking befuddled and exhausted. His thought balloon reads, "Oh fuk...another day..." Throughout frequent breaks in the day's testimony Boldt repeatedly spoke of his patience and restraint, quoting Jesus on the cross, "they know not what they do."

Parker then returned to the stand to describe his observations at SLF's January HUB planning meetings, so critical to the prosecution's case. Pitkin's questions and Parker's responses sparked objections from the defense attorneys, but this time, Boldt more often overruled them. Attorneys on both sides were occasionally confused about what was being stricken and what wasn't. Boldt himself was irritated enough to snap at Pitkin a couple of times, and Pitkin voiced frustration at Parker's persistent inability to avoid embellishing his accounts with his personal interpretation of the defendants' unspoken thoughts. Both Boldt and Pitkin were forced to interrupt Parker's testimony with instructions to answer with a simple yes or no whenever he eagerly began to elaborate.

Pitkin asked Parker if he "participated in the life style of the Weathermen" and if he used drugs. Parker said yes, "Acid, grass, speed, methedrine, coke," and that he was told by the FBI to "do anything that was necessary to protect my credibility." Defense attorneys Holley and Maxey objected to the idea that the FBI was responsible for Parker's drug use, noting "If he uses drugs, he uses them on his own."[10]

Attorney Maxey was the first defense attorney to cross-examine Parker. He established that Parker had heard sharp public disagreements among the very defendants currently on trial for conspiring together. He elicited the information that Parker worked as a sales manager at a paint store and had supplied the paint that had been splashed on the Seattle courthouse walls during TDA, and that he had supplied Robby Stern, Susan Stern's ex-husband, with a tear gas gun in September 1969, even though by then Parker believed Robby to be a dangerous revolutionary.

During this testimony, Susan Stern spoke up to say that Parker seemed to be exchanging messages with an FBI agent near the courtroom door. They denied it, but said that a spectator had signed with Parker, using "language that is common to the Weathermen." Five transcript pages of discussion later, Parker said that the spectator had signed "I hate you. Fuck you," and Parker had replied "Hi, Traitor." All were perfunctorily admonished by a tired Boldt.[11]

Maxey then asked Parker to describe how he came to be in the FBI's employ. He said he called the CIA first, but they told him to call the FBI. Maxey then returned to Parker's drug use:

MAXEY: What kind of a sensation did you get from [smoking marijuana]?

PARKER: Got stoned.

BOLDT: What does that mean?

PARKER: Well, you get high; you feel good.

MAXEY: Does it make you do things you wouldn't do when you are not affected by it?

PARKER: I don't know. I got immune to it.

MAXEY: You got immune to it?

PARKER: After a while. It took quite a bit of grass to get off.[12]

Parker looked uncomfortable and the spectators clearly appreciated it. Maxey then effectively linked an error in one of Parker's FBI reports to the likelihood that Parker had been stoned when he wrote it. In this instance, he had misidentified Michael Abeles in a TDA police surveillance photo.[13]

Boldt ended the session in the late afternoon. Perhaps to give Parker and the prosecution time to re-group, he cancelled the Friday session and gave everyone a three-day weekend.

Monday morning, December 7, in Washington, DC, FBI Director J. Edgar Hoover testified before Congress that there was the "ominous possibility" that Black Panthers were conspiring with "North Korea and Arab terrorists" to hijack airplanes in an attempt to free Bobby Seale. Seale was shortly to be moved from his Chicago jail cell to a New Haven, Connecticut, jail to face more serious charges than those stemming from the antiwar protests at the 1968 Democratic Convention. These new charges were eventually dismissed by the judge because the jury could not reach a unanimous decision, and the prosecution declined to retry the case. This was becoming a pattern: the government would indict protesters with serious criminal charges that it couldn't effectively prosecute, but which provided enough distraction to cripple their protest activity.

Back in the Tacoma courtroom, Maxey moved forward with Parker's reports to the FBI, eventually cornering him into admitting to multiple inaccuracies that he had never subsequently corrected. He also zeroed in on Parker's admission that he'd acted as a drug supplier during the time he was an FBI informer. For his close, Maxey suddenly segued to more serious supply behaviors:

MAXEY: Isn't it a fact, sir, that in 1970 you have offered various people plastic explosives?

PARKER: Would you be more specific?

MAXEY: All right. Do you know whether or not you have offered to give or sell to individuals plastic explosives?

PARKER: No I never sold or distributed any plastic explosives to anybody.

ABELES (INTERJECTS): That's not the question.

MAXEY: Did you offer, is what I said.

PARKER: Not plastic explosives.

MAXEY: Any other type of explosive devices or materials?

PARKER: I have never distributed any explosive devices.

MAXEY: I am talking about offers.

PARKER: Would you be more specific about that, please.

MAXEY: Well, to be as specific as I can; in the year 1970 did you in fact, sir, offer to anyone either plastic explosives or other explosive devices or materials?

PARKER: Yes.[14]

Chip Marshall was next up. Maxey had laid the groundwork for Marshall to conduct a brilliantly orchestrated cross-examination. Marshall reviewed Parker's testimony that almost three years had elapsed between Parker's first contact with SDS in 1967 and his first contact with the FBI in 1969 when he had suddenly realized he hated SDS. Wondering why it had taken so long, Marshall reminded Parker that he'd previously testified to being a political science major for three years in college. Marshall asked, "Would it be fair to say you are fairly interested in public affairs?" and "You read a lot, right?" To both of which, Parker responded "Yes."[15] Marshall allowed the jury to reflect on these facts, and then continued:

MARSHALL: So you felt, then, that you were opposed to these people, and you felt the people of the SDS to be a threat of some sort and, therefore, you went to the FBI, right?"

PARKER: Yes

MARSHALL: And you didn't like, for instance, their violence, and you didn't like the fact that they were using the war in Vietnam, or racism, and you felt they were using these issues, is that correct?

PARKER: Yes.

MARSHALL: Rather than being sincere about it.

PARKER: Yes.

MARSHALL: You felt no compunction yourself about using illegal means to get these people?

PARKER: Sometimes it bothered me a little bit.

MARSHALL: But you were willing to do illegal things, and you were willing to use the same tactics as you deplored from these people, correct, for a higher good?

PARKER: Right.[16]

The two then had a short discussion about Parker being willing to grow his hair long and wear "more casual dress" in order to be credible to SLF members, particularly those he was sure were Weathermen. Marshall suggested that Parker was now trying to be credible to the jury by wearing a suit and tie and having a short, slicked-down haircut.

Continuing to raise questions about the accuracy of Parker's memory, Marshall led him to admit other errors he has made in his reports to the FBI, including misidentifying Tom Hayden, a well-publicized member of the Chicago 7 and co-founder of SDS. In his eagerness to meet the needs of his Weatherman-obsessed FBI handlers, Parker identified a number of people as Weathermen who in fact routinely and publicly objected to Weather tactics.

Marshall then began to approach Parker's provocateur role. First he established that Parker had immunity from the FBI to do illegal acts. Parker said yes, he had immunity, but not to "kill anybody or do anything like that."[17]

MARSHALL: But other things you are allowed to do, for instance, you gave Mr. Stern an illegal weapon?

PARKER: Yes.

MARSHALL: And you knew that was illegal?

PARKER: Right.[18]

Marshall's next step was to get Parker to admit that he not only talked about violence with the SLF members he was infiltrating, he actively pressed them to support "the necessity for armed struggle, violence, et cetera. You yourself? Yes or No." Parker responded, "The answer would have to be yes."[19]

As Marshall moved Parker closer and closer to identifying himself as an agent provocateur who was also a liar and a drug addict, prosecutor Pitkin began to get restive and managed to get the judge to back him up with a flurry of objections, although not enough to stop this exchange:

MARSHALL: Have you ever encouraged people, anyone, since you have become part of the FBI, to violate a law, yes or no?

PARKER: Yes.[20]

Hammering on Parker as liar, Marshall asked if he ever "felt any pressure about lying to people then?"

PARKER: None whatsoever.

MARSHALL: It didn't bother you at all?

PARKER: No.[21]

Marshall asked Parker to describe a time when he took some SLF people target shooting and lied to them about having been a sniper in the Green Berets. When asked if he'd told them that he had been a Green Beret in order "to make yourself look big for these people," Parker responded "Right." Marshall went on:

> MARSHALL: Some of these people had never shot before, isn't that correct?
>
> PARKER: That's very true.
>
> MARSHALL: And you encouraged them. In fact when some of the women protested, you sort of berated them for not wanting to learn how to shoot, isn't that correct?
>
> PARKER: I berated them because I was afraid they would shoot me because they didn't know how to handle a gun. One of the girls almost blew my foot off, as a matter of fact, because she didn't know how to lower the hammer down.[22]

After Parker defended his shooting lesson as a way to find out how much SLF members knew about shooting, Marshall asked if that was his "normal practice, to find out things by pushing people into it?"[23] Then, when Parker said he'd brought a .22 automatic rifle into the Weatherman collective house, Marshall asked, "Can a .22 kill a person?"

> PARKER: Certainly
>
> MARSHALL: I see. And you taught people that you considered dangerous revolutionaries how to use weapons, isn't that correct?
>
> PARKER: Yes.[24]

Marshall then switched over to Parker's role as a drug supplier to people in the movement, and the fact that besides "Red," Parker's other nickname was "Speed." Parker admitted that his drug use had begun prior to his need to protect his credibility with SLF members. He testified that he was so concerned about becoming addicted himself that he had consulted a physician about it. The jurors, who didn't always appear to be engaged, perked up and began to ask questions about the language of drug use—Parker obligingly described terms for them, such as what a nickel bag was, what it looked like, what it cost, and how much he was taking himself.[25]

Marshall re-emphasized Parker's previous testimony about having first gone to the CIA, suggesting that perhaps he did that because it was a more glamourous agency than the FBI. By now, Marshall felt he had created a picture for the jury of a prosecution witness who was personally needy and factually unreliable.

The coup de grace was then delivered:

MARSHALL: It's very important to you that people like us be brought to justice, isn't that correct? I mean you feel very strongly that we are bad people and should be brought to justice?

PARKER: That's one way of putting it.

MARSHALL: All right. So I mean, you would go to almost, not to any length, obviously not killing somebody, but almost any length of trickery to bring us to justice?

PARKER: Yes, any length.

MARSHALL: Any length, and for months and months and months, you took people who thought perhaps that you were their friend, and you were willing to lie to them in order to get us, is that correct?

PARKER: That is absolutely correct.

MARSHALL: You are willing to go, as you say, to any length to get us?

PARKER: That's correct.

MARSHALL: Do you still feel that way?

PARKER: Yes.

MARSHALL: You're willing to lie to get us?

PARKER: Yes.

MARSHALL (TURNING DIRECTLY TO THE JURY): That's what he said.[26]

Marshall sat down. Defendants and spectators were delighted—scripted theater couldn't have topped what had just occurred. They were quite sure that the jury would now understand that the key prosecution witness was a confused drug addict and liar whose personal hatred of the defendants fueled his desire to frame them in any way possible, including lying in his reports to the FBI and in his courtroom testimony.

It was open and shut to the defendants: Parker hated the defendants' politics and he was being paid by the FBI to lie in order to get them locked up. Marshall and Lerner then suggested that Pitkin and Boldt should bring charges against Parker and "the government itself" for their illegal acts. Boldt responded that he was very busy right then, but after the case was concluded, if he did believe that "some criminal offense has been committed by anyone that is within the jurisdiction of this court, I will refer it to the Grand Jury inquiry."[27]

While the defendants enjoyed this win, they didn't see the firestorm of unintended consequences roaring their way. They were naïve to think they were out of the woods.

12

Calm Before the Storm

I have twin interests in life, seeing that people not die in wars nor expire of terminal boredom.

—JEFF DOWD, SEATTLE 7 DEFENDANT

All politics is famously said to be local, but it is even more circumscribed than that. All politics is personal. We are human actors, and to maintain a steely focus on the endgame of radical political or social change through a clutter of personal blind spots and desires is a heroic state found mainly in fiction. Saul Alinsky, who defined and practiced modern community organizing, both despaired of and hoped for the success of the 1960s antiwar and civil rights activists. His 1971 book *Rules for Radicals* railed against their simplistic illusions by drawing a sharp line between the "realistic radical" and the "rhetorical radical." The former is detail-oriented, in it for the long haul, and works with people where they are, not where the radical wishes them to be. The rhetorical radical loves to shout and loves to shock. Both may accurately tell truth to power, as the saying goes, but the realistic radical chooses his or her words, venue, and actions in ways that are more likely to move the cause forward.

In the Alinsky model, the realistic radical starts from where the world is, and incrementally moves the opposition first to a neutral position, and then to a supportive one. Dissidents don't win by converting opponents in one fell swoop—they engage in a stepwise dance that begins with reaching toward, not away from, the people they intend to win over.

While portions of the SLF's organizing work, and the Seattle 7's behavior, fit this realistic radical model, their adolescent anger and energy broke through often enough to scuttle their chance of courtroom vindication.

◆

Tuesday, December 8, dawned foggy and chilly—about ten degrees cooler than the day before. The local papers had had a field day with Parker's Monday testimony. They reported the fact that FBI funding had been used to print SLF literature and to purchase the paint that was used to deface the courthouse during the February TDA demonstration. The news media also highlighted Parker's admission that his drug use had begun long before he had become an FBI informant, and they noted his teaching of reluctant SLF members to fire guns. His willingness to lie also did not go unnoticed.

As the defendants shivered and stumbled into the van for their early morning trip to Tacoma, they were buoyed up by thoughts of the previous day. Maybe the American legal system wasn't so bad after all. Surely the jury could see as clearly as they could that they'd been framed by a lying, drug-addicted nutcase. Dowd told his buddies that yesterday he'd been leaning back in his chair at the defense desk, picking his teeth with a toothpick, and he'd noticed that one of the jurors had then made the same motions, with a quick wink in his direction. Surely a sign, they thought, that the jury was on their side.

Things were looking good, justice-wise, except that Lerner's house had been burglarized again. Again Boldt inquired if Lerner wanted surveillance by the police department. Lerner again equivocated, not wanting the fox to guard the hen house.

Susan Stern was also distracted by events outside the courtroom. She had a painful infection that required surgery, which was scheduled at the University of Washington Hospital for the following day. She would need to be excused from the courtroom for a day or two.

Parker resumed the stand to be cross-examined by Tigar, who noted that Parker had received three times his usual pay from the FBI in April, when the Seattle indictments were announced. Tigar then got a squirming Parker to admit that his most recent payment from the FBI was just two days ago, even though he'd previously testified that he was no longer working for the FBI and hadn't been paid by them for months. This caused an uproar amongst the defense, with Marshall shouting he was being paid by the FBI to lie on the stand.

Tigar pointed out that some of Parker's reports to the FBI were written ten months after the event, some even at the request of prosecutor Pitkin as they were preparing for trial. These reports included complete paragraphs of speeches and conversations in full quotation marks. Parker admitted that he hadn't taken notes at the time of these events. When he needed to confirm a date, he said, he referred to his diary. This caused further uproar—a diary? He had a diary? Why wasn't it entered into evidence? Why hadn't the defense lawyers been told about it? The papers headed their stories that day with news of the missing diary. Pitkin had to admit that he didn't know where the diary was, the FBI had it and it might be in Washington, DC. Boldt, unhappy at this lack of proper protocol, told him to get it, and get it quickly.

This precipitated an ongoing legal tussle, led by Tigar, that Pitkin was not abiding by a federal rule that the government must provide the defense with documents (in this case, both FBI notes and Parker's diary) that prosecution witnesses use to buttress their testimony. Derived from the Jencks Act, this rule was enacted in 1957 in the wake of a Supreme Court decision overturning a case in which a New Mexico labor organizer named Clinton Jencks had been convicted of lying about being a member of the Communist Party on the basis of false information in documents written by paid FBI informers that the government had refused to share with the defense attorneys. The acclaimed 1954 movie *Salt of the Earth* dramatized those struggles, and the vindicated Jencks was one of the many non-professional actors in the cast.

After Tigar sat down, attorney Holley took over, catching Parker in various confusions over the differences between SDS, the Weathermen, and SLF. Lerner then cross-examined Parker, underlining Parker's predilection for impressing his FBI handlers by claiming to know more about the people he was informing on than he actually did. Lerner took Parker through a series of questions trying to get him to admit that he also had committed, in the language of the Seattle 7 indictment: "offenses against the United States, to wit: to willfully and unlawfully injure and aid, abet, counsel and procure others to willfully and unlawfully injure the property of the United States."

Parker continued to be a frustrating witness for all sides. When forced by Boldt to respond "yes" or "no," he would still slip in an ambiguous "to some extent." When Lerner asked Parker to explain the differences between Maoism and Marxism—a critical distinction to political radicals in those days as it implied very different tactics, strategy, and leadership approaches—Parker fumbled his response. Marshall couldn't resist jumping in, "What Mr. Lerner is trying to get at, this person probably doesn't know Mao Tse-tung from Johnny Appleseed."[1]

After the jury recessed for lunch, the attorneys, Boldt, and the defendants had further discussions—Lerner and Marshall asked Boldt to charge Parker with perjury and conspiracy, making the point that the perjury problem couldn't be postponed because, as Lerner noted, "It's not that we want to deny him his liberty. It's that we don't want a perjurer to deny us ours, and we think it is appropriate for you [to tell] the jury… that this witness has at several points perjured himself."[2]

The attorneys then bickered about rules of evidence and documentation of money given or promised to Parker by the FBI or the Department of Justice. The drama and forward progress of the day before was gone. The prosecution was scheduled to put another witness on the stand after lunch, but Pitkin had told him to go home. Boldt, who liked his trials to be tight and fast, dismissed the jurors for the day, and made it clear that he was unhappy with the prosecution's delay. He told Pitkin that he should not have released the witness, and that he didn't want any other schedule changes. Pitkin apologized.

In the absence of the jurors, the defendants once again complained to Boldt about the many people who wanted to attend the trial but weren't let in. They discussed how many inches of bench an average spectator would need. When told the rule was eighteen inches per person, Abeles said, "I really think that the only kind of animals that need eighteen inches have got to be pigs."[3] The defendants framed the issue as an unconstitutional denial of their right to a public trial. Judge Boldt said it was the fire code. Attorney Steinborn responded that fire codes "are the minimum safety standards for a wooden building, and I would suggest that the U.S. Army with all its napalm would have a hard time setting fire to this building."[4]

Steinborn went on to suggest that having an overflow room with the sound piped in was a useful solution that had been used in similar situations. Jeff Dowd conveniently supplied Boldt with a diagram of the microphones and speakers needed to accomplish that, saying that he could provide all the equipment and two technicians to install it, free of charge. With no resolution and everyone dissatisfied, the day ended early. Marshall announced that he and his fellow alleged conspirators would be recessing to the Century Tavern.[5]

Wednesday, December 9, opened with more courtroom bickering among the judge, attorneys, and the defendants (minus Susan Stern, who was home in Seattle recovering from her medical procedure). The spectators had been seated, but not the jury. No government witness was scheduled to appear. Boldt was increasingly tired of the defendants' interruptions of normal courtroom procedure and now it wasn't just the defendants causing trouble—the prosecution also was drifting.

The squabbling began to sound like a tired family quarrel. When Joe Kelly sat on the back of his chair, the Judge said, "Mr. Kelly, get down off the furniture."[6] As both sides mislaid papers, they blamed each other. On the prosecution side, Pitkin was repeatedly reduced to explaining his delays by saying that the FBI hadn't responded yet, or that the documents the judge or the defense attorneys had requested were being held in Washington, DC. It was always the other guy's fault.

The attorneys began a long discussion about the wording of the indictment itself—the defense noting that the agreement to conspire had to precede any of the overt acts supposedly committed in furtherance of the agreed-upon conspiracy, which clearly had not happened and which the prosecution wasn't even trying to prove. It appeared as though the professionals were as flummoxed by the wording of the federal conspiracy law as everyone else. After much discussion and case-citing, Boldt ruled on the side of the prosecution.

Chip Marshall noted that being in the courtroom was like being in elementary school. Grown-ups yammering at you all the time, but never about what really matters, and then there's a recess, and then everyone comes back and it all starts over again.

The main problem, though, from everyone's perspective, was that the prosecution's case seemed to be suspiciously stalled after their key witness admitted to hating the defendants and wanting to get them behind bars badly enough to lie under oath, and who then admitted he was being paid by the FBI at the time of said testimony. Wednesday, day nine of the trial, ended at 5:00 p.m. with no witnesses, no testimony, and everyone frustrated and ill-tempered.

13

Mistrial!

It was all so chaotic—like guerrilla theatre, the best I've ever seen.
—Nick Licata, retired Seattle City Councilman

Thursday, December 10, the defendants ran out of patience. Strategy and cooperation, what there was of it, went out the window. Justice was nowhere to be found. The skies were spraying freezing rain on the defendants' supporters; Judge Boldt refused to address the issue of so many people out in the rain even though a perfectly safe and dry vestibule was available. The prosecution appeared to be dilly-dallying. The defendants had had enough of this legal game.

Early in the morning, Jeff Dowd strode out of the defendant's conference room and down the hall to the judge's chambers, determined to convince Boldt to do right by their cold and wet supporters. He pounded, hard, on the judge's outer door, yelling that he wanted to talk with him. Dowd rarely did anything quietly.

Boldt was taken aback by the ferocity of the pounding, saying later it almost broke the door. When he emerged, with help from marshals, he immediately cited Dowd for contempt, noting his belligerent temperament throughout the trial. The judge said he had no intention of letting any of the spectators in, particularly the "type of people who day after day have been extremely disruptive...I may show my bias but I cannot do anything further about it, and I do not intend to, and if that is error, make the most of it."[1]

Dowd returned to the defense room to tell his alleged co-conspirators the news of his contempt citation, while Boldt entered the courtroom to bemoan yet another late start. Attorney Steinborn, sitting in the courtroom, responded to the judge that "if the marshals [refusing entry to the spectators on the sidewalk] would begin to act like humans, we would have been ready to start at 9:00."[2] Steinborn then left the courtroom to return to the defense conference room.

About twenty minutes later the jury was seated, Pitkin and his staff were present, the judge was there, but Maxey was the only one at the defense table. In retrospect, the defendants commented that it was unprecedented for Boldt to have seated the jury before checking to see that both defense and prosecution were present and ready to begin the day's proceedings. Suddenly, Tigar hurried in to the courtroom, having come from the defense conference room where the defendants were still talking about how to convince the judge to allow their supporters to come in out of the rain.

Addressing Boldt, Tigar attempted to plead the spectators' need to take shelter in the vestibule of the courthouse. The judge would have none of it, and ordered Tigar to bring the defendants into the courtroom. He sent a bailiff along with him to see that it was done. The bailiff returned about five minutes later to say he had notified the defendants to appear but that Lerner had asked for five more minutes to confer. Lerner was trying to convince his fellow defendants that it was not good timing to demand a discussion about the spectators in the rain, or to object to Dowd's apparent contempt citation. "Let's not hold things up for these two procedural issues," he pleaded. The others disagreed. (Years later, Joe Kelly was to note ruefully that they had played perfectly into the judge's and the prosecution's hands by escalating their boisterous demands just as the government's case was falling apart.)

Exactly five minutes later, the bailiff was sent to get the defendants. He quickly returned to the courtroom to report that the defendants' room was locked, but that the three missing defense attorneys were coming down the hall. Tigar explained that the defendants didn't want to return to the courtroom unless those two matters could be discussed first. Boldt refused, saying, "I personally will go there." He ordered the jury and the spectators to stay seated, and told the defense attorneys to come with him. The attorneys, Boldt, and "a large number of marshals" charged down the hallway to the defense conference room.[3] Just as they arrived the door opened, and the defendants poured out.

Boldt demanded that they all return to the courtroom. Abeles interrupted, "We were just on our way."[4] The defendants then raced en masse toward the courtroom. Dowd later said that all the shouting and shoving and running was like participating in a roller derby.[5] The marshals, confused by the sudden motion, chased after them. A newsman in the hallway noticed a marshal hitting and swearing at one of the defendants, who yelled to the judge, "Did you see that?" "The Judge," the newsman wrote, "appeared frightened by the incident."[6]

Reaching his chambers door part way down the hall, Boldt quickly veered off into his room to compose himself. The defendants ran on past and into the courtroom. They noticed, to their surprise, that the jury was seated, listening intently to the commotion in the hallway. Boldt was nowhere in sight. Chip Marshall immediately walked over to talk to the patiently seated jury. Leaning affably against the jury box, he said, "We would like to explain to the jury why we refused to come in at the beginning of this trial. There are a number of people who have been kept outside every day in the rain, people who are getting sick, and all we ask is that the marshals allow these people to come into the lobby, which they have not done."[7]

Boldt then emerged from his chambers, and was shocked to find Marshall speaking directly to the jury, highly irregular and forbidden courtroom behavior in the absence of the judge. "Be silent!" he repeated in louder and louder tones, while Marshall concluded his explanation of the defendants' grievances to the jury. Interrupting Marshall, Boldt abruptly dismissed the jury, and began to harangue the defendants as prologue to issuing contempt citations to one and all: "the sum total of all of this is one of the most inexcusable and outrageous incidents of contempt of court that I have ever read about or learned of in any way, certainly far beyond anything that I have seen."[8] Boldt went on in this vein, detailing how their behavior had constantly frustrated the orderly progress of the trial. He sounded like a father at the end of his rope, who, having first temporized when the children misbehaved, then had escalated to repeated shouts of "if you do that *one more time…*" and then, as the children inevitably continue to test their father's limits, he suddenly lowers the boom.

Marshall and Kelly shouted back that it was Pitkin who was frustrating the orderly progress of the trial, as he hadn't brought in a witness for two days. The defendants had never back-burnered their earlier shock and anger over the skewed jury selection process either; nothing, they said, about the whole process had seemed fair. Boldt, equally angry, repeated his story of how loudly Dowd had pounded on his door. Although he didn't say he was frightened, observers noted he was shaking and pale.

Boldt then dropped his real thunderbolt:

BOLDT: I now have grave doubts that this trial could possibly continue with an unbiased jury by reason of misconduct of the defendants...in these circumstances I hold it to be my duty in the interests of justice to declare a mistrial of this case and I do now and hereby declare—

MARSHALL: The reason you do is you are afraid the jury has seen Mr. Pitkin and his witnesses. We are not afraid of the jury.

KELLY: We think we can get off.[9]

The judge then ordered the courtroom cleared, and repeated "I now declare a mistrial of this case by reason of misconduct of the defendants and, to some extent, their counsel in failing to assist the court in the matter of procuring an orderly trial and in the matter of bringing the defendants into the court."[10] Amidst much shouting from the defendants Judge Boldt loudly repeated "Recess! Recess!" as he backed strategically behind a bailiff into his chambers.

The defendants assumed they were heading back to jail immediately—Kelly slipped out to a hallway pay phone to call Stern to tell her the news. But when nobody came to take them away, they went back to their conference room.

An hour and a half later the attorneys and the defendants were summoned to Boldt's chambers. Boldt said he couldn't get the contempt citations completed for an afternoon session, so he would deliver them in the courtroom the following Monday morning. Lerner asked if they were going to be charged with contempt for things that Boldt had previously said he wouldn't charge them for. In his response, Boldt called him Mr. Marshall. Lerner then explained his view of the morning's events—that they weren't trying to ignore Boldt's order to come to the courtroom—and concluded, "I think it would be a tremendous miscarriage of justice now to compound this [misunderstanding] by sending us to jail."[11] He also raised the point, which would come up later, that Boldt had made no effort to establish whether or not any of the jurors had in fact been prejudiced by witnessing and hearing what they did.

Several newsmen, however, had caught up with most of the jurors as they left the courthouse to ask that question—had the melee of the morning made it no longer possible for them to render a fair judgment? Most said no. The local news director for the NBC affiliate submitted transcripts of his interviews with eight jurors, none of whom felt their opinion was changed by the morning's events, nor were they prejudiced against the defendants. A typical response was from juror Floyd Getchell: "No, I had no prejudice against any of the defendants," and "Yes, quite," when asked, "Were you surprised that you were let go?"[12] Another juror, Robert Owen, said "The outbursts didn't bother us." A third, Robert McNamee, characterized the case as a "run-of-the-mill TV trial." Many jurors voiced disappointment at not being allowed to finish out the trial. One, though, was reported as saying "I think after that incident it would have been hard for us not to be prejudiced. They were sure guilty of one conspiracy. They conspired to stop the trial."[13]

The defendants held a press conference. Chip Marshall compared their situation to a railroad workers' strike that was going on that week, "the railroads are on strike today and we're on strike from this railroad." Stern, after receiving Kelly's call, had stumbled into her clothes and found someone to drive her to Tacoma, where she appeared in the press room, pale and weak. Everyone now assumed they would be sent to jail on Monday. They noted that the prosecution had delayed the trial for almost two days, calling no witnesses since Parker, with only a mild reprimand from Boldt, yet when the defendants delayed the trial for five minutes, Boldt went ballistic. Tigar said what was really happening was that the government was playing a double jeopardy strategy—since the prosecution appeared to be losing the case, the government had decided to end it and start over again.

Stern was in a quandary—since she hadn't been in the courtroom that day, she wasn't held in contempt, but she thought "not to go to jail would have made everything I had claimed about being a revolutionary meaningless. It's not that I wanted to go to jail; it's just that that I wanted the judge to know I was just as contemptuous of him as the boys were, that women could hate just as much, could be just as disruptive and deaf to authority. I was caught up in the drama of it all. To be a defendant of a famous conspiracy case and not go to jail—what a farcical anticlimax."[14] Not surprisingly, she decided to act in as confrontational a way as possible when she returned to court on Monday.

The newspapers speculated whether and where a second trial might take place. The decision to retry the case rested in the U.S. Attorney's office; Pitkin equivocated, citing the unprecedented nature of the case. If it were retried, it would have to occur in the same western Washington federal district and Boldt could again be the judge assigned to the case. The Washington State Bar Association voted "to examine the trial record to determine whether any attorney in the case is guilty of unprofessional or unethical conduct." The *Seattle Times* reporters noted "It is unusual for a judge to order a mistrial because of defendants' conduct. Most mistrials result from actions by the prosecution resulting in charges being dismissed."[15]

Meanwhile, Tigar jump-started his research on declarations of mistrial, instances of double jeopardy, and the finer points of contempt citations in excess of six months. Back in the courtroom for a brief session, Boldt again told the attorneys and defendants that he needed some quiet time to collect his thoughts to document the citations and notice of mistrial. "I need some—what did they use to call it, the MRA people, what was their name? What was it, the Moral Re-Armament? A quiet time."[16] For the newspapers, though, he didn't stint—calling the defendants' behavior a "degrading and outrageous" example of contempt.

Looking for a compromise, a way to defuse the contentiousness, Lerner asked Boldt, "is there any way we can unmiss the mistrial?" "No. There is no way. The jury has been discharged," responded Boldt.[17] He explained that his decision "was not done suddenly in the heat of it; it was done after much thought and soul-searching." Lerner then tried again, explaining the cost and time it had taken to prepare for this trial, that their attorneys likely wouldn't be available for another trial and that the mistrial "is an unfair disaster."[18]

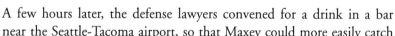

A few hours later, the defense lawyers convened for a drink in a bar near the Seattle-Tacoma airport, so that Maxey could more easily catch his flight home to Spokane. Tigar, who described himself as "riotously drunk" was stopped by a Seattle policeman on his own way back into Seattle:

> With all the bravado of the truly squiffed, I decided to drive back to the home of Michael Rosen, the ACLU lawyer who had lent me a bedroom in his house. I was doing just fine with all the controls and such, but I did not see a stop sign near Rosen's house. A Seattle policeman pulled me over and asked for my driver's license. I saw him register who I was, and I thought I was in serious trouble. The cop looked up from my license

to my face, and said, "You're the lawyer for those defendants in that trial, aren't you?"

I said yes.

"Well, he continued, "is it true what they said in the paper, that the FBI bought the spray paint for people to use in the demonstration, and all the rest of that."

"It's all true," I said. "Their witness admitted it on the stand."

"I'll be damned," the cop said. "That really pisses me off. You know, we local cops had to go down there and wrestle with that crowd, trying to protect that federal building. It was really crappy duty, let me tell you. And now we find out that the goddamn feds were actually helping make it happen. I'm glad you were able to bring that out."

I felt better, but he continued, "Sir, you not only went through a stop sign, but you appear drunker than owl shit, if you don't mind me saying so. How far do you live from here?"

"A couple of blocks." I gave the address.

"OK, I want you to follow me, real slow. There are no stop signs between here and there, but I want you to watch my taillights and take it easy. I'll get you home before you hurt somebody."[19]

Judge Boldt's diary indicates that he spent all day Friday, December 11, and both weekend days, December 12 and 13, in his chambers working on the mistrial and contempt papers. But if he thought declaring a mistrial and invoking contempt charges under Federal Rule of Criminal Procedure 42(a) meant that he had regained control over his courtroom, he was gravely mistaken.

14

A Double Dose of Contempt

We're all probably going to be charged with interfering with the orderly perversion of justice.

—JEFF STEINBORN, SEATTLE 7 DEFENSE ATTORNEY

While Judge Boldt was in his chambers writing up the paperwork to send them all to prison, the defendants held an all-day meeting. Stern admitted that she couldn't "remember much of it, because Joe [Kelly] and I dropped acid and giggled through the entire thing. During that meeting we did decide that all of us including myself would make a statement to the judge concerning the mistrial. We decided that since I was not cited for contempt, my speech could be more vitriolic."[1]

When the defense attorneys arrived at the courthouse on that gray Monday morning, they noted increased security around the courthouse building and in the hallways. Waiting spectators were subject to more intrusive searches and stepped-up intimidation. The dozen or so additional marshals in the courtroom were dressed like ninjas in black turtleneck sweaters, black jackets, and black gloves. A contingent of them hovered protectively around Stan Pitkin and the prosecution table.

Promptly at 9:10 a.m., Judge Boldt entered the contempt sentences according to Rule 42(a) of the Federal Rules of Criminal Procedure, which allows the judge to issue summary judgments (which would send them to jail immediately) on courtroom misconduct that he himself has witnessed. Attempting a modicum of fairness—again perhaps to separate himself from his colleague Judge Hoffman in Chicago—Boldt began by saying that attorney Maxey had in every way been a model attorney, and, although he felt the other three defense lawyers were less than helpful in controlling their clients, he was not going to charge any of them with misconduct. In addition, he would desist from charging Stern with contempt because she had not been in the courtroom the previous Thursday, although he couldn't resist calling out "her serious and repeated misconduct prior to December 9."[2]

157

These conciliatory statements over with, he then threw the book at the six male defendants. He described the events of Thursday from his perspective, characterizing their behavior as: "contumacious conduct," "tumultuous and near riotous conduct," "gross misconduct," "willful, flagrant and totally inexcusable defiance of the court," "long continued and repeated misconduct." [3] When Marshall interrupted, Boldt ignored him and continued to read his document.

If he thought he could get through this final encounter with these defendants without further ado, he was wrong. Again. Receiving paper copies of their contempt citations, each defendant (except Lerner, in his usual jacket and tie and whose mother was said to be present in the courtroom) tore them up and threw the paper bits toward Boldt's raised desk. "Pick up the garbage, Judge," said Marshall.[4]

Trying to ignore them, Boldt asked the attorneys how much time they would like for a response. Tigar noted that there were a "number of legal arguments that are required to be made." Boldt responded "I am not going to hear any legal arguments." The spectators laughed and Boldt doubled down on his control, asking Marshal Robinson "to post your men over here where we can quickly pick up those who are interrupting…Put as many people there as necessary."[5] The courtroom resembled an armed camp.

Each attorney and defendant was allowed twenty minutes to respond. Tigar began with his usual legal acumen—reminding the judge of the long history (back to the infamous Star Chamber of seventeenth-century England) of the requirement to apply summary contempt very narrowly as it gave a single person the power of both prosecutor and judge. Tigar quoted multiple contempt appeals and *Harvard Law Review* articles. He argued that the contempt charges should be heard before a jury. He said that it hadn't been contempt of court that occurred on Thursday, it was a failure of communication. He concluded with a quote from Supreme Court Justice William O. Douglas' recently published *Points of Rebellion* in which Justice Douglas defended dissent, writing that it is usually opposed by "the older generation" who tend to "resist all change in any case."[6]

The literary tone continued as attorney Holley began with, "They have eyes and see not, they have ears and hear not, they are a generation of vipers." Boldt, perhaps understandably confused as Holley had conflated two Biblical quotes, interrupted, "Of whom are you speaking now?" Marshall interjected, "You, Judge." Holley responded, "I am speaking about the established order of this society and the Federal Courts, your Honor."[7] Holley then wandered a bit further afield, discussing the postwar Nuremburg trials and the McCarthy hearings of the 1950s, but he also continued to hammer on the fact that Thursday morning's seating of the jury in the courtroom before the judge, attorneys, and defendants were all present was an unusual and unexpected event.

To this day, the defendants suspect that Boldt may have deliberately placed the jury in the unsupervised courtroom that morning to precipitate a crisis that would then allow him to order a mistrial—which would hide the fact that the prosecution's case had collapsed in the wake of Parker's less-than-stellar testimony and the apparent lack of any other significant prosecution witnesses. Boldt could then send the defendants to prison for contempt and the prosecution could prepare for a retrial. Meanwhile SLF would be crippled.

Maxey was up next, speaking to Roger Lippman's consistent and sincere comments about their supporters being out in the rain day after day: "As a matter of fact, he used to drive me crazy, because I would be preparing for an opening statement and this is all that Roger Lippman [was] ever concerned about. I couldn't believe it...a prudent counsel would have said, 'You need a spectator gallery in this case like you need a hole in the head.' But it was their case and their experience, and they wanted their people to give witness."[8] Maxey also emphasized each defendant's sincerity and integrity, and reiterated the fact that they, unlike the jury, were grappling with the morality of their country's actions in Vietnam.

Lerner spent his twenty minutes underlining his differences from the other defendants. He tried to soften their revolutionary rhetoric, and framed the issues, as Tigar had suggested, as a matter of poor communication. They were late coming into court because they wanted to iron out their disagreement about tactics in the relative privacy of the defense room and not burden the courtroom with their conversation. He himself opposed making a big issue about the spectators out in the rain. He himself did *not* tear up his contempt citation even though the judge attributed that action to everybody. He also noted that "you do read the newspapers, you know that everybody felt that the Government's case was in very bad shape at that particular moment."[9] He said Boldt was "intellectually sloppy" and by defending his mistake, Boldt was only making things worse, just like the U.S. in Vietnam.[10]

Boldt responded, "Mr. Lerner, your time has expired. I am going to let you speak a little further, but would you believe that what I was concerned about is that you people have prejudiced yourself to the jury?...a fair trial was impossible because of your misconduct, and this is what I was concerned about." Lerner responded ruefully, "With such friends, we need no enemies,"[11] and said their trial was a spectacle to "focus attention *here* hoping...that the people will not notice that their problems [unemployment, etc.] are not being solved by the Government."[12]

Dowd went next:

> I don't like the idea of this, you know, elocution before the execution, everybody just getting up and making a little speech, and you are going to throw us in jail, but I guess that's what you're supposed to do. I would like to bring the world into this courtroom...have some Vietnamese child sitting there like you are...400,000 people gathered at Woodstock sitting in this courtroom...I would love to hold this court one day at the unemployment office...I would dare you to try to hold it there and take yourself seriously."[13]

Dowd also addressed the issue of the spectators: "You wonder why we always care about the spectators, these spectators don't consider themselves spectators, they know damned well this is...a trial of all youth."[14]

He then referred to his knocking on the judge's chamber door, demonstrating by knocking on the lectern, "What would have happened if Martin Luther had been sentenced for contempt for knocking on a door that loud? I just wonder."[15]

Ever theatrical, Dowd continued, "the thing that disappointed me most is every day coming in this courtroom and you stand up and you salute that flag [the American flag on the side of the judge's bench]. That flag was born in revolution and, your Honor, I honestly don't think that flag deserves to be up there. The flag that deserves to be up there is this one...the Nazi flag."[16] Spectators then applauded as Dowd pulled out a large Nazi flag from under his shirt and he, Marshall, and Abeles "hurled" it at Judge Boldt.[17] Boldt was visibly shaken.

After the hubbub died down, Roger Lippman asked that the flag be entered as a government exhibit. He then laid out the lengthy sequence of requests and potential solutions for allowing more spectators into the building, along with the court's negative response to all ideas. Switching topics, he next asked for a recess because the Seattle Black Panther Party was being evicted from their house and "all of us ought to be up there supporting them," and secondly, he said he didn't want to be in jail on December 20 because it is "the tenth anniversary of the founding of the National Liberation Front of South Vietnam, and I think that we ought to have a celebration about that...they have inspired us a whole lot, [but] if we're in jail, we'll celebrate it there too. But I would like to be on the street."[18]

Joe Kelly was thoughtful, saying "I'm glad that you used the term contempt of court [as the reason] you sent us to jail for because that's exactly what I feel for you." He pointed out that he wasn't in Seattle during the January and February timeframe of the indictment, but then he realized that "the FBI had made no mistake whatsoever, because if I had been here, I would have been in all those rallies, I would have been in all those

TWO DEFENDANTS HELD UP NAZI FLAG BEFORE JUDGE GEORGE H. BOLDT

Defendant Jeffrey Dowd, in slam at judge, said it should replace American flag in courtroom

Seattle 7 defendant Jeff Dowd smuggled a large Nazi flag into the courtroom on the day the seven were sentenced to prison for contempt. The defendants threw it at the judge's raised desk. *Seattle Post-Intelligencer sketch, December 15, 1970, Bob McCausland, seattlepi.com, image courtesy Seattle Public Library.*

meetings…I would have been in TDA, because TDA was right…and this proves it." It's all a set-up, he said, to intimidate everyone, "we're on trial for being alive, we're on trial for just trying…to support the Vietnamese people in their desire to be alive."[19]

Michael Abeles continued in the same vein, "I'm going to charge you just as responsible for that bombing [in Vietnam] as Sergeant Calley or Westmoreland…because you represent the power structure in this country, and you're just as guilty as them."[20] To spectator applause he raised the ante and promised that all the young people in America were "going to see how crazy you are, and how fascist you are, and more people are going to fight to their death, if they have to, to see people like you out of power."[21]

Chip Marshall said he wasn't worried about going to jail, because he didn't think the judge had the nerve to send them there—"I think what this whole trial is about is fear, and the fear you have and the fear that all those marshals have and the reason they have so many people there to guard your bench, the reason that you have to stand ten feet above everybody is the kind of fear this judicial system has of its people."[22] In addition to fear, Marshall accused the judge of being unaware of the changing world around him. He then referred Boldt to the Bob Dylan song "Ballad of a Thin Man," comparing the judge to the song's refrain about the man who is clueless about what is happening all around him.

Marshall returned to his analogy between the courtroom and the school. It wasn't just about having recesses inserted between older people in power standing up and talking nonstop, it was also the fact that the people in power were also saying "kids, we're only doing this for your own good…it hurts us more than it hurts you." Marshall observed "that does make some sort of sense because every time you do something like this, I'm sure it destroys some of your humanity, if there's any left."[23]

"You couldn't understand what Vietnam has to do with this," Marshall said, and in the end, it didn't matter if the judge sent them to jail, or not, "because you have maintained the structure which maintains injustice, and you have kept the power away from the people."[24]

Marshall concluded by accusing the judge of acting like a "good German." Boldt interrupted and said "I'm not a German, you understand that, my ancestors are Danes."

MARSHALL: Pardon?

BOLDT: My ancestors are Danes and Swedes. I have no German blood whatsoever.

KELLY: You don't even understand what he's talking about.

STERN: There's something rotten in Denmark.

Spectators applauded Stern's Shakespeare reference. Boldt, perhaps because he thought the whole case was mercifully almost over, or perhaps he still did not catch the literary reference, responded almost cheerfully, "for once, I have to agree with you, Mrs. Stern. I was there about a year ago and I know."[25]

Shortly thereafter, Marshall wound down with various references to the Boston Tea Party, the Constitution, and the value of America's immigrants. Boldt sighed, but still believed the worst was behind him.

Then Susan Stern stood up. Boldt repeatedly told her to sit down, as she was not charged with contempt and therefore had no right to speak. He pleaded, "Mrs. Stern, please listen because it is to your advantage… will you listen, please. Please listen, you have not been cited for contempt and, therefore, there is no occasion for you to speak. If you do speak, it may result in you being cited for contempt." He gave up after another full transcript page of pleading, finishing with "if you want to speak in defiance of my order, you may do so."[26]

She then launched into a long and occasionally rambling speech, starting with thanking the attorneys, and then moving on to wishing the jury were more ethnically diverse. She was sorry there were no Vietnamese in the courtroom, but they couldn't be, because they were all being killed, "Judge Boldt, the onus is on you, their deaths are on your shoulders, and not mine."[27]

She likened Boldt to Pontius Pilate, washing his hands of "Vietnam and the ghettos of Seattle and around this country and Latin America, and Africa."[28] Boldt, seeing a quick and tidy ending of this nightmare case vanish in front of him, told her that she had taken more than enough of the court's time. But she continued to talk, and Marshall, Dowd, and Abeles chimed in as well. There was a bit of back-and-forth shouting of "You're in contempt" "No, you're in contempt." Boldt focused on Stern:

BOLDT: Please discontinue right now.

STERN: I'm sorry, your Honor. I prefer to continue with my remarks.

BOLDT: Please do not do so.

STERN: They will have to drag me off to stop me.

BOLDT: If that is necessary—[29]

Marshall got up to walk out, saying if he couldn't get a jury trial, he was going to leave. He said talking to Boldt was like talking to the Sphinx. Some spectators took up a "Kill the kids" chant, led by Dowd who, like many of his generation, firmly believed that youth were the oppressed leaders of the coming revolution. Other spectators stood and waved their fists, shouting that it was the judge who was in contempt of American justice. Everyone was standing; everyone was shouting. The U.S. Marshals were circling.

Boldt had finally had enough: "Clear the audience," he nodded to Robinson, who signaled that Boldt should leave the courtroom, thinking that the disturbance "had proceeded to a point where law enforcement officers might not be able to control it without the use of weapons."[30] Then, as one radio newscaster who was present reported, "All hell broke loose in the courtroom."[31] Boldt, from his chambers retreat, spent the next half hour listening through closed doors as his courtroom became a battlefield.

First, two black-clad marshals seized one-hundred-pound Susan Stern, who was still trying to speak. They jammed her arms behind her back and put her in a chokehold. Tigar ran across the courtroom to unloose her from their grip, yelling "Let her go, she's sick!" Another deputy marshal threw Tigar against a wall and squirted mace in his face. He crumpled and two deputies dragged him out of the courtroom. As the mace was wiped from his eyes, he said, "I can see things much more clearly now."

FBI case agent Louis Harris reported the scene to Director Hoover: "A free-for-all battle ensued between defendants, spectators and Deputy U.S. Marshals in the courtroom which lasted approximately 35 minutes…all defendants with the exception of LERNER were observed physically resisting arrest and causing injury to Deputy U.S. Marshals… Numerous injuries resulted during battle in courtroom but all defendants taken into custody."[32] At a later date, the Department of Justice contemplated bringing charges against the defendants for their attacks on federal marshals.

Kelly described it as a set-up, "The goon squad came in on a prearranged signal, although nothing had happened at all, yet, with any of the defendants. Susan was trying to continue speaking, people were standing there, then all of a sudden [the marshals] grabbed everybody and started dragging people out."[33]

Abeles was attacked from behind by a leather-gloved marshal and put in a hammer lock. Twisting his arm back, the marshal caused additional pain by bending Abeles' fingers backwards. Abeles yelled that he couldn't breathe. Lippman was on his feet, but off to the side. He saw the "marshals swinging away…it looked pretty dangerous." He went out into the hall, where he was taken into custody.[34] Marshall was grabbed when he started to walk out, saying "I'm not going to take any more of this bullshit." Lerner sat down on a chair at the edge of the room and didn't move.

By this time, the reporter for the *Seattle Post-Intelligencer* wrote, "the courtroom looked like a tornado had swept through it. Paper littered the floor, drinking cups were strewn about, counsel tables and spectator benches shoved awry and chairs upset."[35] Ten spectators were arrested, charged with assault, and held on $10,000 bail.

Thirty minutes later, the spectator benches empty and the armed marshals back in place, Boldt emerged from his chambers to read the now doubled contempt citations in the presence of all defendants, who were by this time handcuffed. The defendants were to go immediately to jail; bail would not be set until a later date. Boldt took care to quash any hopes that further deliberations would be held before a different judge—he said this case would remain on his personal calendar "until either the case is finally terminated or my capacity to carry on with it is completely exhausted."[36]

He reminded the defendants that his Christian faith remained strong, saying "I have freely forgiven and forgotten everything….my Christian faith requires it." He viewed nothing that the defendants did or said as "an affront to me personally." He then noted that disruptive court trials were becoming more common, and that the threat of contempt didn't seem to deter their frequency. Boldt expressed his hope that serving their contempt sentences would:

> give the defendants ample opportunity to reflect upon their past misconduct…I pray it will convince defendants [that] disruption in the next trial is not worth what it will cost the defendants…I myself have not the slightest doubt that my daily prayers for strength and guidance to be calm, understanding and patient in this case and to do that which is fair and just, not necessarily in my eyes but in the sight of our Heavenly Father have been answered. I believe Divine Providence may have given

this Court and others guidance to an effective solution of disruptive trials. I pray it may be so.[37]

Attorney Holley responded "I believe that there were some nine thousand witches burned in this country because the particular people burning them knew that they had Divine Providence on their side."[38] He then quoted most of the heavily ironic lyrics to the 1964 Tom Paxton song "What did you learn in school today, dear little boy of mine?"

Tigar did his best to get Boldt to release the defendants on their own recognizance while an appeal of their contempt sentences was heard. He pointed out that all seven had shown up in court every day. He said that each defendant had solid citizens to guarantee that they wouldn't jump bail, including Lerner's parents, Judge and Mrs. Lerner. He quoted a number of federal case precedents and submitted several documents studded with relevant case citations. Maxey added that the judge need not worry about the defendants not showing up, "as a matter of fact, you could almost say, tongue-in-cheek, they show up too frequently."[39]

Lerner argued that they would all show up because they wanted to vindicate themselves before the American people. Marshall said that the reason for their courtroom behavior was that they hadn't been allowed to be heard before an impartial jury. "We were faced with a situation which seems to be very contradictory to one of the basic tenets of the Constitution,"[40] he noted, and now it was doubly true for the contempt proceedings, because they had no jury at all.

Steinborn offered to take personal responsibility for all the defendants if they were remanded to his custody. He then described Stern's medical problems in some detail, having just spoken with her physician—she needed specific postoperative care, including painkillers that wouldn't be allowed in prison (due to their resale value), and a check-in with someone familiar with her condition every other day for several weeks. Lippman and Kelly reminded the judge that they had shown up for trial every day, even though they were demonstrably not even in Washington State during the timeframe of the alleged conspiracy.

Boldt ignored them all. He then handed the defendants over to police custody, saying that Stern could go to the public health hospital in Seattle under guard. He announced he would make his decision regarding bail the following day. Which he did: no bail for any of them. He said their release on bail would threaten members of the court and the community at large. He also thought there was a good chance they "would take

P.I. DEC 15 1970
—*P-I Sketches by Bob McCausland.*

SUSAN STERN TORE UP A PAPER

Other defendants ripped up contempt citations

Seattle 7 defendant Susan Stern tears up her contempt citation and throws it at the judge. With the exception of Michael Lerner, all the other defendants did the same. *Seattle Post-Intelligencer sketch, December 15, 1970, Bob McCausland, seattlepi.com, image courtesy Seattle Public Library.*

flight, go underground, or abroad or…become a fugitive, frustrating a new trial."[41]

They were to serve their prison sentences for contempt of court consecutively, which meant a full year each for Marshall, Dowd, Abeles, Kelly, and Lippman, and six months each for Stern and Lerner. Back in charge, Boldt firmly declared that he would not order a new trial until they had all served their entire contempt sentences.

While their defense attorneys hunkered down to write and submit appeals for bail to the Ninth Circuit Court in San Francisco, Stern was hustled north to the Seattle hospital and the rest of the defendants were hauled off to Tacoma City Jail to await transport to federal prison.

Newsweek magazine, unable to keep up with the fast pace of the activity in Judge Boldt's courtroom, hit the stands that December 14 with an article praising Boldt for being "unusually adept at keeping his cool," and concluding, "So volatile are the issues—and so vague are the Federal laws involved—that the trial of the Seattle Seven is very likely to run into the new year."[42]

PART THREE

Consequences

Cover of an SLF Seattle 8 Defense Fund newsletter.
*University of Washington Libraries, Special Collections,
Vietnam Era Ephemera Collection, UW38749*

15

Jailed Without Bail

Jailtime means time. Endless time...Jailtime means waiting...Jailtime means the blues, black and blue, growing deep and mean out of your soul. Jailtime is life being buried alive.

—Susan Stern, Seattle 7 defendant

It didn't take more than a few days in Tacoma City Jail for Lippman, Marshall, Kelly, and Dowd to organize a prison demonstration. Lippman recalled, "Because the prosecution had built up this huge paranoia about how powerful we were, they separated us and so because we were instinctual organizers, we were able to organize the entire jail."

One hundred or so of their SLF supporters continued their daily trek from Seattle to Tacoma, moving now to march and chant on the sidewalk around the jail instead of the courthouse.

Lippman described the prisoner protest they organized:

We had brooms that we used to close the windows to make them look like they were latched, but they weren't. When we heard the crowd on the sidewalk, we opened the windows and cheered and yelled—regular prisoners joined in. We flew paper airplanes out the windows until guards came back and latched the windows shut. So we broke the windows by throwing bars of soap at them. Then very soon, guards came back, searched each of us, threw us in one disgusting cell and took away all of our clothes. So there were five of us naked in this cell for a while.[1]

Lerner, the fifth man, hadn't participated in the protest. But he was thrown in with the others anyway, freezing and naked and not knowing why:

"What happened?" I asked.
"You know, your riot," the guard answered.
"I had nothing to do with that."
"You can't tell us a bunch of winos got this together on their own."[2]

Chip Marshall wrote a letter addressed to "Brothers and Sisters," which was printed in several underground newspapers: "The abrupt end of the Seattle Conspiracy trial may signal a new pattern for federal repression…The new approach allows the state to fill all functions at once—judge, jury and executioner—thus avoiding the possibility of any embarrassing errors ([such as] acquittal)."

After quoting Boldt's statement that "Divine Providence may have given this court and others guidance to an effective solution of disruptive trials. I pray it may be so," Marshall added, "If 'divine inspiration' was involved in this trial, it was clearly of the same sort which inspired the Inquisition and the Salem witch trials."[3]

Back in Seattle the defense collective was busily raising funds for the day when bail would finally be set while the defense attorneys were working overtime to file an appeal to the Ninth Circuit Court to revoke Boldt's no-bail order. On December 23, two days before Christmas, that court ordered Boldt to immediately set bail for the defendants. Boldt refused, saying "I think the order is wrong."[4] Besides, added the clerk of the Tacoma court, "the court closed at noon today. The next working day will be Monday," which was four days later, after Christmas. When Steinborn called Boldt at home, pleading with him to set bail so the defendants could go home for Christmas, Boldt was angry at the intrusion: "It was well after the Christmas holiday had begun; yet you persisted in annoying me. It greatly disturbed my wife."[5] Attorney Tigar reacted to Judge Boldt's refusal to act by saying that Boldt not only thinks he's God, he also thinks he's the Supreme Court.[6]

Joe Kelly's father had once been a driver for U.S. Rep Richard L. Ottinger, D-NY. On January 6, 1971, Ottinger wrote to defense attorney Maxey:

> I am very concerned about the apparent miscarriage of justice in this case and the implications for the country of the apparent attempt of the authorities to get Joe and his companions in jail regardless of legal niceties—even to the extent, apparently, of the trial judge's ignoring the bail order of the Court of Appeals. If there is any way I can help, please let me know. I spoke of the situation to [U.S. Rep.] Brock Adams [R-WA], who looked into the initial case and determined that it would have been dismissed by the prosecutor but for orders to pursue it from Washington. I am very close to Brock and if there is any way his help could be useful, or mine, please let me know."[7]

After being rebuffed by Judge Boldt and his office staff on December 23, the defense attorneys filed another brief asking the appeals court to enforce its previous ruling that bail be set. Pitkin's office filed a counter argument, saying that the court's previous ruling to grant bail was precipitous and incorrect because it hadn't read the full transcript, nor did it see the elusive videotapes of the courtroom riot.[8] Pitkin buttressed his objection to bail by likening the Seattle 7 to the Black Panthers. Not hesitating to stoke racist fears, he announced that the Seattle 7 were "as dangerous as Eldridge Cleaver and Angela Davis." Boldt, Pitkin, and FBI case agent Louis Harris each submitted affidavits that they feared for their lives if bail were granted.[9]

On Wednesday, December 30, 1970, the Appeals Court judges agreed with Pitkin's argument, and changed their minds about requiring immediate bail, at least until they could read the transcript. It also set February 11, 1971, as a date for a hearing on the contempt sentences themselves.

None of this legal maneuvering prevented the defendants from being transported from the Tacoma jail to federal prison facilities up and down the west coast. Marshall, Kelly, and Lerner, shackled in leg and handcuffs were bundled into a van with several U.S. Marshals who would not answer their questions about where they were being taken, nor tell them whether or not their attorneys knew they were being moved. They drove fast, going south on Interstate 5, crossing the Columbia River at Portland and stopping for the night at a local jail in southern Oregon. They drove again all the next day, still mystified about their destination. They could hear news snippets on the van radio—their attorneys were interviewed saying that they didn't know where their clients were or what was happening to them.

They pulled up the next night at a jail in Salinas, California. Kelly remembers the Salinas jail: "The inmates had just had some kind of rebellion and they had burned their mattresses. The smoky smell still hung in the air, the place was a mess. We met Cesar Chavez, leader of the United Farmworkers of America, as we passed one of the jail cells."[10] Lerner recalls talking with Chavez "about the struggles ahead and the difficulties of dealing with the Nixon administration." Kelly recalls that Chavez "was such a quiet unassuming person. We recognized him through the bars as we were going down a corridor. We said hello and told him who we were, but we didn't have much time to talk with him."[11]

Mostly it was a boring trip, cramped and cuffed in a windowless van. Interstate 5 winds through flat green Oregon farmland and the beautiful Siskiyou Mountains. It skirts Mount Shasta and then zooms straight down California's golden inland valleys. The defendants, though, saw none of this. Searching for ways to pass the time, Lerner found something to "rattle the marshals—I started to sing Hebrew songs and prayers. This upset them because they didn't know what I was saying. Psalm 118 was a favorite, and I told them what it meant: *Open for me the gates of righteousness, I will enter into them to praise God.* I liked the obvious connection to prisons and prisoners."[12]

Kelly had the impression that "the Feds took us much more seriously than we took ourselves. But we were surprised that Boldt could deny the Ninth Circuit Court ruling. I had spent the summer in Chicago's Cook County Jail, so I wasn't all that worried. Cook County Jail was 80 percent black; gang members, not political. Lerner, though, was really worried about the kind of prison we might be going to. Chip and I were kind of making fun of him. We sang the Steven Still's song *Love the One You're With* when it was on the radio—Lerner didn't like that."[13]

The third day, back on the road, still going south, they stopped at a rest area for a bathroom break. They "saw the first people we'd seen who looked like they might be supporters. We asked them to call our lawyers and tell them they'd seen us here."[14]

Kelly was the first to be dropped off. He spent the next month at Lompoc Federal Penitentiary, a medium security prison in Santa Barbara County, waiting for bail to be granted. He didn't think his fellow inmates knew anything about the Seattle 7; they were in for drug offenses, with some fraud and white collar crime mixed in. "Some prisons are known as 'gladiator schools.' Didn't see that. Did see some Hispanics with major tattoos on their backs, Jesus on the cross, and tears and blood; I think that was gang culture."[15] Perhaps he was assigned to this relatively non-violent prison population because by then the prosecution had finally realized he hadn't been in Washington State in the timeframe defined by the indictment.

Kelly, probably the Seattle 7 defendant who had already done the most jail and prison time, was used to the routine, and took advantage of the free time to read a lot. "The better jails had a book cart that came around once a week. Some guys had a stash in their cells and they'd lend them."[16] At Lompoc he read Ken Kesey's *Sometimes a Great Notion.*

After Kelly was left at Lompoc, Lerner and Marshall were driven farther south to Terminal Island Penitentiary in Los Angeles County, where they were greeted by a bevy of guards who shaved their hair and beards. "A big victory" for the government, noted Lerner ironically. He recalled:

They put us both into some form of isolation. And that's where we stayed for the first week or two. Then when the prison administration realized this was not going to be a short stay, we got moved. We could eat with the general population, but Chip and I were not allowed to eat together.

I was terrified to go into this prison. This was not Lompoc. This was hardened criminals. I had been exposed to the view that was popular in the movement at this time that all prisoners were political prisoners. But I didn't believe that for a second. I was well aware of the romanticization of anyone who was oppressed. I'd grown up with an oppressed population—Jews—and I knew that being oppressed doesn't always bring out the best in people.

But I was surprised as I talked with these people that many of them were not hardened criminals. I began to realize that prisons are instruments of repression more than I'd realized. Amazing to me how many decent human beings there were there.

Chip was as usual an inveterate optimist, and I was not. Especially when I heard that Judge Boldt wasn't following the Appeals Court ruling to set bail. These are the sorts of things that don't happen in America, and yet they were happening.

Suddenly I was faced with a new danger—there were a bunch of white supremacists in the jail, and Nazis. They wanted to hurt me. But on the other side, there were a group of people who were either Panthers or supporters of Panthers. They invited me to come talk with them, during the hour they were in the yard. They were extremely supportive; they knew that part of TDA was in support of Bobby Seale, and some of them knew that I knew Huey Newton, Bobby Seale and David Hilliard—the guys in the jail heard about this from the Panther office and they protected me from the supremacists.[17]

Marshall's laconic description of his days at Terminal Island was "Jail was OK—not nearly as bad as ones in the South that I'd been in. Got thrown into solitary pretty soon—lecturing the other inmates about revolution, etc." He did, however, have what he called a "transforming experience":

We got to go out into the yard for one hour a day and there was another prisoner with me—a young black guy who had been a professional fighter and was in for murder. We got along well, and he humored me by sparring around and not knocking me out—I had boxed in college but the Ivy League was not the streets. Had a number of good conversations and as I was leaving I said something like "Sorry you aren't getting out—the system is rigged against you." He suddenly got very serious and looked me straight in the eye and said "Chip, let me tell you something—I killed the guy for no good reason, I was guilty as sin. Yeah, I know minorities get a bad deal, but the truth is there is evil in the world and I'm evil and I can't blame that on anyone but myself. If I ever get out, that will be the sin." Blew my mind and starting me thinking about things in a much different way.[18]

Lippman and Dowd were not sent to California facilities, but were taken by car and ferry to McNeil Island Federal Penitentiary in Puget Sound, south of Tacoma.[19] Lippman tells the tale:

> We get there and the first thing they do is throw us in the hole—a disgusting tower of small floors, several floors high. They left us there all weekend. Guards would come up the stairs to bring food and prisoners would throw things at them on the stairs. Monday morning we're taken into the warden's office. Basically he said you can get along or not. The message was clear.
>
> Then they put us into the regular prison. When you enter McNeil Island as a prisoner, you go into the admission and orientation room, with cots where you sleep, before you go into the cell blocks. You are there for 30 days, partly to check on if you are marked as a target by gangs or whatever—they don't want you to get stabbed on your first day. But during that first month, you could eat with the general population, go to the library, etc. Our uniforms were khaki pants with a belt with a clasp, not a buckle, and there was a tiny space there that was never searched. Just enough room for a hit or two of LSD. This would come in handy later.
>
> We made friends instantly. A lot of people there had been sentenced by Boldt. He was a tough sentencer. Armed robbery got 25 years. The fact that we'd stood up to him was heroic to them. They all knew about the case because of TV, radio. One guy said, "You're never going to get out of here." There were lots of cynics. We knew, though, that we had good lawyers and a whole movement behind us, so we didn't feel as isolated.
>
> We ate three times a day, had friends, visitors, etc. As a federal prisoner, you get free paper, free stamps, free Christmas cards. I sent Christmas cards to everyone I could think of, usually saying 'wish you were here.'
>
> After we'd gotten comfortable and knew how to behave, Dowd and I had some fun. A visitor brought me two tabs of windowpane acid which I concealed in my belt clasp. Jeff and I talked a lot about how we were going to act the day we tripped. We had breakfast, took the acid, weren't sure how we would handle lunch. We got a table with two doper friends

who were cool. Then we went and watched TV, Lost in Space or something, boy, were we lost in space."[20]

Susan Stern was taken to Seattle where she could continue to get the medical care she needed while remaining in custody. Michael Abeles was kept in the Tacoma City Jail—he was still a minor, and the marshals weren't sure where to send him.

The Special Agent in Charge of the Seattle FBI office sent Director Hoover a status memo on February 5, 1971. He highlighted his teams' continuing efforts to further destroy SLF by placing anonymous phone calls implying that one or more of the defendants was in fact an FBI informer. They also opened and recorded the contents of all of Lippman's Christmas cards.

16

"Free," Eventually

When our courts resort to the club and stick method of justice, the fear and power method of justice, the haves and the haves-not method of justice, then our society invites the return of the only remedy left to the victims, out of their frustration, the "club and stick."

—JOE KELLY, SEATTLE 7 DEFENDANT

Despite the government-supplied Christmas cards, the seven prisoners scattered along the West Coast would have preferred to be back on the streets. Their attorneys were not enjoying the holidays either—they were tied to their desks searching for their incarcerated clients and drafting appeals to force Judge Boldt to set bail.

When U. S. Marshal Robinson finally did release the prisoners' whereabouts, Maxey noted that imprisoning them up and down the coast was "very unusual. They are in jail for contempt, not because of a conviction in their trial. It makes it difficult for us to consult with our clients on the appeals when they are all over the world."[1] In fact, the prisoners appeared to have been deliberately placed as far from their attorneys as possible: Joe Kelly was in southern California but his attorneys Steinborn and Maxey were in Seattle and Spokane; yet Roger Lippman and Jeff Dowd, jailed near Seattle, were represented by Michael Tigar, who was based in Los Angeles.

On January 8, 1971, the Appeals Court, having read the trial transcript and all attorneys' briefs, reaffirmed its first ruling ordering Boldt to set bail at $25,000, with 10 percent of that required to post bond. The three-judge court noted that although Pitkin's argument to keep the seven in prison without bail included "voluminous evidence in the form of threats and belligerent statements" by the defendants, he "failed to establish that the appearance bond will not adequately assure" that the defendants would show up in court or that they were a danger to others if released on bail.[2]

With the go-ahead for bail, Steinborn and the defense collective went into high gear, raising money, mostly from the defendants' parents. Susan Stern was the first released, on Monday, January 11. In dark glasses and with her head high, she left the courthouse on Steinborn's arm and responded loudly to the waiting press who asked what her plans were, "I will probably do as much speaking as possible."[3] Lippman and Dowd were next, having been taken by ferry and bus to downtown Tacoma and left to fend for themselves. They scraped together enough money for the bus to Seattle. Abeles, released from Tacoma City Jail, also made his way back north to Seattle.

They didn't waste time. Roger Lippman participated in a protest rally at the Seattle federal courthouse shortly after he was released. It was an ironic moment, doing exactly what he had been falsely accused of doing almost a year earlier at the February 17, 1970, TDA protest: "U.S. Marshal Chuck Robinson was there, keeping an eye on things. He had a certain charm, I don't know if it was Stockholm syndrome or not, but he didn't come across as a thug. He could be cordial—had a nice face, a nice smile. So I went over to talk to him. I said he owed me a couple bucks for a bus ticket. He pulled out some change and offered it to me. I didn't take it."[4]

Just a few weeks later, Jeff Dowd returned to McNeil Island with a group of SLF members to support a widespread prisoner strike there. Attorney Lee Holley was also actively supporting and representing several local prisoners' rights groups.[5]

Earlier, and without waiting for the Los Angeles contingent of Lerner, Marshall, and Kelly to arrive back in Seattle, Stern, Abeles, Lippman, and Dowd held their first post-bail press conference. They appeared energetic and smiling and looked healthier than they had in the Tacoma courtroom. The press made much of the fact that both Dowd and Lippman had had their long hair shorn at McNeil Island and "came back looking very much like the old version of Joe College." Steering the session in a more serious direction, the four affirmed that they would continue the fight. They expected to be re-tried, but because they were sure they would be acquitted, they had no reason to jump bail. Stern was clear she would maintain her revolutionary stance, "it is the only way we can… live in dignity."[6]

Just released from prison, (from left) Jeff Dowd, Michael Abeles, Susan Stern, and Roger Lippman hold an upbeat and relaxed press conference. Both Dowd and Lippman had their hair cut on arrival to prison. Abeles, who remained in Tacoma city jail, did not. *MOHAI, Seattle Post-Intelligencer Collection, 1986.5.53617.13, Phil H. Webber photo*

Lerner, Kelly, and Marshall were released from their California prisons on January 14. It was exactly one month since they had torn up their contempt charges and been taken to jail. They returned to Seattle on plane tickets funded by the defense collective. Kelly recalls, "Chip had already been to a second-hand store and bought himself some jeans and a sweater. I was decked out in what he referred to as my 'Arnold Palmer golf outfit' which was prison-issued lime green shirt and pants. Chip thought it so funny looking that he convinced me to wear the outfit on the plane back to Seattle. Everyone got a big kick out of my clothes and the new short hair look."[7]

Despite the upbeat approach of these returning Seattleites, *The Nation's* reporter saw the city's activist scene in a decidedly downhearted and slightly more realistic light:

> The radical movement in Seattle is wrecked. The Seattle Liberation Front…is all but defunct, with but a few collectives surviving. The rest of the movement, reflecting the current malaise and confusion of activists

across the country, is fragmented, analytical, bickering…the willingness of the government to railroad young activists, here and elsewhere, has had a chilling effect on radical organizing…[forcing] would-be activists into relative quiescence or terrorism…there is also an increase in hard-drug activity among Seattle-area youth, perhaps attributable to [their] retreat from activism into escapism.[8]

For some activists, this slide into apathetic or suicidal behavior could have been due in part to the inability to imagine or implement new ways to fight racism or stop the war. The well-used playbook of street demonstrations, picketing, rallies, and window-breaking appeared to have run its course. Outside of the small Weatherman contingent, it was clear to even the most hardcore radicals that the models of rural guerrilla warfare in Asia, Africa, and South America were not transferrable to the United States. And yet, no other approach that fit the urgency of the situation presented itself. To re-enter the world of incremental change, legal challenges, and electoral politics was still too bitter a pill for many of these dissidents to swallow.

Having won the bail fight, the Seattle 7 attorneys began to tackle Boldt's contempt sentences themselves. The Appeals Court had already enumerated several legal difficulties with Boldt's rulings: they weren't specific enough about who had said or done what and when. Tigar was certain that Boldt had committed other significant legal errors during the contempt sentencing phase of the trial, and he filed a 117-page brief to prove it. Tigar supported his brief with his usual cascade of citations and literary references. He gave the three Appeals Court judges several avenues to choose from to justify a decision to vacate the contempt charges against his clients. He concluded by arguing that whatever the results, they must order that Boldt not be involved in any other hearings or re-trials of the Seattle 7 case.

The thrust of Tigar's argument hinged on legal details. Judges have a choice of using one of two statutes when they cite for contempt: Federal Rule of Criminal Procedure 42(a) or Federal Rule of Criminal Procedure 42(b). Boldt chose 42(a) which covers behaviors so obviously disruptive that the judge who witnessed the behavior can act as witness, prosecutor, and judge. No hearing, no oversight, and immediate incarceration. Rule

42(b), on the other hand, requires a hearing with testimony from witnesses other than the judge, and a jury to decide whether or not the behavior was so contumacious as to require the perpetrator to be sent to prison.

Kelly also submitted a brief to the Appeals Court. Assisted by Jeff Dowd and attorney Holley, Kelly's forty-page brief listed many instances of the judge ignoring defense motions for discovery of illegal surveillance. It noted the many times Boldt had allowed and even encouraged the defendants to speak up in court, until the final day, when he chose to call it contempt. In fact, twenty-four of the twenty-nine specific instances of contempt cited by Judge Boldt occurred without punishment prior to December 10 and 14, when the two sets of contempt citations were issued.

Chip Marshall participated in the February oral arguments to the Appeals Court in San Francisco saying, "Perhaps some of the things we did were not in the proper mode. The judicial system has to be aware that justice and obedience are not the same thing."[9]

Defendant Joe Kelly holding the Vietnamese National Front for Liberation flag, demonstrating in a downtown Seattle hotel against the March 1971 visit by General William Westmoreland. Kelly had been out of prison for only a few weeks and all charges were still pending against him. *Courtesy Paul Dorpat; Doyal Gudgel, photographer*

The following month, with the Appeals Court still deliberating, Guy Goodwin launched another salvo against three of the Seattle 7. In a March 23, 1971, letter to Stan Pitkin, Goodwin wrote: "You will recall that we discussed indicting Susan Stern and Michael Abeles for violations involving assaults on Federal officers arising out of the disturbances at the contempt proceedings, would you let me know on what date that matter may be presented to the grand jury. I will arrange to have an attorney available to assist in the presentation of this matter."[10] He continued, "You mentioned to me that your office has instituted a prosecution against Roger Lippman for some violation of postal laws, would you please forward to me a copy of the indictment and investigative reports in that case."[11] Goodwin apparently was not yet satisfied that he'd adequately obliterated the organizing abilities of the Seattle 7.

In November 1971, eight months after hearing the February oral arguments, the judges of the Ninth Circuit Court of Appeals released their ruling. It was just short of a year after the trial itself had commenced. The defendants had tried to get on with their lives during those months, but reporting to parole officers, being travel-restricted, and living with the notion that they could be sent back to prison on a moment's notice was somewhat dampening. In addition to believing they would be re-tried on their original conspiracy charges, several had other pending felony charges from previous actions to resolve.

The three judge Appeals Court substantially agreed with Tigar's arguments. Boldt had indeed erred in applying Rule 42(a) to both sets of contempt citations. The court agreed that Boldt was not in a position to impose summary contempt sentences, because he had been in his office and not in the courtroom during some of the contumacious events he claimed to have witnessed. If he wished to revisit the contempt charges he could do so, but only after including appropriate witness testimony and decision by jury. The Appeals Court judges also kindly suggested "that the trial judge [Boldt] give serious consideration to the decided advantages of having another judge conduct further proceedings."[12]

By this time, a clear and public majority of the country was in an antiwar and anti-government mood. The Pentagon Papers had made headlines, and files stolen from a Pennsylvania FBI office revealing Hoover's COINTELPRO activities and orders were being published and puzzled over.[13] More than 12,000 demonstrators were arrested at the 1971 May Day antiwar protests attended by over a half million people in

Washington, DC. Present, but not arrested, were Joe Kelly, Chip Marshall, Michael Lerner, and Susan Stern, breaking their bail restrictions by not informing the authorities that they had traveled outside the Western District of Washington State. When they realized their error, they panicked and spent part of the protest in a Washington, DC, courthouse with an attorney, signing in with a local federal marshal.

The prosecution, though, was not quitting. Pitkin responded to the Appeals Court ruling by refiling the contempt charges in a 42(b) format that included witness testimony and a jury. The hearing was scheduled, and the defendants showed up, once again, in court on February 22, 1972, two years and one week after the Seattle TDA demonstration.

The defendants were tired and out of money. They wanted to move on with their lives, although what that would entail was unclear, other than knowing that their choices would be individual, not collective. They hadn't conspired in 1970, and by 1972 there were more dissimilarities than similarities amongst them. They did agree, however, to stop fighting the contempt citations: they all pled no contest. Marshall summarized, "We don't feel we did anything wrong, but we don't want to contest the facts. We're out of money; we've been harassed and we just want to get it over with."[14]

In some ways, the Department of Justice won. Their strategy to interfere with the perfectly legal organizing work of SLF by arresting their leaders on complicated conspiracy charges had succeeded in dismantling the group's forward progress. Guy Goodwin and his superiors probably didn't care if the indicted rebels were found guilty in court or not. Their goal was attrition and distraction—and that they achieved.

By pleading no contest, the defendants waived their rights to a juried hearing without admitting guilt. Judge Russell Smith of Montana (Judge Boldt had by this time been rewarded by President Nixon with a Washington, DC, job) said he would study the facts of the case, and hand down appropriate sentences on the contempt charges. In Seattle, Pitkin had not yet decided if he would re-try the defendants on the original conspiracy charges.

A month later, on Wednesday, March 29, 1972, six of the seven defendants were sentenced to jail for their contumacious actions in the Tacoma courtroom seventeen months earlier. Only Michael Lerner walked free—his new wife and infant son were front and center in the courtroom and his father had flown in to tell the judge that Michael was going to become a rabbi. Marshall, Kelly, Abeles, Dowd, Lippman, and Stern were each given sentences of several months, with credit for the time they'd spent in prison in the winter of 1970–71. This time they were incarcerated in the Washington State prison system.

Stern, depressed, wasn't sure that the political gains of their aggressive trial strategy were worth it. She spent her jail time working on a book about her life on the political, social, and cultural edge of the mid-twentieth century.

By July 1972, they were all out of prison, although they all could be re-tried on the still open original conspiracy charges. Finally, almost a year later, on March 22, 1973, Pitkin's office entered an Order for Dismissal in United States District Court, Western District of Washington on case #51942. The federal conspiracy and intent to riot indictments against Marshall, Dowd, Kelly, Abeles, Lerner, Lippman, and Stern were withdrawn. Pitkin justified his decision to his dissatisfied superiors in Washington, DC, as best he could:

> Four confidential informants were the heart of the case. On the eve of the trial two were necessarily abandoned as witnesses for the government. One was seriously compromised by associating with the defendants' group during defense planning sessions [probably David Sannes] and the other abandoned witness had real veracity problems. Witness Parker was on the stand several days and was very effective, but the mistrial cut off the balance of the cross examination before all the defense points were made. The trial ended without the second confidential informant, who had much less useful testimony…suffice it to say that the chance for conviction on four defendants is one in three, on defendants Lippman and Stern, virtually nil, on defendant Kelly no chance at all.[15]

The Department of Justice was not happy. A return memo told Pitkin "to make no statements to the press regarding the dismissal and to forward all inquiries…to the Office of Public Information at the Department of Justice."[16]

But what of Michael Justesen? His name was not on Pitkin's withdrawal order; the charges against him were not dismissed. There is some evidence that he had tried to surface and work a deal in 1973, but it didn't happen. He remained underground, and his Seattle indictment was not dismissed until a year later, in May 1974. But despite no longer being a fugitive, the FBI continued to look for him.

On June 13, 1974, finally clear of pending trials and jail terms completed, Roger Lippman filed a civil suit against John Mitchell, Guy Goodwin, Louis Harris, and the revolving door of Attorneys General and FBI directors who had taken over from Mitchell and Hoover during Watergate's unwinding of the Nixon presidency. Although it was still a year before the Senate Church Committee report would lay out the full scope of the FBI's COINTELPRO dirty tricks activities, enough had been released by 1974 for Lippman to think his case had standing.

The core of his suit was that he had been illegally wiretapped throughout the late 1960s and early 1970s as he pursued his perfectly legal SDS antiwar and draft resistance organizing. Wiretapping telephone conversations on issues of domestic concern without a court order was affirmed as unconstitutional in a unanimous Supreme Court decision in 1972.[17] The FBI had tapped the phone lines of hundreds of antiwar and civil rights activists in the 1960s and 1970s without obtaining warrants; this is the major reason that federal cases against the national Weather Underground leaders never went to trial when the fugitives finally surfaced in the late 1970s and 1980s. The FBI preferred to drop the charges rather than admit the extent of their warrantless wiretapping and other illegalities.

Evidence of illegal wiretapping peppers the personal files of antiwar activists obtained under the Freedom of Information Act, including those of the Seattle 7 and the author. Lippman's suit alleged not only acts of commission, i.e. wiretapping, but also acts of omission; that is, he said that the people he was suing "had the power to prevent or aid in the prevention of the said [illegal] events, but they neglected or refused to do so; and they further concealed the occurrence of the said events and thereby facilitated their recurrence."[18]

Government attorneys managed to throw enough procedural roadblocks in front of the suit to prevent its progress. Lippman had the assistance of a pro bono attorney, who wasn't able to pursue the case very aggressively. Much of building the case required the government to produce documents that it repeatedly refused to admit it had. What materials it did release was information Lippman already possessed.

Eventually, after a couple of years, the case was dismissed for lack of progress. As Lippman said, "It's not like we thought we were going to win, or get any money, but still…there was good publicity."

It was the mid-1970s. The draft ended in 1973. Vice President Spiro Agnew was forced to resign in 1973 and was jailed for tax fraud. Nixon resigned in disgrace in 1974, and several of his chief staffers were sent to jail. The last U.S. soldier left Vietnam as Vietnamese forces retook Saigon in the spring of 1975. The Seattle Liberation Front was history. The country as a whole was exhausted by riots, assassinations, anger, and polarization. The Seattle 7 defendants needed time and space to make sense of the lessons they had learned. The U.S. government was clearly far more powerful than they had realized, and was more than willing to use that power to disrupt, entrap, and prosecute its own citizens when it felt even marginally threatened. The justice system was neither blind nor rational. The Seattle 7 also had to conclude that most Americans had no objections to any of that. It was a rude awakening.

17

The Years After

I thought activism was something that just happened. You went to college and you joined the movement.
—Bruce Parks, Seattle resident, 8 years old in 1970

The 1970s was a long time ago. The student protesters of the 1960s and 1970s are now in their sixties and seventies. They dissented and there were consequences. Their lives, like everyone's, are particular and individual. They do not claim to represent all activists of their generation, nor do they see themselves as wise advisers to the protesters of today. If their actions have influenced those currently fighting against racist violence or advocating better stewardship of our planet's resources, or any of the other present-day efforts to improve the lives of all seven billion of us, that is a judgment left to others.

Susan Stern

After her release from prison, Susan Stern remained in Seattle, working on a memoir of her political days. Called *With the Weathermen,* published in 1975, it is the only personal account written so close to the times by anyone in or on the fringes of Weatherman. Other such memoirs, notably by Weatherman leaders Bill Ayers, Cathy Wilkerson, and Mark Rudd, were all written decades later, after 2001. The only other first-person books about Weatherman to come out in the 1970s were written by an informant and an FBI undercover agent.[1]

Several weeks before the Seattle 7 trial began, Stern tried to put her mercurial nature into words: "I still think that even for me, too much of my life is not acting out what I feel. In many ways being in the conspiracy has saved me from further action because now I can finally relax and 'they finally got me' let somebody else carry on for a change now."[2] It is hard to tell if she is saying she feels relieved or guilty; if she worries she did too little to end the war or worries that she overdid it, to the detriment of her own life.

Stern gave a copy of her book to attorney Carl Maxey and his wife Lou, inscribing it, "Dear Carl and Lou, I hope you are both happy the rest of your lives. Thank you, Carl especially, for being there when I needed you so many times, so many unthanked times, now finally in ink, thank you, I love you both, Susan."

Stern's book, like her life, generated a storm of critical comment. She wrote with painful openness about her considerable drive for sex and drugs and how that muddied the waters of her political life. People active in the movement, including co-defendant Roger Lippman, were certain that the book would smear them all by leaving readers the impression that every leftist was a self-indulgent child who didn't think clearly about the strategic impact of his or her personal actions. Her publisher's attorneys saw the book as "one big libel problem" as living people's names were linked to "drug taking, extramarital sex, bomb making, thievery, arrests and terms in jail."[3]

Susan Stern, out of prison and on a book tour in Seattle for her book *With the Weathermen*. This memoir of her chaotic rebel days was the first of a string of books by radicals about their days of resistance, protest, love, concern, and jail time. *MOHAI, Seattle Post-Intelligencer Collection, 2000.107.18.01, Cary Tolman photo*

One woman friend and SLF member commented: "Her description of reds, speed, meth, heroin use on a regular daily basis—that was not really part of the movement as I experienced it. A few parties with some tripping, yes, but even pot was not that much of a daily diet... more likely it was just beer! Who had the money?? Or could be that stoned all the time?? Well, stoned, sure. But whacked out, fucked up, downer loaded? No. It's sad. I had so much respect for her strength. Was it all merely a façade of drug-fueled pseudo machismo?"[4]

Another activist recalls Stern as "a bundle of contradictions, smart and talented but she had this air of a self-educated person with a lot of idiosyncratic ideas. Her book seemed kind of childish to me; I couldn't get through it. I felt sorry that she got swept up in the self-dramatization of the whole Weatherman thing."[5]

A woman who was a UW graduate student, protest leader, and part of the women's consciousness raising group in Stern's basement, described Stern's sexual behavior as not so much licentious as controlling. But because she liked sex and wanted to control her own sexual activity, she was regarded by some as pushy and obsessed with sex.[6]

Stern earned rent and food money in those days as a stripper and dancer in clubs and dives. This continued after she got out of jail. One memory of Stern is from a man who briefly managed a Seattle peep show where she worked:

> Susan showed up one day, said she'd danced before. She could be pretty goddamn vivacious. She made an impression. Crazy but fun, then crazy again. I would sometimes overhear her talking to the other dancers about radical feminism. I think it was kind of interesting to some of them; they'd ask "but what should I do to keep my boyfriend from hitting me today?"
>
> My strongest memory of her is that she was very strange when she danced. What I mean is that although "tease" is essential to the "strip," she took the tease into another zone. The fact that the audience couldn't touch her seemed to please her no end. She would laugh, and I don't think many strippers laugh at their audience.
>
> She was a bit of an outsider, no close friends…Then later I heard she'd died.[7]

Returning from work one night in late July 1976, Stern partied with her housemates for a while before going alone into a basement sauna where she was found several hours later, unconscious. Jeff Dowd, one of those present, frantically tried CPR, but was unsuccessful. Six days later she was declared dead of heart failure at the University of Washington hospital. She was thirty-three years old.

MICHAEL JUSTESEN

Michael Justesen immediately fled his Seattle indictment, heading south, where he hooked up with a Weatherman collective in California, first in San Francisco and later in the Echo Park neighborhood of Los Angeles. Two months after he went underground, he sent a flaming and jargon-filled letter to his aboveground comrades, which was printed in several underground newspapers:

> We understand that our place is within the Third World revolution. For too long we acted as the man's stooges—in the schools, the army, in the factories—and accepted his bribes. But no more! Now we are the allies

of the slaves we once possessed; their wars are ours. Our only demand is theirs: that we join in the liberation of mankind.

We don't have to be isolated and desperate; we have a strategy. We can catch the oppressive system in a pincers: the army between Vietnam and ourselves, the pigs between blacks and ourselves.

We have made a beginning in attacking the institutions that are already weakened, to push them towards death. But now we must go on the offensive, all of us struggling as hard as Vietnam, and calling on our people to do the same.[8]

Justesen lived the underground life of day jobs, multiple identities, jolts of fear, and endless planning meetings in California with a small collective for seven years until he was arrested in 1977. He was charged with conspiracy and possession of explosives in a bombing plot against a California state senator who had proposed a bill to fire all gay or lesbian people employed in school settings. Justesen's group had been infiltrated for

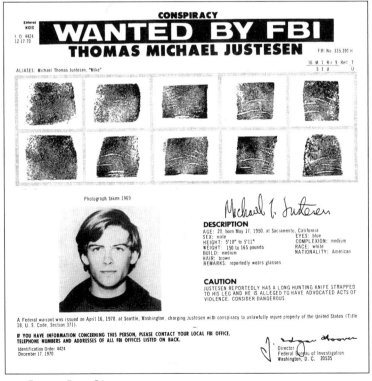

Courtesy Roger Lippman

several years by two FBI agents posing as revolutionary recruits and acting as provocateurs, teaching weapons handling and other paramilitary skills to Justesen and his comrades.

After serving two years in prison, Justesen married and moved to a Midwest college town. He declined to participate in this book project.

MICHAEL LERNER

Michael Lerner did indeed become a rabbi, although not until 1995. His teaching position at the UW was not renewed, and he was unable to secure a long-term teaching job at any other university. After a few years he returned to Berkeley to complete a second PhD in social psychology. There, he founded an organization called the Institute for Labor and Mental Health which researched the effect of the American marketplace on human relationships and the search for personal meaning.

In 1986, he and his wife founded *Tikkun: A Bimonthly Jewish Critique of Politics, Culture and Society*, a print magazine and blog. "Tikkun" is a Hebrew word having to do with healing and restoring the world. Lerner's voice is evident throughout, and he remains its editor-in-chief.

Lerner is also rabbi at Beyt Tikkun synagogue in Berkeley, which describes itself as "neo-Hasidic" because it welcomes "gays and lesbians, and reject[s] every form of chauvinism and affirm[s] the equal value and equal closeness to God of all people on our planet."[9] His goal is to create a "religious left" to counter the influence of the "religious right."

Lerner and boxing champion Muhammad Ali had met and worked together on a few antiwar actions in New York. Before he died, Ali listed Lerner as one of the speakers he'd like at his memorial. Lerner's passionate speech at the June 10, 2016, ceremony laid out the progressive Jewish position, and aligned it with Ali's Muslim faith. He spotlighted Ali's moral integrity in taking an early public stand against the Vietnam War, which led to his being stripped of his heavyweight title. "If Muhammad Ali were here today, I'm sure his message would be this: Don't waste your time on this planet fighting the small battles—put your life energies and money into fundamental systemic transformation." That would be Lerner's message as well.

Lerner lives in a rambling house in the Berkeley hills with his wife and a large friendly dog.

ROGER LIPPMAN

Roger Lippman gradually moved away from his Weatherman politics, parting ways in 1976. Among other things, he studied the horrors of the Khmer Rouge bloodbath and learned more about Chinese interference in Southeast Asia: "This was my first experience with international inter-communist conflict, which my parents' generation had also come to grips with (or not) in 1939–41."[10] His other focus is on environmental issues.

After the trial, Lippman stayed in Seattle, living in the Capitol Hill neighborhood and learning auto mechanics in a backyard garage. With seven mechanic friends, he formed a collective car repair business dedicated to serving the low-income community they all lived in. They fixed cars and taught car owners to take care of their autos. Then, he recalled:

Roger Lippman in his alcohol-fueled vehicle in 1981. He has worked for a company active in carbon fuel alternatives for decades. *MOHAI, Seattle Post-Intelligencer Collection, 2000.107.114.06.01*

As I was getting ready to move on to something else after doing this for about eight years, the second oil crisis hit, in 1979, and I got interested in exploring alternatives to petroleum fuels. I studied alcohol as an alternative to gasoline and built an engine that would run on pure alcohol. In the Jimmy Carter years there was some government support for such ideas. I got research funding from the City of Seattle, and a little development money from a U.S. Department of Energy program that provided small grants for appropriate technology projects. The engine worked well, and I drove the car for five years, but meanwhile Ronald Reagan cancelled funding for alternative energy development.

So I went back to college and completed my bachelor's

degree in energy systems. Soon after, I was hired to work on research into how energy is used in buildings…One such project led to another, and for over thirty years I have worked for the same company on a variety of projects in energy conservation and research.[11]

In 1982, on the leading edge of people waking up to the problems of too much carbon dioxide (CO_2) in the global atmosphere, he wrote a pamphlet describing how to convert gasoline automobile engines into alcohol-fueled engines. In it Lippman succinctly described how the use of fossil fuels contributes to global warming. He acknowledged funding support from the U.S. Department of Energy, noting that, "The opinions expressed herein are those of the author. Unfortunately they are not those of the U.S. Department of Energy."

Lippman is today actively involved in a coalition of regional environmental and political groups working to shut down the one remaining nuclear power plant in the Pacific Northwest. Of his Weatherman-leaning days, he notes, "We had no idea what we were up against. Either politically or militarily. We had no idea how adaptable the system can be."[12] He summarizes, "We were ahead of the game but on the right side of history."[13]

Lippman travels regularly for work and pleasure, and is gradually cutting back his work hours to allow for more family and personal project time. He maintains an extensive personal website documenting his interests. He and his wife live in Seattle.

JOE KELLY

Joe Kelly returned to his rural roots shortly after his release from prison. He married a UW student who was part of the SLF defense collective. They moved to eastern Washington in 1974, and then in the early 1980s, went to Alaska where he was hired by the Alaska Department of Fish and Game.

Coming back to Washington after a few years, they settled in a lovely green valley along a winding dirt road in eastern Washington, where there is plenty of room for horses and hayfields and the life he loves. He began work as a fisheries biologist at the Bureau of Land Management (BLM), analyzing the effects on fish and their habitats for all BLM projects in eastern Washington. He maintained a friendship with attorney Carl Maxey—they would watch boxing matches, and Carl would reminisce about his own boxing days.

Recently retired, Kelly and his wife have two grown daughters. He still fishes, hunts, rides horses, bales hay, hikes, and loves the outdoors. In retrospect, he wishes they had taken Maxey's advice and played it straight in the courtroom. Maxey was sure they could win, and Kelly now agrees. But, he acknowledges, they were young, feeling helplessly railroaded, and were crazed by the terror and devastation caused by the war being waged in their name.

When asked what words he would want to leave for posterity, he was unhesitating, "Don't be afraid, stand up for what you believe in. Don't worry about what people think of you. Have lots of sympathy for those who have less than you do."[14] He added, "I think the time is right to be demanding broad-based progressive ideas: minimum wage, single payer health insurance, a new tax system that does not contain loopholes that primarily benefit the rich, possibly a guaranteed income for poor people."[15]

MICHAEL ABELES

Michael Abeles had headaches. They became increasingly worse after the trial. One day, in so much pain he couldn't see straight, friends took him to the Country Doctor clinic. Diagnosed with a possible brain tumor, Abeles was quickly referred to a hospital for care. Surgery removed the tumor, although some tissue damage remained.

Abeles stayed in Seattle, working odd jobs as a tile-setter, painter, and contractor, making friends, and being an all-around well-liked guy. His business card and his truck displayed his tagline "Abeles to do it." Clients said he was always friendly, cheerful, prompt, and a fun conversationalist. He had an artistic talent that he exercised in stone carving. Like Kelly, he maintained a friendship with defense attorney Carl Maxey. Maxey's widow recalls Abeles' sweet temper, and treasures a strikingly haunting stone head that Abeles sculpted as a gift to them.

Abeles was clear that his antiwar work was the most important thing he'd done in his life, but he was not blind to the overreaching nature of SLF's goals. "We made mistakes, but I'm proud of what we did…I think the slogan for today has got to be 'think global, act local.'"[16]

The tumor, though, had impaired him, along with the heavy drugs he'd indulged in during the 1970s. (He acknowledged his drug use, and was proud of having been in recovery for almost thirty years.) After moving home to live with his sister in Buffalo, New York, he had his good days and his not-so-good days. He died August 24, 2016.

JEFF DOWD

Once out of prison, Jeff Dowd spent the summer of 1973 traveling in South America with his then-girlfriend, an SLF member. While traveling, he wrote a long letter to Special Prosecutor Archibald Cox and Senator Sam Ervin, both of whom were leading investigations into President Nixon's Watergate burglary. The eleven-page, typed letter covers his own political history, that of SLF, the TDA demonstration, the trial, and its aftermath. An internal Department of Justice memo attached to Dowd's letter summarizes its hectic and somewhat rambling content, and disputes Dowd's accusation that White House special assistant John Ehrlichman offered Judge Boldt his federal job with the National Pay Board in return for declaring a mistrial in the Seattle 7 case when it had become clear that a conviction was unlikely.

Dowd closed his letter, "I am doing this all for the same reasons I have done all other political actions in my life—to make a better USA which I consider to be analogous to a situation if the Miami Dolphins lost all their games. WASTED POTENTIAL WITH BEAUTIFUL POSSIBILITIES" [Dowd's capitalization].[17]

When Dowd returned to Seattle, he maintained his interest in producing effects that shock, entertain, and educate people. He worked with a chain of movie theatres in Seattle to bring in interesting movies. One was *Blood Simple*, Joel and Ethan Coen's first feature film, released in the fall of 1984. It didn't do well nationally, but did very well in Seattle. The Coen brothers, curious, flew to Seattle to talk with theatre people to find out why. They were told that it was because a guy named Jeff Dowd had loved it and had vigorously promoted it. They met Dowd, were charmed, and subsequently fashioned The Dude character in their 1998 film *The Big Lebowski* on some of Dowd's personality and actions. There is a line in the script that refers to The Dude's history with the Seattle 7 ("me and uh, six other guys") conveniently ignoring Susan Stern. In another line of dialogue, The Dude claims authorship of SDS' foundational Port Huron Statement.

Although Jeff Bridges played The Dude role in the movie, Jeff Dowd has made his association with the character into his persona: there are *Big Lebowski* festivals around the country almost annually, and Dowd is usually the keynote speaker. A 2013 Huffington Post interview noted, "Dowd is everything a 'Lebowski' enthusiast would hope. His speech is muddled and, at times, inaudible. He laughs often and refers to himself as The Dude. He goes on long-winded tangents, speaking with intelligence, but randomness, on everything from the Irish revolution to his past friendship with Jane Fonda to Boy George's given name."[18]

Dowd's penchant for touting his connections with celebrities perhaps comes from living and working in Los Angeles' entertainment industry. He's been there since the late 1980s, and has produced several films, including *FernGully: The Last Rainforest* and *Zebrahead*. Most recently, he has launched an indie film consulting business and is pitching a series of classic, entertaining stories designed to help people live better lives. He is active on Facebook and continues to pepper friends and acquaintances with emails outlining plans to amuse and save the world, being as focused as ever on avoiding terminal boredom. He maintains a love of overarching conspiracy theories and the enthusiasm, if not the ability, to solve the world's biggest problems.

CHIP MARSHALL

Marshall views his prison time as "a good experience in the end. Sobered me up, which is what it's supposed to do right? Not because it was scary or anything, but because I had a lot of time to myself which I'd never had before and it gave me time to reflect, away from the mania of the last throes of the movement."[19]

When he got out of prison, Marshall hitchhiked across Europe and Asia, where he "met all kinds of people and realized that in most of the countries I was traveling through, if I'd done what I'd done in the U.S., I'd have been shot. So it didn't make me think the U.S. was just wonderful, but it did make me realize that it wasn't the root of all evil either."[20]

Marshall then came back to Seattle, where he twice ran for city council. He wasn't elected, and decided to look at the private sector for opportunity and challenge. He began working in real estate development in the suburbs east of the city, a move that caused some to say he'd sold out to "the system" he'd once tried to overthrow. His own view is that SLF oversimplified issues enormously, but was right about many of them, and he's proud of what they did. "At certain times in history, it serves a constructive function to be outside the system."[21]

In 1983, Chip Marshall was thirty-eight years old and about to leave Seattle for Hong Kong and a master's program in Asian studies. Although he planned to return to the Pacific Northwest to work in international

Chip Marshall handing out campaign literature on a Seattle bus. He ran for a seat on the Seattle City Council twice, but didn't win. *MOHAI, Seattle-Post Intelligencer Collection, 2002.46.1620.9*

trade after his stint in Hong Kong, he instead lived and worked in land and building development in China. He has spent most of his life living and working outside the United States.

Marshall believes the causes of the late 1960s and early 1970s were good ones, that some of their efforts have paid off, and, although "racism remains the deepest-seated problem, I can say unequivocally that America is the least racist developed country in the world." He also worries about the "intolerance and narrow-mindedness that…has now become mainstream in our universities and the media…Just as we were called 'dirty communists,' now any contrasting view is branded 'racist,' 'sexist,' 'fascist.' We need debate, not 'safe' spaces that only serve to stifle learning. If we don't change our approach, progressivism will suffer." [22]

In 2016, he retired. He and his wife now live in Malta.

Human lives are threaded with good and bad, kindness and thoughtlessness, intelligence and waste, consistency and conflict, optimism and pessimism. The aging leaders of the Seattle Liberation Front are the first to admit that utopia is not right around the corner for anyone or any place. But to the extent they have any regrets about either their protest or their trials, it is only about tactical missteps, not about the causes they championed or the risks they took.

The Harmony of Dissonance

*Conflict is the essential core of a free and open society. If one were to project
the democratic way of life in the form of a musical score, its major theme
would be the harmony of dissonance.*
—SAUL ALINSKY, 1971

Observing the violence and turmoil of the 1960s, Supreme Court
Justice William O. Douglas observed, "The dissent we witness is
a reaffirmation of faith in man."[1] Dissent, protest, and political activism
are nothing new in the United States, a country that empowers its citizens
with a library of liberties and legal rights with which to participate in
governing.

Securing those liberties and those rights began with active protest and
resistance by small groups of people. These efforts to increase individual
freedoms and enhance community safety have been answered historically
and currently by concerted pushback from the seated government, from
corporations, from those who fear that any change will take something
away from them.

After pushback, dissent may escalate to more protest, then more
defense of the status quo, and so on, volleying back and forth until, often,
the dissidents' position becomes the new normal. Perhaps because these
efforts take such a long time we forget that many of the protections and
liberties we take for granted today originated from a few lone dissenters
who were labeled in their day as criminals and crazies.

For instance, in the nineteenth century deadly street battles were waged to
end child labor, to enforce the eight-hour workday, to be paid a living wage. It
took a brutal civil war to abolish slavery. It took seven decades of active effort
for women in the United States to win the right to vote. Struggles continue
today for women's rights to equal pay, equal employment opportunities, and
reproductive choice. Fights to expand and enforce civil rights among ethnic,
racial, and gender minorities continue.

Public health and safety requirements are another battleground, as we seek to protect citizens from contaminated food and drinking water, shoddily constructed buildings, and unsafe highways and bridges. Requiring and regulating health information about heavily advertised products such as tobacco, highly sugared or fatty foods, and automobiles has saved thousands of lives. Public health today encompasses community safety, which includes efforts to end minority profiling and targeting, and to reduce gunshot injuries and deaths by promoting firearms regulation.

One of the errors of the 1960s antiwar movement was the dissenters' unrealistic expectation that they could quickly convince the U.S. government to end the war. In fact, progress often comes in tiny increments, with compromising strings attached, requiring yet more attention by the next generation.

How, in the charged environment of the early twenty-first century, has dissent grown and diverged from that of the 1960s and 1970s? Beyond the obvious changes in communication, coordination, and publicity allowed by cell phones and social media, and a vastly more sophisticated use of the courts as instruments of change, today's protesters have a more realistic appraisal of the scope and power of the opposition than existed in the 1960s. There appears to be an understanding among many (but not all) that truly revolutionary changes can indeed blossom from reformist strategies.

Four key concerns of today's activists are the health of our U.S. democracy, racism, the environment, and the preservation and expansion of personal liberties and freedoms.

All four of these issues, clothed in different language with different emphases, were at the core of the protests of the 1960s and early 1970s. The topics haven't changed in the intervening decades, but dissenters and protesters, as well as the government and other organizations supporting the status quo, have both retained and refined their tactics and tools.

The government, for example, continues to use the grand jury as a major tool to eviscerate active dissent. In 2012, several protesters at Seattle's annual May Day rally in support of immigrant rights became a grand jury target. Three of the subpoenaed protesters spent several months in solitary confinement when they refused to testify. One of the jailed protesters described his grand jury experience: "It became incredibly difficult to separate fear from reality. Am I being followed or am I just losing it? Once I was driving to work and I heard a noise in my car—a ticking sound. I let my imagination get away from me. It was a time of being pretty freaked out about a lot of stuff."[2]

When the local FBI office requested a warrant to search the protesters' homes, the charges on the search warrant were identical to those on the Seattle 7 indictments some forty years earlier: "Conspiracy, Destruction of government property; Interstate travel with intent to riot."[3] This time the FBI wasn't chasing Weathermen, but so-called anarchists.

In the end, no indictments came from this grand jury, no federal charges were made, and the prisoners were released. Their protest movement, however, was slowed and hindered, just as it had been for the SLF forty years earlier.[4]

Looking beyond the Pacific Northwest to each of these four concerns of contemporary dissenters, we see that the details have shifted since the heyday of the Seattle Liberation Front, but the purpose, motivation, and guiding principles of the efforts are recognizably similar. The activism of the 1960s is not as exceptional as it may appear.

DEMOCRACY

Contemporary concern for the health of democracy in America is expressed in projects to enlarge and protect the right to vote, to improve the quality of information provided to voters, and to encourage citizens to pay closer attention to what their government is actually doing. Many organizations, from the venerable American Civil Liberties Union and the League of Women Voters, to newer groups such as Fix Democracy First, MOVI: Money Out Voters In, MoveOn, and Common Cause, are working on issues such as legislative reform at all levels of government, overturning the Supreme Court's 2010 decision defining corporations as people (*Citizens United v. Federal Election Commission*), gerrymandering, and voting rights.

Advocates pursue these issues on the streets, in the offices of elected officials, in meeting rooms, and on the web. These groups work well within the law, since that is their point: democratic means are the best way to strengthen democracy.

In 2011 the Occupy movement criticized President Obama's response to the financial meltdown as a highly undemocratic example of capitalism run amuck. Camping in public spaces, creating small self-governed units, running educational sessions and planning meetings, they embraced the slogan "We are the 99 percent," in opposition to the "one percent" who own a hugely disproportionate (and growing) share of America's wealth.[5]

Seattle's Occupy action began just ten days after Occupy Wall Street was launched. Once again the federal courthouse was the meeting point, but camp-ins were moved over the next few months to several sites, including the plaza in front of City Hall at Mayor Mike McGinn's invitation. The overall message from Occupy and similar groups is that democracy is fragile. Democracy thrives only if its citizens have access to relevant, fact-based information, which they then use to evaluate and react to their government's actions, either supporting or changing them in such a way as not to harm the underlying balance that maximizes personal freedom and community security for all.

Racism

Black Lives Matter, the brainchild of three black women, was a movement born in 2013 when a white Florida man was acquitted for killing an unarmed black teenager. The organization has refocused national attention on the unfinished business of eliminating racial prejudice and has become an advocate for all Americans fighting racial discrimination.

Evidence of racism can be seen in multiple instances of police violence leading to the deaths of unarmed black people; data showing the highly disproportionate rates of arrest and incarceration of blacks for the same crimes committed by whites; state-level laws making it harder for poor, mostly nonwhite people to vote; and continued disparities in income and health status across color lines. The meme "driving while black" represents the ubiquitous nature of today's racism.

Washington State has one of the most restrictive laws preventing police who have killed in the line of duty from being criminally charged with mistaken use of force. One Seattle attorney, responding to reactions over recent national cases of black men killed by police and retaliatory shootings of policemen, urged local, legal action: "My advice to people is to start locally…Get active, read, research and know the law…demand our legislators change this law. It's not as sexy as taking to the streets and pumping your fist in the air, but we can channel our anger into making policy change that matters."[6]

Black and white dissenters today are approaching racism from multiple practical angles. They are building strategies to reform prison and sentencing practices, to expand educational and employment opportunities for blacks (especially men), to enact stricter and more evenly enforced gun and drug laws, and many other efforts to root racism out of our institutions and daily practices.

THE ENVIRONMENT

Despite overwhelming scientific documentation that the global climate is undergoing a change, calls to address this environmental crisis have been met by outright opposition, and, like racism, by denial that any problem exists at all.

A comfort level with the status quo is always the first hurdle a dissenter must breach; in this case the complacent denial of the existence of a global climate-related problem is fueled by distrust of scientists and a failure to understand the scientific method. This is a problem in itself; climate change activism now includes a significant effort to support scientists and to explain to skeptics the underlying methods, purposes, and successes of science. For example, thousands of people in over 600 cities around the world celebrated Earth Day, April 22, 2017, with a March for Science. Barely two weeks later a Climate March drew tens of thousands more people to Washington, DC, to advocate for climate research and action. As if to make the point, the day of the march saw the hottest temperature ever measured for that day in the DC area.

An active, multi-organizational movement exists today to pressure both corporations and the government to reduce CO_2 levels. The methods used by these organizations range from civil disobedience to street protests to legislative lobbying at all levels. Proposed solutions also lie in changing the behavior of large corporations through legislation, regulation, and consumer pressure.

The grandmother of all environmental activist groups, Greenpeace, advocates cutting carbon pollution, growing non-fossil-fuel energy alternatives, promoting sustainable agricultural practices, and other environmental protections, using a wide range of tactics, from lobbying to civil disobedience.

In a powerful echo of the 1960s, both the U.S. government and privately contracted security companies are today actively using the methods of COINTELPRO against environmentally-focused dissenters. In May 2016, the Bureau of Land Management in Colorado paid local police to go undercover and inform on the activities of anti-fracking groups.[7] In Texas, the "FBI breached its own internal rules when it spied on campaigners against the Keystone XL pipeline, failing to get approval before it cultivated informants and opened files on individuals protesting against the construction of the pipeline in Texas."[8]

Among dissenters, civil disobedience tactics have been used to underline the urgency of the need to decrease atmospheric CO_2 levels. In 2015 a group of "kayactivists" took to the water in their kayaks to try to prevent a Shell oil-drilling ship from reaching its destination in the Alaskan Arctic. Later when the same ship was damaged (not by the kayakers), and towed to Portland, Oregon, for repairs, Greenpeace protesters with technical climbing experience dangled below bridges so the ship couldn't pass. It was a twentieth-century sit-in tactic brought up to date.

In 2016-17 the Sioux tribes of North Dakota garnered much attention and support for their protests against construction of an oil pipeline planned to run near their reservation and under one of their primary sources of water. Protesters, many from other tribes around the county, are taking new, creative organizing tactics and cross-tribal personal contacts from their North Dakota experiences back to their own tribes.

Personal Liberties and Freedoms

Freedom of religion, freedom of speech, and freedom from warrantless search and seizure are hallmarks of the United States Constitution's Bill of Rights. Americans, however, are certain that their founding documents guarantee many other freedoms, but because the Bill of Rights doesn't specifically mention them, we don't all agree on which those are. Currently, three of the most contentious of those unmentioned freedoms are: 1) the freedom for a woman to choose when in her life to give birth; 2) the freedom to marry a person of the same sex; and 3) the freedom to own and carry firearms including military-grade assault weapons.

All three have a history of decades of debate punctuated by intense lobbying, demonstrations, civil disobedience, and deadly violence. All three have had lengthy days in court, have been on innumerable legislative agendas, and have been the subject of reams of press material and infinite online postings. The fierceness on all sides resists attempts to predict a final outcome. Only the second of the three, the battle for same-sex marriage rights, is considered here because the overall arc of this struggle, which currently has reached new levels of guaranteed personal liberty, might help set the strategic stage for the resolution of the other two.

As in the civil rights movement, it took a dramatic confrontation for mainstream America to pay attention to the struggle of homosexual people to obtain equal personal liberties and rights. The 1969 six-day Stonewall riots in New York City are considered the genesis of the fight for recognition and equal rights in the LGBTQ (Lesbian, Gay, Bisexual, Transgender, Queer) community.

In addition, the AIDS crisis of the 1980s and 1990s sparked a new militancy among gay men. ACT-UP (AIDS Coalition to Unleash Power), a national organization, used confrontational tactics to bring scientific attention and medicine to people suffering from the HIV virus. In part because of their work, HIV testing is easily obtainable today, and AIDS itself, thanks to activist pressures to increase research funding and decrease pharmaceutical prices, has become treatable as a chronic, not catastrophic, disease.

Some forty-six years after the Stonewall riots, same-sex couples won the national right to all the legal benefits of marriage in the 2015 Supreme Court decision *Obergefell v. Hodges.* In Seattle, same sex marriage was legally recognized in 2012, first in the state legislature and then by statewide referendum. Three years earlier, a state referendum had given domestic partners of the same or different sexes the same rights as married couples, particularly with respect to health benefits and tax issues.

Today, annual gay pride parades are held in many cities across the country. (The word "parade" was deliberately chosen over the word "march" to indicate celebration and fun as opposed to controversy or belligerence.) Seattle's first gay pride parade was held in 1977. Today, the city has painted many street crosswalks in the inclusive rainbow colors of the LGBTQ rights movement, and Pride posters and flags adorn buildings throughout the city during the now week-long festivities.

Effective American dissent is a multi-step process of observation, thought, and action. It may not always be a conscious process, but dissenters first recognize a problem, weigh how much they care about it, and consider its significance, both personally and to the wider community. Depending on their conclusions, they might move on to action.

Dissent is practiced in many ways: individual acts of civil disobedience, street marches, protests and demonstrations, boycotts and petitions, street theatre, strikes, physical occupations, civil suits, and electoral activity. Individuals enter and leave the fray as their energy, understanding, resources, and competing commitments wax and wane. Individuals coalesce into groups and organizations which sometimes collapse under factional infighting and sometimes grow into large united fronts.

Most dissenters, like the Seattle 7, are not movie heroes or villains. They are always a minority of the population. They are individuals with their own energy levels and their own sense of patriotism. Their timing might be ill-advised, they may misjudge the strength and rootedness of the problem they wish to fix, and they may have only a partial grasp on the consequences of their actions. Still, they choose to step beyond a life of family, home, and career in order to engage with others in some of our world's greatest challenges. Protest is risky, because as one activist put it, "when you expose a problem you pose a problem."[9]

The underlying belief common to the Seattle 7 and many dissenters is that human society should trend over time toward greater freedom for its members and greater safety for its communities. Activists have a profound discomfort with not trying to live according to their principles or seeing their country failing to do the same. They feel a need to personally respond, no matter how small the act may be, to express those principles and ameliorate those failures.

Stories of the Holocaust and the post-war Nuremberg trials were front-and-center in the upbringing of many who grew up to be the protesters of the 1960s. They did not want to be "good Germans," meaning German citizens who sat on the sidelines while their country's armies set out to destroy European civilization.

The Seattle 7 believed that a good society holds itself together by recognizing people's common need for food, shelter, safety, personal affection, and meaningful activity, now and for future generations. That is, of course, the American dream. We live today neither in the worst of times or places, nor in the best of times or places. Much is left to be done; our relatively greater freedom to dissent comes with greater responsibilities to exercise that right. The problems out there to be solved today are surely as great as they were in 1970. The tools available today are more numerous, and the opportunities for creative engagement are broader as well. Dynamic, thoughtfully focused dissent is even more American than apple pie, and is both the foundation and the scaffolding of a more just and free future.

The 1999 World Trade Organization meetings in Seattle were disrupted by people protesting the economic impact of so-called free trade on the less developed nations of the world. Here, protesters are hanging a sign from a construction crane in Seattle, a harbinger of the 2015 event where protesters hung off a bridge in Portland Oregon to prevent and publicize further oil exploration in Alaska. *Photo by Barry Sweet*

Author's Note

The secret of being a bore is to tell everything.
—Voltaire, 1738

As the reader has undoubtedly observed, the author is not an unbiased bystander on the topic of dissent in a democracy. I was born and raised in Seattle in white, middle-class comfort and general oblivion. I left the city in 1964 to attend college in the East. While there, I studied hard and learned a lot about my country's strengths and blunders. Clearly, there was much to be done and I was eager to get started.

I launched our campus Students for a Democratic Society chapter to help end our horrific war in Vietnam, joined a Tom Hayden/SDS project investigating the needs of people in the nearby black ghetto, and led an unsuccessful attempt to unionize the all-black, all-female dormitory staff at my school. When I graduated with a degree in political science I went to Chicago to work in the national office of SDS, where I helped produce the weekly *New Left Notes*. While there I met several of the Seattle 7 as they came through Chicago on various SDS organizing trips.

When SDS shattered, I sided with Weatherman, and spent the next several years in cloak-and-dagger collectives around the country, never in Seattle, vainly trying to figure out how to wage war against the U.S. government. Eventually, I returned safely to aboveground antiwar and anti-capitalist work, but belatedly realized I also needed to earn a living. I found myself back in Seattle in 1977 working as a pediatric oncology nurse, long after the Seattle 7 trial.

Warp speed to the twenty-first century when I ran into Seattle 7 defendant Roger Lippman at a party. We got to talking about the old days, and he mentioned that no one had yet documented the full story of the Seattle 7. Having written a couple of other books, I said I'd take a crack at it.

Over the next six years, I recorded dozens of interviews with each of the defendants (except the deceased Susan Stern), their attorneys, FBI agents, journalists, jurors, the U.S. Marshal, students, SLF members, and both supporters and critics of the Seattle 7. Those personal communications, along with the trial transcript, appeals briefs, depositions, mountains of contemporary newspaper clippings, magazine articles, flyers, memoirs and histories, and pamphlets and other ephemera of the times form the bedrock of this account.

Errors, of course, undoubtedly exist, some due to the mutability of memory, including my own. As F. Scott Fitzgerald observed, "Nonfiction is a form of literature that lies halfway between fiction and fact."[1] Because we all tend to recast our pasts to fit present needs, this version, while it has the advantage of multiple perspectives, will likely not match any one person's individual memories of those days. I expect dissent.

In addition to Roger Lippman, thanks are particularly due to Joe Kelly, who provided years of context, information, and encouragement. Lengthy conversations with defendants Chip Marshall, Michael Lerner, Jeff Dowd, and Michael Abeles also were critically important. Special Collections librarians from the University of Washington, the UW Law Library, the Seattle Public Library, Federal Archives including FOIA staff, the Wing Luke Museum, the Seattle Museum of History and Industry, and the Seattle Municipal Archives, were invaluable, as were Professors Linda Watts, Barbara Winslow, and Arthur Eckstein. James Gregory, professor in the UW history department, maintains a wide-ranging and helpful website, depts.washington.edu/civilr/site_map.htm, on a wide variety of Seattle's civil rights and labor struggles, as do the busy staff at HistoryLink.org.

Attorneys Michael Tigar and Jeff Steinborn were articulate and generous sources, as was U.S. Marshal Charles Robinson, retired UW policeman David Wilma, and Judge George Boldt's daughter Virginia Riedinger. Carl Maxey's widow Lou provided memories and encouragement. High school teacher Ron Green gave me boxes of materials from his 1970s course on extremism. Author Bruce Dancis came through several times with prompt advice and valuable information.

Many SLF supporters, members, and critics chimed in with just the right piece of needed material or personal observation. To name just a few who were particularly unstinting with their memories and their photos: Steve Hudziak, Thurman Fremstad, Pat Tonnema, Todd Cameron Miller, Zels Johnson, Peggy Dow, Kathy Ingalls-Severn, Jane Smith, Joan Sharp, Linda O'Toole, Paul Wick, Robby Stern, Paul Dorpat, Nan Faessler, Bob Kaplan, and Patrice Demombynes.

Helpful readers, early and late, include Lynn and Brian Grant, Stephanie Kallos, Lorraine McConaghy, Peter Russo, Ken Mankoff, and Tess Russo. On the production side, Barbara Sjoholm provided exquisitely valuable editorial assistance and Penny and David Miller contributed their expert transcription and formatting skills. Grateful kudos to the WSU Press staff: Ed Sala, Bob Clark, Beth DeWeese, Caryn Lawton, and Kerry Darnall. They have been delightful partners in every way.

Eternally thankful nods to my husband Peter, who cheerfully, patiently, and supportively lived with this project—not an easy task.

I cannot thank all of them enough for the privilege of documenting this piece of history and its connections to the present. May hopeful energy reign as the work continues.

Notes

Introduction

1. My Lai is a village in Vietnam that was the scene of a civilian massacre. U.S. Army infantry troops killed between 350 and 500 unarmed women, children, and men in spring 1968. Women were gang raped and bodies were mutilated. The event was covered up and didn't come to light until fall 1969. Judicial punishment was light—only one soldier was convicted; he served three and a half years under house arrest. Soldiers who had tried to stop the carnage were denounced as traitors in the U.S. press and by the chairman of the U.S. House Armed Services Committee.

2. Using an oral history approach, this book is based on dozens of face-to-face, transcribed interviews bolstered by many telephone and email conversations. I have very lightly edited some of these conversations for ease of reading on the page. I have done the same with some of the lengthier extracts from the trial transcript.

Chapter 1: The Lay of the Land

1. The term "red diaper baby" was commonly used to describe a child raised by parents who were in or sympathized with the U.S. Communist Party. For more, see Judy Kaplan and Linn Shapiro, eds., *Red Diapers: Growing up in the Communist Left* (Chicago: University of Illinois Press, 1998), and Thai Jones, *A Radical Line* (New York, NY: Free Press, 2004).

2. Wording from the Civil Rights Act of 1968, 8 U.S.C. § 2101, was quoted by U.S. Attorney Stan Pitkin in his Government's Trial Brief for the Seattle 7 case.

3. The words "liberation front" were commonly used in those days to indicate solidarity with third world struggles, such as the National Liberation Fronts in Vietnam and Algeria.

4. For example, the Country Doctor Community Health Centers, Northwest Immigrant Rights Project, and others (see Chapter 5).

5. Paul Potter, "The Incredible War," in *Rebels with a Cause: A Collective Memoir of the Hopes, Rebellions and Repression of the 1960s*, Helen Garvy (Los Gatos, CA: Shite Press, 2007), 49.

6. "List of Bombs in the Vietnam War," en.wikipedia.org/wiki/List_of_bombs_in_the_Vietnam_War.

7. Daniel Walker, Chicago Study Team, National Commission of the Causes and Prevention of Violence, "Rights in Conflict," December 1, 1968, chicago68.com/ricsumm.html.

8. Susan Stern describes her experiences and thoughts at the 1968 Chicago Democratic National Convention in her book, *With the Weathermen: The Personal Journal of a Revolutionary Woman*, Susan Stern and Laura Browder, ed. (New Brunswick, NJ: Rutgers University Press, 2007), 28-44.

9. Many of the Port Huron Statement's basic ideas were originally drafted by Tom Hayden while he was in jail in Georgia for protesting against segregation. Hayden was to become one of the Chicago 7. Much later, he settled in California and served in state government, always maintaining his left-leaning political views. He died in 2016.

10. For SDS numbers, see Kirkpatrick Sale, *SDS* (New York, NY: Vintage Books, 1974), 479; and James Miller, *Democracy is in the Streets: From Port Huron to the Siege of Chicago* (Cambridge, MA: Harvard University Press, 1994), 259.

11. Quotes from "Port Huron Statement," Students for a Democratic Society (1962), en.wikisource. org/wiki/Port_Huron_Statement. The Student Nonviolent Coordinating Committee grew out of the 1960 Greensboro, North Carolina, lunch counter sit-ins, and a meeting called by Ella Baker. Its members played a large role in the 1964 Mississippi Freedom Summer's voter registration drives and were sometimes known as the "shock troops" of the civil rights movement. Its leadership included Stokely Carmichael, John Lewis, and Rap Brown.

12. The life and break-up of SDS has been covered by many, including Kirkpatrick Sale, Todd Gitlin, David Gilbert, and Helen Garvy (see Bibliography). The short analysis is that an irreparable factional split occurred between two groups within the organization, partly encouraged by FBI manipulation and partly because of members' frustration over their inability to stop the war.

13. Robby Stern, personal communication with author, December 16, 2011.

14. United States Senate, "Final Report of the Select Committee to Study Governmental Operations with Respect to Intelligence Activities," Rep. No. 94-755, April 23, 1976 (often called the Church Committee Report after committee chair Sen. Frank Church [D-ID]).

15. There are many references to the FBI's warrantless searches and seizures from this time period. One of the most detailed is Arthur Eckstein, *Bad Moon Rising: How the Weather Underground Beat the FBI and Lost the Revolution* (New Haven, CT: Yale University Press, 2016).

16. Jon Leland, "Free the Seattle Eight", KRAB-FM 107.7, Seattle, October/November 1970, audiofile, www.krabarchive.com/player/1970-11-00.html.

17. Founded in 1905, the IWW remains active today, see iww.org.

Chapter 2: Meet the Seattle 8

1. Susan Stern, *With the Weathermen*, 11.

2. David T. Courtwright, *No Right Turn: Conservative Politics in a Liberal America* (Cambridge, MA: Harvard University Press, 2010), 103.

3. Stern, *With the Weathermen*, 13.

4. Ibid., 20.

5. Roger Lippman, personal communication with author, February 23, 2015.

6. Ibid., November 9, 2015.

7. Almost 175,000 people were granted conscientious objector status during the Vietnam War. Nearly 600,000 refused to be drafted but only a third were formally charged with evading the draft, and only a small minority of those were ever convicted. www.swarthmore.edu/library/peace/conscientiousobjection/co%20website/pages/HistoryNew.htm.

8. Lippman, to author, August 16, 2011. Also see Chapter 1, note 12, above.

9. Nan Faessler, personal communication with author, May 21, 2017.

10. Michael Lerner, personal communication with author, August 26, 2012.

11. Pat Tonnema, personal communication with author, January 22, 2014.

12. Faessler, to author, May 21, 2017.

13. FBI Agent Giannotti memo to Director Hoover, June 9, 1977, Clayton van Lydegraf papers, University of Washington Libraries Special Collections, 1341-004, Box 7.

14. Robby Stern, to author, March 13, 2014.

15. Mark Perry, personal communication with author, January 21, 2014.

16. Jeff Dowd, personal communication with author, October 17, 2013.

17. ROTC, or the Reserve Officers' Training Corps, is a college-based military program for training commissioned officers for the U.S. military. These programs and their attendant campus buildings were frequent targets for sit-ins and firebombings by the antiwar movement, forcing many colleges to close their ROTC programs or to cancel academic credits for ROTC coursework. Today, many schools have re-opened their ROTC offerings.

18. Joe Kelly, personal communication with author, February 4, 2016.

19. Ibid., October 23, 2011.

20. Patrice Demombynes, personal communication with author, February 12, 2014.

21. Sunny Speidel, personal communication with author, August 26, 2014.

22. Joe Kelly, to author, October 23, 2011.

23. Demombynes, to author, February 12, 2014.

24. Stern, *With the Weathermen*, 235.

25. Michael Abeles, personal communication with author, July 20, 2011.

26. Demombynes, to author, February 12, 2014.

27. Speidel, to author, August 26, 2014.

28. Dowd, to author, March 30, 2012.

29. Chip Marshall, personal communication with author, February 8, 2013.

30. Volunteers in Service to America (VISTA), originally suggested by President Kennedy as a domestic version of the Peace Corps, was funded as part of the War on Poverty during Lyndon B. Johnson's presidency. It is now called AmeriCorps. Saul Alinsky (1909-1972) is generally known as the father of American community organizing and is the author of *Rules for Radicals* (see bibliography). The irony of the U.S. government hiring Alinsky to train VISTA workers did not escape Marshall.

31. Faessler, to author, May 21, 2017.

32. Marshall, to author, February 8, 2013. But one woman who worked at the Blue Moon flatly denies that there was ever any naked dancing on the bar.

Chapter 3: Seattle Needs Liberating

1. Basically a rout, the Days of Rage drew only about four hundred people and resulted in almost three hundred arrests. The author was among those arrested.

2. Joe Kelly, to author, October 23, 2011.

3. Harry Cheadle, "A Former Weather Underground Member Explains Why Anti-Trump Violence Won't Work," www.vice.com/en_us/article we-asked-a-former-60s-radical-whether-violence -against-trump-is-justified.

4. Joe Kelly described the run-up to this arrest: "Very tough Chicago cops got us in the van, took us to the police station, took us into a freight elevator, closed the door and locked it in at one floor. They started beating us with blackjacks, and stuck a gun in my friend's mouth. I was able to get my hands and arms up so I never got hit in the face, but poor [another friend] showed no ability to protect himself and they really beat him badly." Kelly, to author, April 23, 2015.

5. Jane Smith, personal communication with author, March 19, 2014.

6. David Aikman, "In Seattle: Up from Revolution," *Time*, April 14, 1980, content.time.com/ time/magazine/article/0,9171,923945,00.html.

7. Linda O'Toole, personal communication with author, March 31, 2014.

8. Lippman, to author, August 16, 2011.

9. Py Bateman, personal communication with author, November 1, 2011.

10. Stern, *With the Weathermen*, 223.

11. The trial of the Chicago 7 began with eight defendants when it opened on September 24, 1969. Several weeks into the trial, defendant and Black Panther Bobby Seale was gagged and shackled to his chair. This lasted several days before he was severed from the trial, and it became the Chicago 7. Seale was treated this way partly because he loudly and repeatedly demanded a delay in the trial until his attorney could be present.

12. Lerner, to author, August 26, 2012.

13. Marshall, to author, February 8, 2013.

14. Jeff Stevens, "January 17, 1970: Jerry Rubin Brings the Chicago Noise to Seattle," *The Seattle Star,* January 17, 2013, www.seattlestar.net/2013/01/january-17-1970-jerry-rubin-brings-the-chicago-noise-to-seattle.

15. Dowd, to author, March 30, 2012.

16. Marshall, to author, February 8, 2013.

17. Lerner, to author, August 26, 2012.

18. Ibid.

19. Michael Stanton Papers, Special Collections No. 3978, Box 2, #3978-001. Seattle, WA: University of Washington Libraries. Referred to hereafter as Stanton Papers.

20. Demombynes, to author, February 12, 2014.

21. Peggy Dow, personal communication with author, April 29, 2014.

22. Paul Wick, personal communication with author, August 2, 2011. This group sex approach to collective bonding is described in several memoirs by Weather people including Cathy Wilkerson's *Flying Close to the Sun.* It was part of Weatherman's "smash monogamy" strategy. In retrospect, participants do not recommend it as an organizing technique.

23. Karen Kelly, personal communication with author, May 13, 2017.

24. Lerner, to author, August 26, 2012. The fifteen-point SLF program for action mirrored portions of a similar declaration written in part by Lerner in mid-1969 during Berkeley's People's Park demonstrations.

25. Don Hannula, "Seattle Liberation Front Agreed on Goal, Not Means," *Seattle Times,* February 22, 1970, B7.

26. *United States, Plaintiff, v. Charles Clark Marshall III, Jeffrey Dowd, Joseph Kelly, Michael Abeles, Michael Lerner, Roger Lippman, Susan Stern, and Michael Justesen,* Case No. 51942, United States District Court, Western District of Washington at Tacoma, Transcript (author's copy), 2. Referred to hereafter as *United States v. Marshall et al.,* 682.

Chapter 4: TDA—The Day After

1. Defense attorney William Kunstler received the longest sentence, four years and thirteen days.

2. Stanton Papers, Box 2.

3. Richard Larson, "Buechel and Lerner: What They Think," *Seattle Times,* February 22, 1970, B6.

4. Lerner, to author, August 26, 2012.

5. Ibid.

6. John Repp, personal communication with author, April 16, 2015.

7. David Brewster and Ardie Ivie, "Right On!," *Seattle Magazine,* May 1970, 49.

8. Charles Robinson, personal communication with author, February 20 and 28, 2014.

9. Stern, *With the Weathermen,* 237–39.

10. Zels Johnson, personal communication with author, January 24, 2014.

11. Ibid., July 18, 2017.

12. Mike Nemeth, personal communication with author, August 25, 2014.

13. The police were to make the same mistake twenty-nine years later during the 1999 World Trade Organization (WTO) protests, known as "the Battle in Seattle."

14. Lerner, to author, August 26, 2012.

15. Kevin Castle, personal communication with author, August 29, 2011.

16. Dan Smith, personal communication with author, July 14, 2015.

17. John Chambless, "My Arrest at the Seattle Federal Courthouse," audiofile of KOL-FM radio report, February 1970, provided to author by Ron Green. od.lk/s/NTlfNDI3MTE0Xw/John_Chambless_KOL-FM_February_1970.mp3

18. "Police Use Tear Gas With Demonstrators Outside Courthouse," *Seattle Times*, February 17, 1970, A1.

19. Don Hannula and Richard Larson, "Revolution Wears a New Face in Seattle," *Seattle Times*, February 22, 1970, A1.

20. City of Seattle, *Municipal Archives*, Folder 5, Box 139, #5287-02, 1970.

21. Ibid.

22. Ibid.

23. "TDA," *Discover America*, March 1970 (single-issue newspaper printed by SLF member Bobby Oram, lent to author by Steve Hudziak).

24. Larson, "Buechel and Lerner: What They Think," *Seattle Times*.

25. "Fifty Are Denied Admission Here," *Seattle Times*, February 20, 1970, A2.

Chapter 5: Action and Reaction

1. "Memo to J. Edgar Hoover from Will Wilson," Stanton Papers, Box 1.

2. Stanton Papers, Box 2.

3. Karsten Prager, "Seattle Under Siege: The Troubles of a Company Town," *Time*, January 4, 1971, 28.

4. Dowd, to author, September 17, 2013.

5. Prager, "Seattle Under Siege," 28.

6. Dan Smith, to author, July 14, 2015.

7. Don Hannula, "Seattle Liberation Front Agreed on Goal, Not Means," *Seattle Times*, February 22, 1970, B7.

8. From an unidentified student's paper for Michael Lerner's Philosophy 410 course, provided to author by Thurman Fremstad.

9. Stanton Papers, Box 1.

10. Judge Wachtler is also known for making spousal rape a criminal offense, and for serving a fifteen-month prison sentence after being convicted of threatening his lover and her daughter.

11. "Thirty Years Later…and Still Chasing Witches," Jack Anderson, United Features Syndicate column, *Prescott Courier*, June 9, 1976, 4, news.google.com/newspapers?nid=886&dat=19760609&id=9r-paAAAAIBAJ&sjid=I1ADAAAAIBAJ&pg=7255,5425317.

12. Michael Tigar, personal communication with author, March 7, 2014.

13. Robinson, to author, February 20, 2014.

14. Paul Marcus, "Conspiracy: the Criminal Agreement, in Theory and in Practice" (1977), *Faculty Publications,* Paper 558, 936, scholarship.law.wm.edu/facpubs/558.

15. Dee Norton, "2 to Defend Themselves in Conspiracy 'People's Trial'," *Seattle Times*, May 16, 1970, A4.

16. Stanton Papers, Box 1, May 15, 1970.

17. Bernard Weiner, "What, Another Conspiracy?" *Washington State Bar Association News*, December 1970, 9.

18. U.S. Department of Justice, untitled press release, April 16, 1970, author's copy.

19. Don Carter and Larry McCarten, "Indicted 8 Linked to 2 Named in U Post Office Bombing," *Seattle Post-Intelligencer*. April 17, 1970, B.

20. "SLF: Seattle Is the Target of Revolutionaries," *Seattle Post-Intelligencer*, April 5, 1970, 4.

21. "Fiery Credo Mirrors All Discontent," *Seattle Post-Intelligencer*, April 6, 1970, 10.

22. "P-I Series Hit by SLF," *Seattle Post-Intelligencer*, Friday, April 10, 1970, 14.

23. United States of America v. Charles Clark Marshall, III, Jeffrey Dowd, J. H. Kelly, Michael Abeles, Michael Lerner, Roger Lippman, Susan Stern and Michael Justesen, United States District Court, Western District of Washington Northern Division, *Grand Jury Indictment*, signature lines for Stan Pitkin, Guy Goodwin, and the grand jury foreman, April 16, 1970, author's copy.

24. Lerner, to author, August 26, 2012.

25. Carter and McCarten, "Indicted 8 Linked to 2 Named in U Post Office Bombing."

26. Stern, *With the Weathermen*, 257.

27. Ibid., 259.

28. Marshall, to author, February 8, 2013.

29. Lippman, to author, February 23, 2015.

30. Ibid., August 16, 2011.

Chapter 6: Spring into Summer

1. Larry Ward was a black veteran, recently returned to Seattle from Vietnam, where he'd been wounded. He was lured by a police informer into a plan to bomb a racist real estate office, then shot in the back by Seattle police. The jury at the coroner's inquest ruled 3–2 that Ward's death was a "death by criminal means" but the prosecutor declined to bring the case to trial.

2. "What's Going On Here," Seattle Liberation Front flyer, 1970, author's collection.

3. They were still called the Seattle 8 at this point. When the trial convened and Michael Justesen was still uncaptured, most news media then called them the Seattle 7.

4. Bernard Weiner, "The Seattle Eight: What, Another Conspiracy?," *The Nation*, November 2, 1970, 424–27.

5. "DO IT!," Seattle Liberation Front flyer, 1970, author's collection.

6. Don Carter, George McDowell, Rick Anderson, "Peace March Day 'Almost a Love-in,'" *Seattle Post-Intelligencer*, May 2, 1970, B.

7. Roy Reed, "F.B.I. Investigating Killing Of 2 Negroes in Jackson: Two Negro Students Are Killed In Clash With Police in Jackson," *New York Times*, May 16, 1970:1. en.wikipedia.org/wiki/Student_strike_of_1970#cite_note-Reed.2C_NYT.2C_5.2F16.2F1970-5

8. Scott L. Bliss, ed., *Kent State/May 4: Echoes Through a Decade*, Kent State University Press, 1982. This is a collection of oral histories from participants, including students, university officials, and National Guard troops. The editor wrote, "The dead were surrogates for the radical leaders whom the guardsmen could not reach," 59.

9. James McDonald, personal communication with author, March 18, 2014, and December 5, 2014.

10. Don Hannula, "More Protests Due: 4,000 Rally at UW," *Seattle Times*, May 7, 1970, A1.

11. "Unruly Bands Roam U. District; 8 Injured," and Marty Loken, "Students Clubbed by Vigilantes," *Seattle Times*, May 8, 1970, A1.

12. Charles Odegaard, "Telegram," *UW Daily*, May 6, 1970, 11.

13. "Nixon Impeachment Studied," *Seattle Times*, May 4, 1970, A10.

14. Joe Kelly, to author, October 23, 2011.

15. John Kifner, "Seattle FBI Spy Tells of Actions," *New York Times*, June 13, 1971, 41.

16. Sannes' stories over time do not clearly answer the question of whether he first became an informant and then became publicly critical of the FBI, or whether he always intended to be, in essence, a "double agent" who would eventually attack the FBI and support the dissidents he was spying on.

17. "Seattle Police Communication to Attorney General John Mitchell and the Federal Communications Commission," in Gerald Slater Papers, University of Maryland Special Collections, Series 1, Box 1, Folders 1 and 2. College Park, MD.

18. "PBS Denies FBI Censorship," *Television Digest*, October 11, 1971, 6.

19. "David Sannes statement," in Gerald Slater Papers, Series 1, Box 1, Folders 1 and 2, University of Maryland Special Collections, College Park, MD.

20. Ibid.

21. Thurman Fremstad, deposition, July 6, 1971, author's collection.

22. Ibid.

23. Jeff Desmond, signed deposition, July 12, 1971, 2, author's collection.

24. Ibid.

25. Ibid., 3.

26. Stanton Papers, Box 2.

27. Ibid.

28. Stern, *With the Weathermen*, 21–22.

29. Pat Sullivan, "Hell Hath No Fury—Hideout Tavern catches it," *Puget Sound Partisan*, Vol. 1, No. 2, August 3, 1970, 12.

30. At least one woman I spoke with felt that the term "gang rape" was not intended to be taken literally, but was used to forcibly underline the intensity of the machismo and sexism that they felt from the male SLF leadership.

31. Fanshen is a village in China that was touted as an example of Maoist revolutionary success in the 1966 book *Fanshen: A Documentary of Revolution in a Chinese Village*, by William Hinton. The women in the village were said to be able to address their own oppression while still giving full attention to the country's overall struggles. Seattle 7 defendant Roger Lippman responded to the Seattle women's document by reminding them of Hinton's remarks.

32. "Fanshen Statement," hand-typed copy supplied to the author by female SLF members. It has also been published in various places, including *Socialist Revolution*, September/October, 1970, 117, and *Ain't I a Woman*, October 9, 1970, 2–3. The *Socialist Revolution* version varies from the other two in that it omits the names of the SLF men, but refers to them generically; for instance, the name Michael Lerner is replaced by "a radical Marxist professor from Berkeley," and Chip Marshall, Joe Kelly, Jeff Dowd, and Michael Abeles are referred to as "the Sundance crowd from Cornell SDS."

33. Sky River was a large outdoor rock festival held for several years running near Seattle. The first one predated the more famous Woodstock, and was organized by a group of Seattle counter-cultural cognoscenti, many of whom worked on the city's underground paper *The Helix*. SLF thought of it as a good organizing tool, as well as a lot of fun. In fact, the 1970 version failed on both counts. Bikers tried to steal the cash box and the participants were not very interested in hearing from SLF organizers about Bobby Seale or the revolution.

34. "Fanshen Statement," author's collection.

35. Ibid.

36. Ibid.

37. Deane Rink, personal communication, October 17, 2013.

38. O'Toole, to author, May 18, 2017.

39. These women in their early twenties were among the first to have relatively easy access to contraception, and HIV was yet to arrive. Other STDs were rampant, however, and visits to public health and women's clinics for penicillin and other treatments were common.

40. Tonnema, to author, May 23, 2017.

41. *Ain't I a Woman*, October 9, 1970, 2.

42. "KRAB Programs Spoken Word," recorded between September and November 22, 1970, www.krabarchive.com/player/1970-11-00.html.

43. Ibid.

44. Ibid.

45. Ibid.

46. Ibid.

47. Stern, *With the Weathermen,* 275.

Chapter 7: Gearing Up for Trial

1. Name withheld, personal communication with author, February 12, 2014.

2. James McDonald, to author, March 18, 2014.

3. Ibid.

4. Michael E. Tigar, *Fighting Injustice* (Chicago, IL: Section of Litigation, American Bar Association, 2002), 181.

5. Jeffrey Toobin, "Annals of Law: The Man with Timothy McVeigh," *New Yorker*, September 30, 1996, 48-54; *Law and the Rise of Capitalism (*New York, NY: Monthly Review Press, 1978).

6. Anarchists in Chicago in 1886 were demonstrating in Haymarket Square for an eight-hour work day when a bomb was tossed into the midst of the police. Eight men were charged and convicted of conspiracy, seven were sentenced to death.

7. Jim Kershner, *Carl Maxey: A Fighting Life* (Seattle: University of Washington Press, 2008), 166.

8. Ibid., 17.

9. Robert Thomas Jr., "Carl Maxey, 73, Spokane Civil Rights Lawyer," (obituary) www.nytimes.com/1997/07/20/us/carl-maxey-73-spokane-civil-rights-lawyer.html.

10. Lee Holley, personal communication with author, June 22, 2014.

11. Dow, to author, May 19, 2014.

12. Holley, to author, June 22, 2014.

13. Jeff Steinborn, personal communication with author, July 28, 2011.

14. Ibid.

15. "Who will pick up the pieces," *Sabot*, October 30, 1970, 7.

16. Boldt is best known for his decision in the 1974 fishing rights case, in which he affirmed the treaty rights of Washington's Native Americans to fish in their traditional places. This decision to support tribes and take partial fishing rights away from white commercial fishermen surprised

and angered many. It was appealed to the 9th Circuit Court which affirmed Boldt's decision in 1975; the Supreme Court let the lower court ruling stand. Decades later, Pacific Northwest tribes continue to honor Boldt for his ruling.

17. Virginia Reidinger, personal communication with author, March 31, 2014.

18. Robby Stern, to author, January 13, 2014.

19. "'Seattle 7' echo of Chicago trial," *New York Times*, November 1, 1970, 34.

20. Don Hannula, "Judge refuses to disqualify self in trial of conspiracy 7," *Seattle Times,* November 7, 1970, A4.

21. Michael Tigar, "A New Challenge to Our Court System: The Spirited Lawyer Representing Political Defendants," edited transcript of a discussion at a 1970 American Bar Association meeting in St. Louis, *Washington State Bar News*, September 1970, 12.

Chapter 8: Let the Circus Begin

1. Egil Krogh, "The Break-In That History Forgot," Op-ed, *New York Times*, June 30, 2007, www. nytimes.com/2007/06/30/opinion/30krogh.html.

2. Don Hannula, "Judge refuses to disqualify self in conspiracy trial of 7," *Seattle Times*, November 7, 1970, A4.

3. Don Hannula, "Judge ousts two at conspiracy trial," *Seattle Times*, November 23, 1970, D6.

4. William Blackstone, *Commentaries on the Laws of England*, 4th ed. (T. Cooley, 1896), 349–350.

5. *United States v. Marshall et al.*, 3.

6. Ibid., 10.

7. Lerner, to author, August 26, 2012.

8. David Dellinger, a lifelong pacifist, was one of the Chicago 7. Born in 1915, he was 55 when he attended the Seattle 7 trial in 1970. In his obituary in 2004, the *New York Times* described him as "a child of patrician privilege, he had since his days at Yale learned and practiced strategies of civil disobedience in a variety of causes, steadfastly showing what he called his concern for 'the small, the variant, the unrepresented, the weak,' categories he cited from the writings of William James." See Michael Kaufman, "David Dellinger, of Chicago 7, Dies at 88," *New York Times*, May 27, 2004. www.nytimes.com/2004/05/27/us/david-dellinger-of-chicago-7-dies-at-88. html?pagewanted=all&src=pm.

9. *United States v. Marshall et al.*, 98.

10. Mark Gillespie, "Americans Look Back at Vietnam War," Gallup, November 17, 2000, www. gallup.com/poll/2299/americans-look-back-vietnam-war.aspx.

11. Stern, *With the Weathermen,* 291.

12. *United States v. Marshall et al.*, 125.

13. Ibid., 155.

14. Ibid., 157.

15. Ibid., 385.

16. Ibid., 385.

17. Ibid., 208–209.

18. Ibid., 207–208.

19. Ibid., 223–224.

20. Ibid., 321.

21. Ibid., 357–358.

22. Ibid., 358.

Chapter 9: A Peerless Jury is Seated

1. Dean McNee, personal communication with author, December 20, 2012.

2. Mason Moriset, editor, "Personal Appearance: May a Student Wear His Hair as He Pleases?," Washington State and Seattle King County Bar Associations, *Youth and the Law*, February 1971, 2.

3. *United States v. Marshall et al.*, 333.

4. Ibid., 360.

5. Ibid., 362.

6. Ibid., 363.

7. McNee, to author, December 20, 2012.

8. Don Hannula and Stephen Dunphy, "Jury is Empaneled in Seattle Conspiracy Trial," *Seattle Times*, November 26, 1970, H4.

9. *United States v. Marshall et al.*, 486.

10. Ibid., 487.

11. Ibid., 488.

12. Ibid., 343.

13. Ibid., 537–38.

14. Ibid., 60.

15. Ibid., 500.

16. Hannula and Dunphy, "Jury is Empaneled," *Seattle Times*, H4.

17. *United States v. Marshall et al.*, 571.

18. Ibid., 575–76.

19. Ibid., 576–77.

20. Hannula and Dunphy, "Jury is Empaneled," *Seattle Times*, H4.

21. *United States v. Marshall et al.*, 578.

22. *United States v. Marshall et al.*, 579-80. Because the trial transcript only rarely records behaviors such as laughter, clapping, standing, etc., and cannot capture the chaos of multiple voices shouting, scuffling, chairs falling over as people jump up, marshals entering the courtroom, etc., the attorneys verbally state these events to ensure they appear in the transcript.

23. Ibid., 582.

24. Audrey Waldorf, personal communication with author, July 12, 2012.

25. *United States v. Marshall et al.*, 587.

26. Ibid., 589–90.

27. Ibid., 591.

28. Ibid., 592–93.

29. Ibid., 597.

30. Ibid., 599.

31. Ibid., 614.

32. Statistical information about casualties of the Vietnam War, National Archives. www.archives.gov/research/military/vietnam-war/casualty-statistics.html.

33. *United States v. Marshall et al.*, 757.

34. Lippman, to author, August 16, 2011.

35. Chip Marshall, "Letter from Tacoma City Jail," *Socialist Revolution*, September/October 1970, 139.

Chapter 10: Jail Them, Not Us

1. Waldorf, to author, July 12, 2012.

2. *United States v. Marshall et al.*, 1494.

3. "Swanson Opens Seattle 8 defense," *UW Daily*, November 19, 1970, 6.

4. *United States v. Marshall et al.*, 664.

5. Tigar, *Fighting Injustice*, 181.

6. Michael Lerner, "Letter to the Movement, Conspiracy in Seattle," *Liberation*, July 1970, 36.

7. Jack Wilson and Robert Boxberger, "Proof 7 Are Guilty Pledged by Pitkin," *Tacoma News Tribune*, November 30, 1970, 3.

8. *United States v. Marshall et al.*, 671.

9. Waldorf, to author, July 12, 2012.

10. Jane Smith, to author, March 19, 2014.

11. *United States v. Marshall et al.*, 756.

12. Ibid., 757.

13. Ibid., 786.

14. Ibid., 789, 792.

15. Ibid., 809.

16. Ibid., 813.

17. Ibid., 820.

18. Ibid., 833.

19. Ibid., 849.

20. Ibid., 854.

21. Ibid., 880.

22. Daniel Walker, The National Commission on the Causes and Prevention of Violence, "Rights in Conflict," December 1, 1968, chicago68.com/ricsumm.html.

23. *United States v. Marshall et al.*, 1091.

24. Ibid., 1094.

25. Kim Reich, "U Plainclothesman Questioned at Trial," *UW Daily*, December 2, 1970, 4.

26. *United States v. Marshall et al.*, 1058.

27. Ibid., 1059.

Chapter 11: The Rise and Fall of an FBI Provocateur

1. *United States v. Marshall et al.*, 1122, 1129.

2. Ibid., 1176.

3. Ibid., 1219.

4. Ibid., 1264.

5. Ibid., 1266.

6. Ibid., 1268.

7. Ibid., 1273.

8. "Miscue Triggers More Trial Pandemonium," *Seattle Post-Intelligencer*, December 4, 1970, 11.

9. The following day, Boldt reported that he had spoken with Jane Smith in his chambers and had realized that perhaps he was wrong and that she hadn't spoken. He apologized, she accepted, and she was allowed back into the courtroom. *United States v. Marshall et al.*, 1505–6.

10. *United States v. Marshall et al.*, 1323–24.

11. Ibid., 1418–22. Also Don Hannula and Stephen Dunphy, "Obscene sign language charged at trial," *Seattle Times*, December 4, 1970, A5.

12. Ibid., 1449.

13. Ibid., 1455.

14. Ibid., 1513–14.

15. Ibid., 1569.

16. Ibid., 1573–74.

17. Ibid., 1597.

18. Ibid., 1598.

19. Ibid., 1600.

20. Ibid., 1617.

21. Ibid., 1624.

22. Ibid., 1644.

23. Ibid., 1644–45.

24. Ibid., 1647.

25. Ibid., 1623. (It is highly unusual for jurors to directly ask questions of a witness, and it appears to have only occurred in the Seattle 7 trial this one time.)

26. Ibid., 1649.

27. Ibid., 1704. (Boldt never did refer Parker's case to a grand jury.)

Chapter 12: Calm Before the Storm

1. *United States v. Marshall et al.*, 1807.

2. Ibid., 1826.

3. Ibid., 1784.

4. Ibid., 1843.

5. Ibid., 1850.

6. Ibid., 1880.

Chapter 13: Mistrial!

1. *United States v. Marshall et al.*, 1945.

2. Ibid., 1951.

3. Mike James, Deposition, January 18, 1971. (Submitted as part of defense appeal to Ninth Circuit Court for dismissal of contempt charges. Copy loaned to author by interviewee.)

4. *United States v. Marshall et al.*, 1967.

5. Dowd, to author, September 17, 2013.

6. James, Deposition, January 18, 1971.

7. *United States v. Marshall et al.*, 1967.

8. Ibid., 1969.

9. Ibid., 1973–4.

10. Ibid., 1973–4.

11. Ibid., 1984.

12. Michael Tigar, Brief for Defendants-Appellants, United States Court of Appeals, Ninth Circuit v. Charles Clark Marshall, III, et al., No. 26889, (undated), 12. (author's copy)

13. "Juror feels defendants planned to stop trial," *Seattle Times*, December 11, 1970, A16.

14. Stern, *With the Weathermen*, 325.

15. Don Hannula and Stephen Dunphy, "The New Issues: Mistrial; Contempt Citations Against 6," *Seattle Times*, A16.

16. *United States v. Marshall et al.*, 1993.

17. Ibid., 1994.

18. Ibid., 1999.

19. Tigar, *Fighting Injustice*, 189.

Chapter 14: A Double Dose of Contempt

1. Stern, *With the Weathermen*, 325.

2. *United States v. Marshall et al.*, 2006.

3. Ibid., 2006, 2010–12. "Contumacious" is used frequently in discussions about judicial contempt; it means disobedient, unruly, defiant, and insubordinate to the extent of disrupting normal courtroom decorum.

4. Ibid., 2013.

5. Ibid., 2016.

6. Ibid., 2026.

7. Ibid., 2029.

8. Ibid., 2041–42.

9. Ibid., 2069.

10. Ibid., 2057.

11. Ibid., 2069–70.

12. Ibid., 2074.

13. Ibid., 2077.

14. Ibid., 2080.

15. Ibid., 2081.

16. Ibid., 2082.

17. "Seven Get Six to Reflect," *Daily Olympian*, December 12, 1970, 1.

18. *United States v. Marshall et al.*, 2087–88.

19. Ibid., 2088, 2089, 2091.

20. Ibid., 2092. Lieutenant William Calley Jr. was the only soldier tried and convicted for the massacre and war crimes committed in the Vietnamese village of My Lai. General William Westmoreland was Army Chief of Staff during much of the Vietnam War. His military strategy focused on fire power and air bombing. He declared every battle a U.S. victory and repeatedly told Americans that the war was winding down, starting as early as 1967.

21. Ibid., 2094.

22. Ibid., 2094.

23. Ibid., 2095.

24. Ibid., 2096–97.

25. Ibid., 2098.

26. Ibid., 2015–17.

27. Ibid., 2113–14.

28. Ibid., 2114.

29. Ibid., 2120.

30. Judge Alfred P. Murrah, United States v. Charles Clark Marshall III, et al., 451 F.2d 372 (Court of Appeals for the 9th Circuit November 18, 1971), 13.

31. Jon Leland, KOL Radio, news audiofile, December 14, 1970. od.lk/s/NTlfNDI3MTk4Xw/Jon_Leland_Bear_Facts_News_Tacoma_Courtroom_Fracas_December_14_1970.mp3, provided to author by Ron Green.

32. Stanton Papers, Box 2.

33. *United States v. Marshall et al.*, 2139–40.

34. Ibid., 2144.

35. Larry McCarten, "Chaos in Court As 7 Get Contempt Terms," *Seattle Post-Intelligencer*, December 15, 1970, 1.

36. *United States v. Marshall et al.*, 2123.

37. Ibid., 2126, 2128–29.

38. Ibid., 2137.

39. Ibid., 2159.

40. Ibid., 2164–65.

41. Larry McCarten, "7 Conspiracy Defendants Ordered Held Without Bail," *Seattle Post-Intelligencer*, December 16, 1970, 1.

42. "Radicals: The Seattle Seven," *Newsweek*, December 14, 1970, 57.

Chapter 15: Jailed Without Bail

1. Lippman, to author, November 1, 2013.

2. Lerner, to author, October 29, 2013.

3. Marshall, "Letter from Tacoma City Jail," 138.

4. "Bail for Seattle 7 is Stayed by Court," *New York Times,* December 30, 1970, 23.

5. Larry McCarten, "Judge Boldt Refuses to Grant 7 Bail," *Seattle Post-Intelligencer,* December 29, 1970, 1.

6. Lippman, to author, November 1, 2013.

7. Original provided to author by Joe Kelly. The content of this letter lends additional credence to the probability that the Seattle 7 indictments were managed by the Department of Justice in Washington, DC.

8. When the defense team asked for the videotapes as part of their contempt hearing preparation, they were told that nothing in fact had been recorded because the lens cap hadn't been removed from the camera. Memos in the Michael Stanton Papers between Pitkin and Department of Justice staff indicate the video existed, and copies had been made and sent to Washington, DC. This author was unable to track them down.

9. Bernard Weiner, "The Orderly Perversion of Justice," *The Nation,* February 1, 1971, 148.

10. Cesar Chavez (1927-1993) co-founded with Dolores Huerta the United Farm Workers of America and led important grape and lettuce strikes and boycotts that greatly improved the working conditions of farm workers. The union (ufw.org) remains active in promoting farmworkers' health and welfare with campaigns over insecticide use, working conditions, immigration crack-downs, and other issues.

11. Joe Kelly, to author, October 29, 2013.

12. Lerner, to author, October 29, 2013.

13. Joe Kelly, to author, October 30, 2013.

14. Ibid.

15. Ibid.

16. Ibid.

17. Lerner, to author, October 29, 2013.

18. Marshall, to author, October 29, 2013.

19. It was at McNeil Island that Robert Stroud, the "Birdman of Alcatraz," was incarcerated in the early 1910s, and where he killed a guard in 1916. He wasn't moved to Alcatraz until 1942; he died in 1959 in a prison hospital in Missouri, having lived forty-two-years in solitary confinement.

20. Lippman, to author, November 1, 2013.

Chapter 16: "Free," Eventually

1. Don Hannula, "Conspiracy-Case Seven: Transfer of Defendants Criticized," *Seattle Times,* December 21, 1970, B4.

2. "Bail Ordered for Seven in Conspiracy Case Here," *Seattle Times,* January 9, 1971, A8.

3. Dick Young, "Bail Raised for Contempt Defendants; One Released," *Seattle Post-Intelligencer,* January 12, 1971, 1.

4. Lippman, to author, November 1, 2013.

5. Don Hannula, "The Situation at McNeil Island: Conspiracy Faction Active," *Seattle Times,* February 24, 1971, C1.

6. George McDowell, "Free on Bail, 4 Vow Fight for Revolution," *Seattle Post-Intelligencer,* January 13, 1971, 4.

7. Joe Kelly, to author, October 30, 2013.

8. Weiner, "The Orderly Perversion of Justice,"148.

9. "Seattle Conspiracy Defendants Argue Contempt Appeals," *Seattle Times,* February 11, 1971, C9.

10. Memo from Guy Goodwin to Stan Pitkin, March 23, 1971, Department of Justice files, 146-1-61-465, Doc ID 70001945, 300. FOIA request, file concerning Roger Lippman.

11. Ibid. Neither of these attempts at further prosecution were pursued by Pitkin's office.

12. United States Court of Appeals, Ninth Circuit, United States of America v. Charles Clark Marshall, III, et al., No. 26889, 451 F2nd 372, November 18, 1971.

13. Betty Medsger, *The Burglary: The Discovery of J. Edgar Hoover's Secret FBI* (Waterville, ME: Thorndike Press, 2014).

14. Don Hannula, "Seven Plead No Contest," *Seattle Times,* February 23, 1972, B8.

15. Stan Pitkin memo to superiors at Department of Justice. "Dismissal recommended as to All defendants except Michael Justesen, fugitive. Upon apprehension, we would re-indict for violation of 18 U.S.C. 1361," Stanton Papers, Box 1.

16. Memo from Department of Justice to Stan Pitkin, Stanton Papers, Box 1.

17. The case, 407 U.S. 297, also known as the Keith case, overturned district court rulings in Michigan against the leaders of the White Panther Party, an anti-racist and counterculture group founded in 1968.

18. United States District Court for the Western District of Washington, Roger Lippman v. John Mitchell, et al., Civil Action #C74-342S, June 13, 1974, terrasol.home.igc.org/wiretap2.htm.

Chapter 17: The Years After

1. Larry Grathwohl, *Bringing Down America: An FBI Informer with the Weathermen* (New York, NY: Arlington House, 1976); and Cril Payne, *Deep Cover: An FBI Agent Infiltrates the Radical Underground* (New York, NY: Newsweek Books, 1979).

2. Susan Stern, "KRAB Programs Spoken Word" (recorded sometime between September and November 22, 1970), www.krabarchive.com/player/1970-11-00.html.

3. Laura Browder (editor) in Susan Stern's *With the Weathermen,* xxxii.

4. Tonnema, to author, February 11, 2014.

5. Dan Smith, to author, July 14, 2015.

6. Barbara Winslow, personal communication with author, January 6, 2014.

7. Nick Morrison, personal communication with author, May 21, 2015.

8. Michael Justesen, letter to *Puget Sound Partisan*, July 15, 1970, 3.

9. "About Us," Beyt Tikkum Synagogue, www.beyttikkun.org/index.php?topic=aboutus.

10. Lippman, to author, November 9, 2015.

11. Ibid., October 22, 2015.

12. Ibid., February 23, 2015.

13. Ibid., April 18, 2017.

14. Joe Kelly, to author, October 27, 2015.

15. Ibid., April 22, 2017.

16. Abeles, to author, July 20, 2011.

17. Jeff Dowd, letter to Archibald Cox and Sen. Sam Ervin, July 31, 1973, National Archives, Record Group # 460: Records of the Watergate Special Prosecution Force; Plumbers Task Force; Investigations of Other Illegal Activities, 1973-1976, Record entry 128289 (A1 103), box 12, 11. (Obtained by author through Freedom of Information request).

18. Madeline Boardman, "Jeff Dowd, Real 'Big Lebowski' Dude, Talks White Russians, Jeff Bridges and Bowling," *Huffington Post*, March 6, 2013. www.huffingtonpost.com/2013/03/06/jeff-dowd-real-big-lebowski-dude_n_2814930.html.

19. Marshall, to author, October 29, 2013.

20. Ibid.

21. Joel Connelly, "A Radical Departure: Bye, Marshall & Dowd," *Seattle Post-Intelligencer*, August 11, 1983, A3.

22. Marshall, to author, July 17, 2017.

Epilogue: The Harmony of Dissonance

1. William O. Douglas, *Points of Rebellion* (New York: Vintage Books, 1969), 31.

2. Name withheld, personal communication with author, July 12, 2015.

3. Geoffrey Maron, Special Agent, FBI, Application for a search warrant, United States District Court for the Western District of Washington, Case No. MJ12-534, October 3, 2012, 2. Document provided to author by interviewee.

4. Seattle's May Day marches continue: the 2015 May Day march began at the federal courthouse where TDA was held 45 years earlier, and one of the keynote speakers was the head of the Northwest Immigrant Rights Project, one of the efforts that was birthed by SLF members in the early 1970s.

5. Chad Stone, et al., "A Guide to Statistics on Historical Trends in Income Inequality," Center on Budget and Policy Priorities, Washington, DC, updated November 7, 2016, www.cbpp.org/research/poverty-and-inequality/a-guide-to-statistics-on-historical-trends-in-income-inequality; Drew DeSilver, "U.S. Income Inequality, On Rise for Decades is Now Highest since 1928," Pew Research Center, December 5, 2013, www.pewresearch.org/fact-tank/2013/12/05/u-s-income-inequality-on-rise-for-decades-is-now-highest-since-1928.

6. Lewis Kamb, "Seattle Activist: 'We Can Channel Our Anger' to Make Change that Matters," *Seattle Times*, July 8, 2016, www.seattletimes.com/seattle-news/seattle-activist-we-can-channel-our-anger-to-make-change-that-matters.

7. Lee Fang and Steve Horn, "Federal Agents Went Undercover to Spy on Anti-Fracking Movement, Emails Reveal," *The Intercept*, July 19, 2016, interc.pt/29J5Of1.

8. "FBI Spied on XL Opponents," *The Guardian,* May 12, 2015, www.theguardian.com/us-news/2015/may/12/revealed-fbi-spied-keystone-xl-opponents#img-1.

9. Sarah Ahmed, "The Problem of Perception," feministkilljoys (blog), February 17, 2014, feministkilljoys.com/2014/02/17/the-problem-of-perception.

Author's Note

1. F. Scott Fitzgerald, "The I.O.U.," *New Yorker*, March 20, 2017 (originally published in the *New Yorker*, 1929).

Bibliography

"A New Challenge to Our Court System: The Spirited Lawyer Representing Political Defendants," edited transcript of a discussion of a 1970 American Bar Association meeting in St. Louis, *Washington State Bar News*, September 1970, 5–15.

"About Us." Beyt Tikkum Synagogue. www.beyttikkun.org/index.php?topic=aboutus.

Alinsky, Saul D. *Rules for Radicals: A Practical Primer for Realistic Radicals.* New York, NY: Vintage Books, 1989.

Anderson, Rick. *Seattle Vice: Strippers, Prostitution, Dirty Money, and Narcotics in the Emerald City.* Seattle, WA: Sasquatch Books, 2010.

Ayers, Bill. *Fugitive Days: Memoirs of an Antiwar Activist.* Boston, MA: Beacon, 2009.

_____. *Public Enemy: Confessions of an American Dissident.* Boston, MA: Beacon, 2014.

Berger, Dan. *Outlaws of America: The Weather Underground and the Politics of Solidarity.* Oakland, CA: AK Press, 2006.

Bingham, Clara. *Witness to the Revolution.* New York, NY: Random House, 2017.

Blackstone, William. *Commentaries on the Laws of England.* (T. Cooley, editor). Chicago, IL: Callaghan and Company, 1884.

Boardman, Madeline. "Jeff Dowd, Real 'Big Lebowski' Dude, Talks White Russians, Jeff Bridges and Bowling," *Huffington Post*, March 6, 2013. www.huffingtonpost.com/2013/03/06/jeff-dowd-real-big-lebowski-dude_n_2814930.html.

Boykoff, Jules. *The Suppression of Dissent: How the State and Mass Media Squelch US American Social Movements.* London: Routledge, 2006.

Burrough, Bryan. *Days of Rage: America's Radical Underground, the FBI, and the Forgotten Age of Revolutionary Violence.* New York, NY: Penguin Press, 2015.

Byers, Tom. "Seattle Legal Defense," *New York Review of Books,* February 11, 1971, 46.

City of Seattle, Municipal Archives, Folder 5, Box 139, #5287-02.

Courtwright, David T. *No Right Turn: Conservative Politics in a Liberal America.* Cambridge, MA: Harvard University Press, 2010.

Dancis, Bruce. *Resister: A Story of Protest and Prison during the Vietnam War.* Ithaca, NY: Cornell University Press, 2014.

Dixon, Aaron Floyd. *My People Are Rising: Memoir of a Black Panther Party Captain.* Chicago, IL: Haymarket Books, 2012.

Douglas, William O. *Points of Rebellion.* New York, NY: Vintage Books, 1969.

Dowd, Jeff. Letter to Archibald Cox and Sen. Sam Ervin. July 31, 1973. National Archives, Record Group # 460: Records of the Watergate Special Prosecution Force; Plumbers Task Force; Investigations of Other Illegal Activities, 1973–1976, Record entry 128289 (A1 103), box 12, 11.

Eckstein, Arthur M. *Bad Moon Rising: How the Weather Underground Beat the FBI and Lost the Revolution.* New Haven, CT: Yale University Press, 2016.

Fang, Lee and Steve Horn, "Federal Agents Went Undercover to Spy on Anti-fracking Movement, Emails Reveal." *The Intercept.* July 19, 2016. interc.pt/29J5Of1.

"FBI Spied on XL Opponents." *The Guardian.* May 12, 2015. www.theguardian.com/us-news/2015/may/12/revealed-fbi-spied-keystone-xl-opponents#img-1.

Foster v. Chatman, 578 U.S., No. 14-8349. May 23, 2016. www.supremecourt.gov/opinions/15pdf/14-8349_6k47.pdf.

Garvy, Helen. *Rebels with a Cause: A Collective Memoir of the Hopes, Rebellions and Repression of the 1960s.* Los Gatos, CA: Shire Press, 2007.

Gilbert, David. *Love and Struggle: My Life in SDS, the Weather Underground, and Beyond.* Oakland, CA: PM Press, 2011.

Gillespie, Mark. "Americans Look Back at Vietnam War." Gallup News, November 17, 2000. www.gallup.com/poll/2299/americans-look-back-vietnam-war.aspx.

Gitlin, Todd. *The Sixties: Years of Hope, Days of Rage.* New York, NY: Bantam, 1987.

_____. *The Whole World is Watching.* Oakland, CA: University of California Press, 2nd ed., 2003.

Hayden, Tom. *Hell No: The Forgotten Power of the Vietnam Peace Movement.* New Haven, CT: Yale University Press, 2017. (Includes an excellent further reading list.)

Healy, Thomas F. *The Great Dissent: How Oliver Wendell Holmes Changed His Mind and Changed the History of Free Speech in America.* New York, NY: Metropolitan Holt, 2013.

Historylink.org. www.historylink.org. The Free Online Encyclopedia of Washington State History.

Industrial Workers of the World. www.iww.org.

Ingraham, Christopher. "Republican lawmakers introduce bills to curb protesting in at least 18 states." *Washington Post.* February 24, 2017. www.washingtonpost.com/news/wonk/wp/2017/02/24/republican-lawmakers-introduce-bills-to-curb-protesting-in-at-least-17-states/?utm_term=.4c488b6bbada.

Jacobs, Ron. *The Way the Wind Blew: A History of the Weather Underground.* New York, NY: Verso, 1997.

Jones, Thai. *A Radical Line: From the Labor Movement to the Weather Underground, One Family's Century of Conscience.* New York, NY: Free Press, 2004.

_____. *More Powerful than Dynamite: Radicals, Plutocrats, Progressives, and New York's Year of Anarchy.* New York, NY: Bloomsbury, 2012.

Joseph, Peniel E. "The Black Power Movement: A State of the Field." *The Journal of American History,* December 2009, 751-756.

Juris, Jeffrey, "Reflections on #Occupy Everywhere, Social Media, Public Space, and Emerging Logics of Aggregation." *American Ethnologist.* May 2012, 259–79.

Kaufman, Michael. "David Dellinger, of Chicago 7, Dies at 88," *New York Times,* May 27, 2004. www.nytimes.com/2004/05/27/us/daviddellinger-of-chicago-7-dies-at-88.html?pagewanted=all&src=pm.

Kershner, Jim. *Carl Maxey: A Fighting Life.* Seattle, WA: University of Washington Press, 2008.

King, Martin Luther, Jr. "The Other America." www.crmvet.org/docs/otheram.htm. Speech given several times in various venues throughout 1967.

Krugman, Paul. "We Are the 99.9%." *New York Times.* November 24, 2011.

Leland, Jon. KRAB FM Radio, *Free the Seattle Eight* (audiofile). October/November, 1970. www.krabarchive.com/krab-programs-spoken-word-1970s.html.

Lerner, Michael. Letter to Departmental Peers. Department of Philosophy. Box 1, Folder 11. Seattle, WA: University of Washington Libraries Special Collections.

_____. "Letter to the Movement: Conspiracy in Seattle." *Liberation.* July 1970, 36–42.

Levi, Margaret. *Consent, Dissent, and Patriotism.* Cambridge, MA: Cambridge University Press, 1997.

Licata, Nick. *Becoming a Citizen Activist.* Seattle, WA: Sasquatch Books, 2016.

Lippman, Roger. terrasol.home.igc.org/trial.htm. (Seattle 7 defendant maintains a website about his political interests, including the Seattle 7 trial.)

MacIntosh, Heather. Interview with Dotty DeCoster. "The Women's Movement and Radical Politics in Seattle, 1964–1980." www.historylink.org.

Maron, Geoffrey, Special Agent, FBI. Application for a search warrant. United States District Court for the Western District of Washington, Case No. MJ12-534, October 3, 2012.

Marshall, Chip, "A Letter from Tacoma City Jail." *Socialist Revolution.* September/October 1970, 137–142.

McMillan, John Campbell. *Smoking Typewriters: The Sixties Underground Press and the Rise of Alternative Media in America.* Oxford, UK: Oxford University Press, 2011.

McRoberts, Patrick and Kit Oldham, "Fort Lawton military police clash with Native American and other protesters in the future Discovery Park on March 8, 1970." www.historylink.org.

Medsger, Betty. *The Burglary: The Discovery of J. Edgar Hoover's Secret FBI.* Waterville, ME: Thorndike Press, 2014.

Michael Stanton Papers, Special Collections No. 3978, #3978-001. Seattle, WA: University of Washington Libraries. (This three-box collection of FBI memos and letters, obtained through Freedom of Information Act requests, is a treasure trove of documentation of Seattle-based FBI COINTELPRO activities.)

Murrah, Judge Alfred P. *United States v. Charles Clark Marshall, III, et al.,* 451 F.2d 372. Court of Appeals for the 9th Circuit. November 18, 1971.

National Aeronautics and Space Administration. "NASA, NOAA Data Show 2016 Warmest Year on Record Globally." www.nasa.gov/press-release/nasa-noaa-data-show-2016-warmest-year-on-record-globally.

Payne, Cril. *Deep Cover: An FBI Agent Infiltrates the Radical Underground.* New York, NY: Newsweek Books, 1979.

Ragovin, Helene. "Black Power Revisited." *Tufts Journal.* February 3, 2010. tuftsjournal.tufts.edu/2010/02_1/features/01/.

Rosenfeld, Seth. *Subversives: The FBI's War on Student Radicals, and Reagan's Rise to Power.* New York, NY: Picador, 2013.

Rudd, Mark. *Underground: My Life with SDS and the Weatherman Underground.* New York, NY: William Morrow, 2010.

Sannes, David. Statement. In Gerald Slater Papers, Series 1, Box 1, Folders 1 and 2. College Park, MD: University of Maryland Special Collections.

Shames, Stephen, Eric Himmel, and Bobby Seale. *Power to the People: The World of the Black Panthers.* New York, NY: Abrams, 2016.

"Statistical information about casualties of the Vietnam War." National Archives. Data as of April 29, 2008. www.archives.gov/research/military/vietnam-war/casualty-statistics.html.

Stern, Susan, and Laura Browder, ed. *With the Weathermen: The Personal Journal of a Revolutionary Woman.* New Brunswick, NJ: Rutgers University Press, 2007.

Thomas, Robert McG., Jr. "Carl Maxey, 73, Spokane Civil Rights Lawyer." *New York Times*, July 7, 1997. www.nytimes.com/1997/07/20/us/carl-maxey-73-spokane-civil-rights-lawyer.html.

Tigar, Michael. *Brief for Defendants-Appellants*. United States Court of Appeals, Ninth Circuit v. Charles Clark Marshall, III, *et al.*, No. 26889. (Undated; copy provided to author by Michael Tigar.).

_____. *Fighting Injustice*. Chicago, IL: Section of Litigation, American Bar Association, 2002.

TigerSwan Inc., www.tigerswan.com/about-tigerswan. (International security firm founded by retired members of the U.S. Army's Delta Force in 2007 operating in 46 countries and headquartered in North Carolina.)

Toobin, Jeffrey. "Annals of Law: The Man with Timothy McVeigh." *New Yorker*, September 30, 1996. 48-54.

Turse, Nick. *Kill Anything That Moves: The Real American War in Vietnam*. New York, NY: Picador, 2013.

United States Court of Appeals, Ninth Circuit. *United States of America v. Charles Clark Marshall, III, et al.* No. 26889, 451 F2nd 372. November 18, 1971.

United States District Court for the Western District of Washington. *Roger Lippman v. John Mitchell, et al.*, Civil Action #C74-342S, June 13, 1974. terrasol.home.igc.org/wiretap2.htm.

United States Senate, Senate Committee on the Judiciary. *The Weather Underground: Report of the Subcommittee to Investigate the Administration of the Internal Security Act and Other Internal Security Laws of the Committee on the Judiciary, United States Senate, Ninety-fourth Congress, First Session*, 94th Cong., 1st sess., S. Rept. Washington, DC: U.S. Government Printing Office, January 1975.

United States Senate. *Final Report of the Select Committee to Study Governmental Operations with Respect to Intelligence Activities*. Rep. No. 94-755, Washington, DC: U.S. Government Printing Office, April 23, 1976. (Often called the Church Committee Report, this is the investigation that revealed the FBI's illegal COINTELPRO activities.)

United States v. Charles Clark Marshall III, Jeffrey Dowd, Joseph Kelly, Michael Abeles, Michael Lerner, Roger Lippman, Susan Stern and Michael Justesen. Transcript. Case Number 519342, U.S. District Court, Western District of Washington at Tacoma, Records of the U.S. District Courts (RG 21), National Archives at Seattle, WA.

University of Washington. Seattle Civil Rights & Labor History Project. depts.washington.edu/civilr/. (Excellent site of research reports, oral histories and photographs from Seattle's civil rights movements through the 20th century.)

Varon, Jeremy. *Bringing the War Home: The Weather Underground, the Red Army Faction, and Revolutionary Violence in the Sixties and Seventies*. Berkeley, CA: University of California Press, 2004.

Walker, Daniel. Chicago Study Team, National Commission of the Causes and Prevention of Violence. *Rights in Conflict*. December 1, 1968. chicago68.com/ricsumm.html.

Weiner, Barnard. "The Orderly Perversion of Justice." *The Nation*. February 1, 1971. 145-148.

_____. "What, Another Conspiracy?" *Washington State Bar Association News.* December 1970. 424–427.

Wilkerson, Cathy. *Flying Close to the Sun: My Life and times as a Weatherman.* New York, NY: Seven Stories Press, 2011.

Zinn, Howard. *A People's History of the United States.* New York, NY: Harper, 1980.

―――――――◆―――――――

Fiction writers have also tried their hands at evoking the characters and events of the 1960s and 1970s:

Banks, Russell. *The Darling.* New York, NY: Harper Perennial, 2005.

Gordon, Neil. *The Company You Keep.* New York, NY: Penguin Press, 2003. (Made into a 2012 film of the same name directed by and starring Robert Redford.)

Lessing, Doris. *The Good Terrorist.* New York, NY: Harper Collins, 1985.

Nunez, Sigrid. *The Last of Her Kind.* London, UK: Picador, 2006.

O'Brien, Tim. *The Things They Carried.* Boston, MA: Houghton Mifflin Harcourt, 2010.

Roth, Philip. *American Pastoral.* New York, NY: Vintage Press, 1998.

Spiotta, Dana. *Eat the Document: A Novel.* New York, NY: Scribner, 2006.

Index

239

About the Author

Photo by Natalia Dotto

Believing that the freedom to publicly dissent is the lifeblood of a functioning democracy, Kit Bakke was active in Students for a Democratic Society at Bryn Mawr College in the 1960s, and later joined Weathermen's national antiwar, anti-racist and anti-capitalist efforts. Born and raised in Seattle, she returned to work as a pediatric oncology nurse. She has bachelor's degrees in nursing from the University of Rochester and political science from Bryn Mawr College, as well as master's degrees in nursing and public health from the University of Washington. Now retired, she writes and volunteers in local philanthropic organizations. In addition to *Protest on Trial* (2018), she is the author of *Miss Alcott's E-Mail* (2006), and *Dancing on the Edge* (2015).